Case Studies for Teacher Problem Solving

Case Studies for Teacher Problem Solving

SECOND EDITION

Rita Silverman

Professor of Teacher Education
School of Education
Pace University

William M. Welty

Professor of Management
Lubin Graduate School of Business
Pace University

Sally Lyon

The McGraw-Hill Companies, Inc.

New York   St. Louis   San Francisco   Auckland   Bogotá   Caracas   Lisbon
London   Madrid   Mexico City   Milan   Montreal   New Delhi
San Juan   Singapore   Sydney   Tokyo   Toronto

McGraw-Hill

A Division of The **McGraw·Hill** Companies

This book was developed by Lane Akers, Inc.

This book was set in Palatino by Graphic World, Inc.
The editor was Lane Akers;
the production supervisor was Diane Ficarra.
The cover was designed by Wanda Siedlecka.
Project supervision was done by Tage Publishing Service, Inc.

Library of Congress Cataloging-in-Publication Data

Silverman, Rita (date).
    Case studies for teacher problem solving / Rita Silverman, William
M. Welty, Sally Lyon.—2d ed.
        p.   cm.
    ISBN 0-07-057655-6
    1. Teaching—Case studies.   2. Problem solving—Case studies.
3. School psychology—United States—Case studies.   4. Teachers—
Training of—United States.   5. Case method.   I. Welty, William
M., (date).   II. Lyon, Sally,   III. Title.
    LB1025.3.S55   1996
    371.1′ 02—dc20

About the Authors

RITA SILVERMAN is Professor of Education at Pace University and Co-Director (with William M. Welty) of the Pace Center for Case Studies in Education. She came to Pace in 1984 as Chairperson of the Department of Teacher Education. Prior to that, she was on the faculty at Rutgers University. She teaches courses in learning and development, tests and measurement, teaching diverse students, and special education. She is the author of several book chapters and journal articles, and she coauthored *Assessment for Instructional Planning in Special Education*. She has been the Co-Director of two federal grants funded by the Fund for the Improvement of Postsecondary Education (FIPSE) to develop cases in teacher education and faculty development and to research their efficacy. With William M. Welty she has developed and presented workshops for faculty in case method teaching at more than 50 colleges and universities.

WILLIAM M. WELTY is Professor of Management at Pace University's Lubin School of Business, Director of the Pforzheimer Center for Faculty Development, and Co-Director of the Center for Case Studies in Education. He has been a member of the Pace faculty since 1964 and has also served as Director of Executive Programs and Associate Dean of the Graduate School. He teaches courses in business policy, business and its environment, and public policy in the MBA program and a college teaching seminar for Pace doctoral students. The author of a number of cases studies on the environmental and ethical aspects of business, he has with Rita Silverman co-directed two grants funded by FIPSE to develop case studies for use in teacher education and faculty development programs, co-authored several articles on the use of cases, and developed and presented workshops for faculty on case method teaching nationally and internationally.

SALLY LYON received her masters in teaching from Pace University where she was a Senior Research Associate. She is currently an elementary school teacher in the Midwest. Prior to pursuing her interest in education, she worked for twelve years in marketing and management positions for the IBM corporation, where she gained experience with the case method in a business context. She is a graduate of Northwestern University, where she was a member of Phi Beta Kappa, and the mother of two young children who give her experience as a consumer as well as a provider of educational services.

Dedicated to the teachers and students who told us their stories

Contents

PREFACE   xvii

TO THE STUDENT   xxi

Part One
CLASSROOM MANAGEMENT

Behavior learning theory | Behavior management | Classroom climate | Classroom organization | Rules and procedures | Rewards and punishments | Social learning theory

Case 1   Marsha Warren   3

A teacher is overwhelmed by the problems created by her students, including eight children who have unique home problems and personal situations that are affecting their schooling.

Case 2   Karen Lee   8

A teacher takes over a class in mid-year and faces a group of students with behavior problems. One student, in particular, seems determined to make her miserable by cheating on the tests and undermining her authority.

Case 3   Maggie Lindberg   13

A teacher is afraid to take her class on a nature walk because the children's behavior is so poor that she does not believe they can be controlled outside the classroom. Her students exhibit behavior problems during her instruction.

Case 4 Barbara Parker 17

A teacher meets "the class from hell" and manages the students by becoming extremely firm and autocratic. Her instruction is pedantic and traditional; she has come to hate the class and is sure that the students hate her.

Case 5 Christie Raymond 27

A mature woman in the first month of her first full-time position teaching music in an elementary school loves the work as long as the children are singing, but dislikes the school's emphasis on and her part in disciplining the students. The case describes Christie's classroom teaching in detail as well as her after-school bus duty.

Case 6 Melissa Reid 37

An enthusiastic young student teacher struggles to gain the respect and improve the behavior of her senior-level composition class and is devastated by one of her student's papers which is full of vindictiveness and hatred toward her.

Part Two
TEACHING AND LEARNING

Constructivist teaching / Curriculum / Discovery learning / In-class grouping / Managing the teaching-learning process / Meaningful learning / Motivation / Questioning / Preparing to teach / Promoting social awareness / Teacher expectations / Tracking / Working with parents

Case 7 Therese Carmen 45

A second-year teacher is presented with a new district-wide science curriculum that she finds difficult to teach because she relies on the objectives found in the teacher's manual.

Case 8 Joyce Davidson 49

A teacher is not making much progress with a remedial English class and is particularly concerned about an extremely shy student who is not responding to her teaching methods and style.

Case 9   Alice Peterson   56

A teacher is having problems with a class into which every student brings unique and difficult problems into the classroom, leading her to wonder if she is reaching anyone. Her instruction does not seem to match her students' needs.

Case 10   Ken Kelly   70

A teacher having trouble with questioning and with discussion teaching visits a teacher who is holding a Socratic discussion with a fourth-grade class. He questions the applicability of her methods to his situation.

Case 11   Molly Clark   77

A first-year teacher in a private all-girls high school teaching eleventh-grade English plans and executes a unit on *Macbeth*. The case reveals in detail her unit and lesson planning, several teaching sessions, and her thoughts about her instructional decisions.

Case 12   Frank Oakley: The Classroom   92

A teacher plans a unit in metric measurement for his students, reflecting on what he has tried in previous years and why those plans didn't work. He tries to develop a teaching strategy given the needs of the students and the inadequate materials. (NOTE: May stand alone or be used with Frank Oakley: The Lab.)

Part Three
DIVERSITY

Ability grouping / Affective development / Curriculum / In-class grouping / Moral development / Motivation / Social context of teaching / Teacher expectations / Working with parents

Case 13   Carol Brown   99

A teacher, after socially integrating a diverse class, sees her efforts threatened when a child's pencil case disappears and is thought to have been stolen. Her students' reactions are not what she had expected.

Case 14   Mary Ewing   104

An experienced teacher has problems with grouping in a remedial math class where each of the eleven diverse students is working at a different level. She solves her problem by planning for individualized instruction only.

Case 15   Mark Siegel   109

A teacher is irritated by a parent who visits him regularly, demanding better instruction for her son. The teacher believes that he has tried everything he can and that the problems rest with the child and the demanding mother.

Case 16   Maxine Korns   112

A teacher is having problems coping with her students, many of whom come to school with emotional problems. The number of difficult students has increased recently, and the school district has instituted rules and procedures for dealing with behavior problems.

Case 17   Jim Colbert   120

A third-grade teacher in an inner-city school is trying his best to teach language arts using basal readers and a district-required curriculum. He is especially concerned about one Spanish-speaking child who appears to want to learn but who speaks English only at school.

Case 18   Janice Heron   125

A teacher does some sizing-up assessments early in the school year and concludes that four of her students will probably be eligible for special education services, although she is reluctant to refer them.

Part Four
CLASSROOM ASSESSMENT AND EVALUATION

Formative/summative | Grading | Identification of differences | Role of standardized tests

Case 19   Sarah Hanover   133

A teacher is confronted by a student's angry parents who challenge her grading system when she gives their son, an outstanding student, a lower grade than expected because he never turned in any homework.

Case 20   Diane News   137

In a school district beginning a gifted and talented program, a teacher must choose four students to recommend for the program from her class, but she has five potential candidates. The parent of one of the students has threatened her if she does not recommend his daughter.

Case 21   Melinda Grant   142

A teacher who has developed an innovative curriculum is concerned because another teacher continually warns her that she will be held responsible for her students' end-of-year standardized test scores.

Case 22   Leigh Scott   147

A teacher gives a higher-than-earned grade to a mainstreamed student on the basis of the boy's effort and attitude and is confronted by a black student with identical test scores who received a lower grade and who accuses her of racism.

Case 23   Anita Underwood   150

An experienced and enthusiastic third-grade teacher describes in detail her plans and her activities for the first day of class for the new school year and shares her sense of excitement and her fears. *Developed by Mary Endorf.*

Part Five
MAINSTREAMING

Classification—Special education | Consultation skills | Emotional disturbance | Identification | Learning disabilities | Resource rooms

Case 24   Allison Cohen   157

A teacher opens a resource room at a school that has never had any special education classrooms and believes the teachers are colluding to make the mainstreaming program fail.

Case 25   Lynn Collier   162

An experienced resource room teacher is confronted by a frustrated classroom teacher who wants an emotionally disturbed student who has outbursts in his classroom to be removed.

Case 26   Laura Conway   166

A resource room teacher is surprised and saddened to discover that one of her favorite sixth-grade students hates the resource room and wants to stop coming.

Case 27   Joan Martin, Marilyn Coe, Warren Groves   168

A classroom teacher, a special education teacher, and a principal hold different views about mainstreaming a boy with poor reading skills. The dilemma comes to a head over the method of grading him at the end of the marking period.

Case 28   Cassie Stern   176

An experienced LD teacher is assigned responsibility for a new resource room at an elementary school and finds her most difficult problem to be how to handle a particularly difficult child newly referred for services as learning disabled. His regular fourth-grade teacher seems unable to cope with his problems, and Cassie fears he will be passed on to fifth grade where the teachers are very resistant to mainstreaming.

Part Six
STUDENT-TEACHING ISSUES

Philosophy of teaching / Social context of teaching / Teaching as a career / Understanding the work place / Working with cooperating teachers / Working with diverse populations

Case 29   Patricia Barnes   183

A student teacher who enters teaching after a career in the private sector finds herself unsure of her decision to change careers when she does not find immediate gratification in teaching.

Case 30   Steve Chandler   187

A student teacher placed in a second-grade class substitutes for his cooperating teacher when her father dies. He decides to discuss the death with the class. One child reacts to the discussion by disrupting the class so seriously that Steve must send him to the principal's office. He then has an unsatisfactory meeting with the child's angry mother after school.

Case 31   Jennifer Gordon   196

A mature woman beginning a second career as an elementary school teacher struggles during her student-teaching experience with how to deal with her cooperating teacher who treats her very badly and corrects her in front of the class.

Case 32   Lauren Ross   204

An enthusiastic young student teacher gets her first chance to "fly solo" for a full day with her fifth-grade class. Her cooperating teacher is very upset when she learns that Lauren has reported a mainstreamed student in her class for misbehavior during a fire drill. *Developed by Janet Stivers.*

Case 33   Emily Smith   209

An energetic student teacher requests and is assigned to student teach social studies in an inner-city high school. Her cooperating teacher gradually lets her assume control of the most difficult survey class, and she succeeds in reaching them until they find out her student-teaching assignment with them will soon end.

Part Seven
CONTEMPORARY TEACHING ISSUES

Ethical issues / Maintaining a professional role / Organizational climate / Working with colleagues, parents, and administrators / Understanding the school as a system

Case 34   Ellen Norton   221

A teacher whose concern for a shy, underachieving student has led to the student becoming her 'shadow,' learns that another student may be the victim of child abuse at home. The teacher has to decide if she should become involved.

Case 35   Debby Bennett   227

An experienced high school English teacher on hall duty during final exams challenges an obstreperous student in the hall without a pass. She is offended by the actions of an assistant principal who cajoles the student into leaving by minimizing his offenses and remarking on her need to "hassle" students. *Developed by Mara Goldstein and Janet Stivers.*

Case 36   Kate Sullivan   230

A principal faces the problems endemic to the students served by her school, which is located in a very low socioeconomic area. Issues of drugs, poverty, neglect, hunger, and homelessness are compounded by the underfunding for the school.

Case 37   Chris Kettering   238

A teacher finds to his dismay that his white, middle-class students are not interested in social activism and that he is unable to promote awareness and openmindedness in them.

Preface

Case method is a relatively new phenomenon in teacher education. This book was prepared to provide case material in textbook form so that teacher educators can easily begin to use cases in their classes. Based on the business school model, most of the cases in this collection are problem-centered stories about teaching situations, developed from the actual experiences of elementary and secondary school teachers. Most end with a dilemma or a problem the teacher must resolve. The educational value of case method is in the identification of the problems, in the analysis of those problems, in the development and evaluation of possible solutions to these problems, and in the application of appropriate educational theory to the problem identification, analysis, solution, and evaluation. Case studies are designed for use in a discussion class. The goal is to encourage student-generated analysis rather than teacher-generated solutions.

We are convinced that case method is an appropriate pedagogical technique for teacher education for the same reasons that it is appropriate for management education. Because it is an active learning process, because it requires that the learner understand and apply theory rather than receive it passively, case method prepares the teacher education student for the real world of teaching. Real world teaching requires problem analysis and decision making on a daily (some would say minute-to-minute) basis. Seldom is there time to consult textbook theory. Rarely is one problem exactly like another. Teachers must be prepared to assume responsibility for dealing with their problems rather than seek external causes beyond their control. They must learn to identify real problems and analyze the situation that may be causing them, and to develop and evaluate action plans. Teachers need to internalize theory and to understand its applications and adaptations. Teachers must learn how to be self-reflective and to think critically about their craft. They must learn how to adapt to change. Case method pedagogy is intended to encourage this.

This book is designed as a supplement to standard textbooks for courses in teacher preparation. Though the cases are independent and may be used in any order, we have imposed an organization that sorts the cases into topics that seem appropriate for a pre-service teacher education curriculum. Part One includes a group of cases that center on classroom management issues; Part Two cases emphasize teaching and learning; Part Three, diversity; Part Four, classroom assessment and evaluation; Part Five, mainstreaming; Part Six, student teaching issues; and Part Seven, contemporary teaching issues. The sections on mainstreaming and student teaching issues are new to this edition.

While it is possible to match specific educational theories to each case, keep in mind that these are all true stories, with names of teachers, students, and schools disguised to protect individual privacy. So, these are not single-issue situations that neatly illustrate textbook problems. Real teachers and students are complex characters, not all good or all bad. Problems are not obvious and unidimensional. No solution can be suggested that is without drawbacks. Indeed, like real life, cases are "messy" documents and are intended to be so. Without the messiness of reality, cases would not stimulate the kind of independent and critical thinking that teacher educators want to encourage in their students.

It is important to understand, as well, that cases are written as pedagogical documents; they are written to be taught in a carefully organized discussion class. That class discussion is at the heart of the case method, for it is here that the power of building individual analyses into a class analysis becomes apparent. From this perspective, case method is a compelling way to encourage and develop effective listening skills and group learning habits.

We think that case method is an exciting way to learn. We think it is a powerful way to prepare teacher education students for the classrooms of the twenty-first century. We hope you agree.

Acknowledgments

The original twenty-eight cases in the first edition of this book, nineteen of which are included in this collection, were developed with the help of a grant from the Fund for the Improvement of Postsecondary Education (FIPSE) and the cooperating support of the School of Education and the Lubin School of Business at Pace University. Our next thirty-three cases, eighteen of which are included in this edition, were developed under the auspices of the Center for Case Studies in Education at Pace University. The Center has been supported by royalties from the first edition of this book and by Pace University. We wish to acknowledge especially the role of the University in its support of the Center and for encouraging a research effort that required crossing disciplinary boundaries to an extent almost unheard of in higher education.

Graduate research assistants from the Masters of Science in Education program in the Department of Teacher Education—Phyllis Carr, Keith Eddings, Susan Gould, Peter Miller, Neil Shultz, Robert Sim, and Andrey Wax—played vital roles in this project. They interviewed teachers, observed in classrooms, gathered information, wrote rough drafts of cases, and graciously endured the difficulties of working on a project breaking new methodological ground. As well, other graduate students brought us stories about their student teaching and first-year teaching experiences and allowed us to craft them into cases.

We have profited from the thoughtful criticism and good ideas of a number of colleagues in the business education, teacher education, and higher education communities. The introduction of case method to teacher education owes a great debt to the work of C. Roland Christensen, Robert Walmsley University Professor *Emeritus*. His seminars at Harvard, his book, *Teaching and the Case Method*, and his personal encouragement and example have been an important impetus to our work both as case writers and case teachers. The President's Forum on Teaching as a Profession, sponsored by the Carnegie Foundation and based at the American Association of Higher Education (AAHE) was responsible for bringing together a number of teacher educators interested in case method for two conferences several years ago. These interchanges were very helpful in sharpening our understanding of cases. We wish to thank Russell Edgerton, President of the AAHE and Pat Hutchings, Director of the AAHE Teaching Initiative, for encouraging that effort and for their support in the years since. And we want to acknowledge the colleagues brought together by those conferences who have shared their ideas with us and whose work has influenced us, especially Helen Harrington, University of Michigan; Judith Kleinfeld, University of Alaska, Fairbanks; Katherine K. Merseth, Harvard University; Anna Richert, Mills College; Judith H. Shulman, Far West Laboratory for Educational Research and Development; and Lee S. Shulman, Stanford University. In addition, for their interest, encouragement, and helpful criticism we are grateful to our colleagues at Pace University, particularly Sandra Flank, Carol Keyes, Carol Rhoder, Ann Spindel, and Mary Williams.

Our editor at McGraw-Hill, Lane Akers, saw the value of cases in teacher education and encouraged our work long before the current interest. We are indebted to him for his vision and his support.

Students in our graduate and undergraduate teacher education classes at Pace University have endured with good spirit and hard work the introduction of a new way of learning. Most of the cases in this book have been "reality-tested" in a Pace University teacher education class. That experience helped improve the cases enormously.

Finally, we wish we could identify each of the classroom teachers and student teachers whose stories form the reality base of the cases. But, for obvious reasons, their names and the physical locations have been disguised. They are the most important people behind the spirit that empowers this book—to improve the education of future classroom teachers—and for that reason we have dedicated this book to them.

Rita Silverman
William M. Welty
Sally Lyon

To the Student

For many of you this collection will be a new experience in education. It is a series of case studies describing the experiences of elementary and secondary school teachers in the United States. Based on the concept of case study developed in schools of business, these cases present stories told by practicing teachers about their experiences. The stories introduce problems teachers have encountered and require that students preparing to be teachers use their analytic- and critical-thinking skills, their knowledge of educational theory and research, and their common sense and collective wisdom to identify and analyze problems and to evaluate possible solutions.

At first, case method may seem a strange way of learning. For one thing, cases present stories about real teachers in real schools and ask that *you* go to the theory and apply it to understand the stories and the problems they present. Part of the reason for using cases is to help you understand educational theory more completely by thinking about how it applies in actual situations. Case method requires that you interact with the theory and decide how to use theory to analyze classroom situations in order to solve problems. As well, case method asks you to go below the surface of a situation—to probe into the presenting problem or problems to understand the deeper or more pervasive events of the case in order to offer solutions. Case method eschews immediate responses, facile answers, single solutions. The process of case analysis requires students to get beyond the obvious to practice thinking like a teacher and deciding what you would do if you were the teacher in the case under discussion.

Deciding for yourself—that is really the heart of case-method pedagogy. It is based on the understanding that the most important learning, the most meaningful learning, the most long-lasting learning comes from the work the learner does on his or her own—active learning.

Problem-solving cases require that the learner be active in both the preparation for class and the participation in class. Your preparation for a case class will not be limited by the normal "I've got fifty pages to read tonight." Instead, it will be determined by how much work *you* want to put into the analysis, by the limitations you put on yourself. Usually the cases can be read in a relatively short time, since few are more than ten pages long. But for cases to have any lasting educational value, you must expend much more effort than simply reading them. Because these cases are problem-centered, there will be a more or less obvious presenting problem. But there will be, as well, some more subtle problems, problems the teacher telling the case story may not have recognized. It will be up to you, in your preparation to discuss the case, identify the problems, apply relevant theory, and develop solutions. There will never be one right solution; often there will be many possible solutions. For sure, there will be better or worse solutions, but better or worse will depend on the analysis you used to understand the problem. That analytic process is the heart of case method. This experience can be both frustrating and exhilarating, as it was for the student who describes her introduction to case method in the following excerpt:

I entered the battle of the case method unarmed. The routines and tools that had allowed me to survive years of schooling no longer helped me; my old study habits were useless—counterproductive, in fact. For example, I had always been a diligent student, priding myself on completing the assignments I was given. If I was expected to read pages 200-256 of a book, I read them. As a student in a case class, though, my assignments were open-ended: prepare the case and develop recommendations. I was supposed to decide how to approach the material, but it was hard to know how much to do, hard to know where to stop. Was I supposed to consider two alternatives or six? Was I supposed to consult outside sources (textbooks, class notes, the library)? I had always been an outliner, finding that outlining helped me see the structure of the material. But cases by their very nature could not be outlined. They were not books, logically organized by the author to facilitate my understanding. Just because a particular aspect of the case situation occupied the first three pages of the case booklet did not mean it was more important than an aspect mentioned in one small paragraph on page 17. Just because certain data was not provided did not mean it was not necessary.

Like a "real" [teacher] in a "real" [teaching] situation, it was now my job to impose a meaningful framework on the unruliness of case facts. I had to search for the key nuggets of data, distinguishing central facts from peripheral ones. I had to sort out the conflicting explanations and alternatives presented to me, and arrive at a reasonable recommendation for action.

I understand the importance of these skills in the real world. But that understanding didn't make the skills any easier to develop. . . . Every time I needed to make an assumption, . . . I hesitated and thought, How would I defend my assumption? How could I know what was reasonable? I rarely could walk into class secure in the knowledge that I had "cracked" the case. The uncertainty was frightening. [Robin Hacke, *The Case Method: A Student Perspective,* unpublished working paper, Harvard Business School, 1986, quoted in C. Roland Christensen, "Teaching with Cases at the Harvard Busienss School," in C. Roland Christensen and Abby Hansen, *Teaching and the Case Method,* Harvard Business School (Boston, 1987), pp. 29-30.]

Cases require active learning in the classroom, as well. Do not expect your instructor to prepare a neat lecture that summarizes the main points of the case, points out the relevant theory, provides a list of sources, and details the correct solution. Instead, the class will be a discussion. You will be asked questions designed to get you and your classmates to compare and build your individual analyses into a collective one. You will be challenged to defend your analysis and your solutions, to listen to and challenge others, and to take away from this collective process a deeper understanding of the case situation than you, your classmates, or your instructor could ever have done alone.

All of this is designed not only to make you an active participant in your own education but to prepare you for the *real* world of the elementary and secondary school teacher. That real world is one of constant action, of making decisions day in and day out. Seldom is there time to consult theory; seldom is one situation exactly like another. Real teachers, therefore, need to be prepared to analyze situations for themselves and to build and evaluate action plans on their own. They need to know how to go to colleagues and friends for assistance—again, not in seeking the single right answer, but in seeking help in problem analysis. They need to learn to take responsibility for the problems encountered in teaching and, by taking responsibility, to develop a proactive attitude toward those problems. In short, they need to develop critical-thinking skills for their profession. Case-method education provides a basis for developing these skills and for continuing to use them during one's professional teaching career.

How Do I Prepare a Case?

For the teacher education student encountering cases for the first time, the following are some concrete, step-by-step suggestions for case preparation:

1. *Understand the assignment in context.* Your instructor will probably assign one case at a time and include in the assignment some study questions or issues to think about while you are preparing it. As well, each case will most likely be accompanied or preceded by traditional textbook assignments. These may alert you to theoretical concepts related to the case. So before you begin to read the case, be sure you understand the overall framework within which the case is being used and the points your instructor may want to emphasize.
2. *Read the case for an overview.* Try reading the case first rather quickly, to get a general idea of what it is about: what happened, who the main characters are, what the problems are, and how the issues in the case relate to the overall assignment.
3. *Analyze the case.* Go back and read the case again, this time much more carefully. Begin to try to make sense of the study questions assigned by your instructor. Make notes of main characters and their relationships with each other. Try to understand the problems, both obvious and subtle. Try to understand the point of view of the case; that is, determine who is providing the information. Identify what impact this perspective may have on the information in the case. Make a list of questions you have about the material, and identify any other information you would like to have. At the end of this stage you should have a list of problems and an understanding of the causes of these problems.
4. *Seek outside information.* At this point you should turn to outside sources for help in understanding the problems you have identified and to develop solutions. Go to the textbook, specifically the chapter(s) assigned to accom-

pany the case. In addition, you should use any material that helps you understand the case better.

5. *Develop solutions.* Ultimately, cases call for solutions to problems, not to determine the one right answer but to focus analysis and to prepare you for a real world of teacher action and decision making. Relate your solutions to your analysis of the problems. Since there are no perfect decisions, be sure you understand both the weaknesses and the strengths of your solutions. Every good solution has a downside; it may not negate the solution, but you should at least always understand the negatives as well as the positives of what you are proposing. Prepare to argue for your ideas in class. Come armed with the relevant theory that supports your position. Be ready to take risks. The case class is a teaching laboratory. The case is the lab experiment, and you are the social scientist seeking to test your ideas.

How Do I Participate in Class Discussion?

Thoughtful participation in case discussion has two components: you should state your own informed ideas and analysis, and you should listen actively to the contributions of your classmates. The case class is a learning community; collectively you and your classmates are proceeding toward a more complete understanding of the case situation and possible solutions. No one person can do it all. Your instructor will guide the class toward this collective understanding but your active participation and active listening are necessary to further this process. You must listen actively in order to understand where the discussion is going and where the group is in the process of the case analysis so that your contributions are relevant to the discussion of the moment.

After the discussion is over, go back over your analysis of the case and think about how the discussion changed or added to what you understood. Be sure you understand how and where the case related to theory. Think about the questions you still have relating to the case or the general assignment and about the ways you might begin to answer them.

Case method is an exciting new venture in teacher education. Our experiences using case-method teaching have demonstrated that new teachers go into their own classrooms more ready to deal with the myriad of problems they must face if as students they have prepared seriously for case discussions by taking the time to analyze the cases and to develop solutions based on the educational theory and have taken part in case discussions with both thoughtful contributions and active listening.

The Setting for the Cases

The cases that follow are the true stories of practicing teachers. Each tries to capture an event or experience that was particularly significant or memorable in the teacher's life. As you read the cases and then analyze them, you will need some information about the settings in which they occur. Knowing the socioeconomic, ethnic, and racial makeup of the communities and having information about class size and availability of ancillary services will help you make decisions about the cases. On the other hand, since the cases are true stories, for privacy reasons we have disguised the names of all individuals, both teachers and students, and of all actual places.

Most of the cases in this collection are set in a school district we have named "Littleton," a suburb of a large northeastern city with a population of 75,000. It is large enough to be classified by the state as a small city district, and is made up of neighborhoods with a wide range of incomes. While many homes in the area are valued at more than $350,000, the city is also plagued with the problems faced by most urban centers: poverty, decaying public housing, crime, and a recent increase in the homeless population.

Once primarily a bedroom community of its core-city metropolitan area, Littleton has in the last twenty years become a business and local government center. Many residents still commute to the city, but others work in local corporate and government offices. Several companies have moved into the Littleton area, taking advantage of the more affordable space and small-town amenities. In addition, over the past ten years, Littleton has become a major shopping hub, and this has created new jobs in the retail and service industries.

There is wide ethnic representation in the district and that diversity is reflected in the school population: approximately 50 percent of the students are white, 30 percent are black, nearly 20 percent are Hispanic, and about 2 percent are Asian.

The district serves more than 8,000 children in six K-6 elementary schools, one middle school (serving grades 7 and 8), and one high school. The average class size is twenty-four students. There are 500 teachers, 60 school administrators, and more then 300 ancillary (nonteaching) staff. Teachers average fifteen years of experience. Salaries in Littleton are well above the national average, starting at more than $35,000 and reaching $85,000.

The Littleton school budget is more than $85 million. The district spends well above the state average per student per year. As a result of its operating budget, the district is able to offer some unique features. Class sizes are smaller than average. Teacher aides are available in the buildings to work with teachers and small groups of children. There are a variety of services for English-as-a-second language (ESL) students and for high school students who function best in a smaller, less structured environment. Most students classified as eligible for special education services either are served in self-contained special education classes or receive support in a resource room for no more than two periods a day. There is a pilot inclusion program in kindergarten and first grade. Prereferral services are available for students whom teachers identify as having problems in the classroom. These students are seen by a Child Study Team (CST) made up of a school psychologist, a learning consultant, and a social worker. Three CSTs serve the six elementary schools (each team is responsible for two schools), and there is a team at the middle school and one at the high school. Students determined by the CST to need further intervention are seen by the Committee on Special Education (CSE) which determines if the students are eligible for special education services.

Gifted students in the elementary schools are served in a pull-out program of enrichment activities for two half-days a week. Teachers of the gifted students also work with teachers in regular classrooms, offering enrichment options for all students.

The high school tracks the students into four levels: honors, above average, average, and remedial. Students typically enter one of the tracks in ninth grade and usually remain at the same level throughout their four years of high school.

There is a great deal of cooperation between the school system and the education-oriented local government. Joint programs such as after-school play groups and summer day-camps have been successfully established and now operate in the community.

The district also maintains close ties with the local universities. Teachers in all the schools accept student teachers and field placement students each semester. Some of the Littleton teachers and administrators are adjunct professors at the local colleges, and faculty from the colleges are involved in several innovative programs and action research efforts in the schools.

Some of the cases in this book are set in neighboring districts that contrast sharply with Littleton. Raddison is a homogeneous, upper-socioeconomic community with a district budget that reflects a per-pupil expenditure of $17,000 (second highest in the state) and the two elementary schools and the junior-senior high school have the equipment, physical plants, and staffing to prove it. Parental support in Raddison is very strong; for instance, more than 80 percent of the parents attend Open School Night each year. Secondary school students are grouped beginning in seventh grade, and movement among the skills, average, and AP honors tracks is minimal. Parental pressure is the most likely reason for a student to be moved across tracks. More than 95 percent of the high school graduates attend post-secondary programs, most at four-year institutions.

Alton represents the other extreme—a school district where more than 70 percent of the students are eligible for the free or reduced lunch program. The racial and ethnic make-up of the community, which is approximately 50 percent white and 50 percent black and Hispanic, is not reflected in the schools; fewer than 25 percent of the students are white. When a school desegregation order required the district to bus children across town to achieve racial balance, many white parents chose instead to put their children in private, often parochial, schools. The town of Alton does not have a strong tax base, passing a school budget every year is difficult, and the schools are underfunded. The per-pupil expenditure is less than $10,000, and teacher salaries in the district are close to the bottom of the pay scale for the area, with starting salaries just above $23,000 and maximum salaries at $60,000.

The cases that do not take place in Littleton, Raddison, and Alton are clearly identified, and background information for each setting is provided within the case itself.

Case Studies for Teacher Problem Solving

PART ONE

Classroom Management

Marsha Warren

An experienced third-grade teacher is overwhelmed by the problems created by her heterogeneous class, which includes eight students who have unique home and personal situations that are affecting their schooling.

José glared at Tyrone. "Quit looking at me, you jerk!"

"I wasn't lookin' at nothin', creepy," replied Tyrone vehemently.

Marsha Warren looked up sharply at the two boys and made a cutting gesture through the air. "That's enough from both of you. You should both be looking at your books, not each other."

"I *was* lookin' at my book!" protested Tyrone.

"Just stop!" repeated Marsha. "Please continue reading, Angela."

Angela rolled her eyes at no one in particular and resumed reading aloud in a bored, expressionless tone. Her progress was slow and halting.

Marsha Warren was a third-grade teacher at the Roosevelt Elementary School in Littleton. She was trying to conduct a reading group with the eight slowest readers in her class of twenty-two while the other children worked in workbooks at their seats. But each time an argument erupted among the children in the reading group, most of the children at their desks snapped to attention to watch the sparks fly.

"You can stop there, Angela," interrupted Marsha as Angela came to the end of a paragraph. "Bettie Ann, will you read next?" As she spoke, Marsha also put a hand out to touch another child, Katie, on the shoulder in an attempt to stop her from bouncing in her chair.

Bettie Ann didn't respond. She was gazing out the window at the leafless November landscape, sucking her thumb and twirling her hair with her other hand. "Bettie Ann, I'm talking to you," repeated Marsha.

"Your turn," yelled José as he poked Bettie Ann's shoulder.

"Shut up, José," interjected Sarah. Sarah often tried to mediate between the members of the group, but her argumentative streak pulled her into the fray as often as not.

"Quiet!" insisted Marsha in a hushed, but emphatic, tone. As she spoke, she turned her head to glance over her shoulder at the rest of the class. The hum of conversation was growing in the room. Tension crept into her voice as she addressed the reading group. "We're distracting the other children. Do we need to discuss rule 3 again? Everyone pull out the class rules from your notebook, now."

The chemistry in the reading group—and in the class in general—had been so explosive since September that Marsha had gone beyond her normal first-of-the-year review of rules and procedures. All the children in the class had copied the four class rules into their notebooks, and she had led long discussions of what they meant. Rule 3 was "Be considerate of other people."

Loud groans from the reading group greeted Marsha's mention of rules. Simultaneously, a loud BANG sounded in the back of the room. Marsha turned and saw a student reaching to the floor for a book as his neighbor snickered. She also noticed three girls in the far-left row leaning into a conversation over a drawing, and she saw most of the students quickly turn back to their work, as if they were not enjoying the entertainment of the reading group once again.

"That's it!" Marsha exclaimed. She slammed her hand down on the reading-circle table and stood to face the entire class. "Put your heads on your desks, and don't say another word—everyone!" By the time she finished the sentence, Marsha realized she had been shouting, but she didn't care. Her class gazed at her in stunned disbelief. Mrs. Warren had always been so gentle! "Now!"

Marsha quickly turned and walked from the room, not bothering to look back to see if her command had been obeyed. She closed the door to her classroom, managing not to slam it, and tried to control her temper and collect her thoughts. "What in God's name am I going to do with this class?" she asked herself. "I've got to calm down. Here I am in the hallway with twenty-two kids inside who have driven me out—they've absolutely won." Marsha suddenly felt paralyzed.

Marsha tried to remember if there was ever a time in her eleven years of teaching when discipline and control were such a challenge. "It's not as though I were a rookie. I ought to know what to do!" she agonized. But Marsha had tried everything she had ever learned or done before to interest and control this group, and the class as a whole, yet there she was, standing in the hall.

Marsha's third-grade class was indeed a difficult group of children. There were a few students who liked school and really tried to learn, but overall it was a class full of children who were just not focused on learning. It was impossible to relax with them. If Marsha let down her guard and tried to engage them on a more friendly or casual level, the class would disintegrate. Marsha's natural inclination in teaching was to maintain a friendly, relaxed manner; she usually enjoyed her students and her enjoyment showed. But with this class she constantly had to be firm and vigilant ("witchlike," she thought) in order to keep the students under control.

Academically the class was fairly average, but Marsha did have two instructional challenges: There were three really bright students, whom Marsha tried to encourage with extra instruction and higher expectations, and there were three students (besides the Hispanic children in her slow-reading group) who spoke little or no English. The most remarkable characteristic of the students, though, was their overall immaturity. Each child seemed to feed off the antics of the others, and every issue was taken to its extreme. For example, whenever one child laughed, the entire class would begin to giggle uncontrollably. The students' behavior was simply inappropriate for their age and grade.

The core of Marsha's problem was the lowest-level reading group. This group provided the spark that set off fireworks in the entire class, day after day. The slow readers were rude and disruptive as a group, and they were instigators on their own.

When Marsha thought of each child in the lowest reading group individually, she was usually able to summon some sympathy and understanding. Each of the eight had an emotional or academic problem that probably accounted, at least in part, for his or her behavior.

José, for instance, topped her list of troublemakers. He was a loud, egocentric child. His mother, Marsha thought, probably had surrendered long ago, and his father did not live with them. José had little respect for or recognition of authority; he was boisterous and argumentative; and he was unable to take turns under any condition. When something didn't go his way, he would explode. This low flash point, Marsha felt, was just one of many signs of his immaturity, even though José was repeating the third grade and was actually older than his classmates.

José had a slight learning disability in the area of organizational skills, but Marsha didn't think this justified his behavior. His mother spoke only Spanish, and—although José was fluent in both Spanish and English—when Marsha sent notes home, she would first have to find someone to translate for her. Conferring with José's mother on the telephone was out of the question.

Angela was also repeating the third grade, and Marsha thought the child's anger over this contributed to her terrible attitude in class. The child just refused to learn. She could be a low-average achiever if she would apply herself, but it was clear that Angela's agenda was not school. She was concerned with her hair, her looks, her clothes—preoccupations that Marsha found inappropriate for a third-grader. Angela came from a middle-class black family, and her parents were also angry that she had been held back; consultations with them were not usually fruitful. Angela seemed truly upset if Marsha asked her to do any work, and Marsha was sure her frustration with the child was occasionally apparent.

Tyrone, on the other hand, was a very low-average learner, but he, at least, worked to his capabilities. He even tried to mediate arguments among the members of the group. But Tyrone had a very stubborn streak, which was typical, Marsha thought, of slow learners. If he was on the wrong track, he just would not get off of it. She frequently asked him to redo work and helped him with his errors, but when he presented it to her the next day as though it were different, it would contain the same mistakes.

Sarah, too, knew right from wrong and generally wanted to do her work, but she was easily pulled into the fray. Sarah had appointed herself protector of Bettie Ann, an overweight, emotionally insecure child who had difficulty focusing on the topic at hand. Bettie Ann was the baby of her family, with several near-adult siblings at home. Marsha wondered if Bettie Ann's position in the family was the reason she assumed no responsibility for her own actions and no control over her own fate. Bettie Ann seemed hungry for Marsha's attention, but she exhibited no independence or initiative at all.

Katie was one of the brighter students in the reading group, but her hyperactivity caused her to be easily distracted and argumentative. She could neither sit still physically nor pay attention mentally. Katie had a rich home background, full of books and middle-class aspirations, but Marsha thought she also encountered pressure at home to perform, perhaps to levels beyond her capability.

Rhea, another child with at least average intelligence, was one of the more heartrending cases. Her mother was an alcoholic who neglected her, and Rhea had to do the housework and care for her older brother, who was in a special education class. She had no time for homework, and there were no books or even conversations at home. Rhea had been held back in the second grade, and while she tried to do her work, the language deficit at home was so severe that she kept falling further behind.

Finally, there was Maria, a petite, immature native of El Salvador. She had average intelligence and a cooperative spirit, but Spanish was spoken in her home and her limited English vocabulary severely limited her progress.

Marsha tried to analyze what it was among these children that fostered such animosity. Not a day passed that they didn't argue, fight, or insult one another. The reading group was not the only arena for these combatants; they fought in the playground, in line, on the bus, and in the cafeteria. They were troublemakers in previous grades, and some of the teachers at Roosevelt called them the "Infidels."

They tended to be at their worst as a group, and so Marsha had tried separating them, but with little improvement. Three weeks before, in early October, she rearranged and reorganized all three reading groups, distributing the students in the lowest section among three new groups. But she found that the inappropriate behavior did not stop; it only spread. Now all three of her reading groups, rather than one, were disrupted, and mixing her slow and her average readers dramatically reduced the pace of both groups. Finding this arrangement unfair to her other students, she reorganized back to her original group assignments last week.

Marsha also tried other remedies. She introduced popular reading material for the reading groups and tried innovations such as having the children act out the stories they read. She wrote a contingency contract with the groups when she reconstituted them last week, promising that they could use the school's audiovisual equipment to make filmstrips illustrating their current book if they behaved, but so far that wasn't working either.

Marsha did not think she was generally too lax. She had procedures for incomplete work (the students had to come to her room during lunch hour or after school to finish); she had rules for appropriate behavior in school; and she never hesitated to involve parents. She praised the children for completing work, and she sent positive notes home when they did so. She also sent home disciplinary cards (much more frequently, unfortunately), which parents were supposed to sign, and she telephoned parents when she thought it would help.

Marsha also tried punishment. She sent individual troublemakers to the office, and she held detention during lunch. She isolated children for misbehavior by separating their desks from the rest of the class, and she used denial of privileges (the children really liked using the class computer, so she withdrew that privilege frequently). Marsha even tried talking honestly with the children, giving them pep talks about the value of education and their need to read and write and think in order to participate in life. But nothing was fundamentally altering the course of the class's behavior.

Besides having the desire to teach the "Infidels," Marsha knew that the progress of the rest of the class was being slowed because of the time she was forced to spend on policing. Her patience, her ideas, and her fortitude were fast evaporating, and she knew she had to solve the problem even though she felt like giving up.

Marsha stood on tiptoe to look through the window of the classroom door. The children were sitting in their places looking at each other uneasily and at the door, clearly wondering what would happen next. With a sigh, Marsha turned the knob.

Karen Lee

A first-year Spanish teacher takes over a high school Spanish III class in midyear and faces an unruly group of students. One student in particular seems determined to make her miserable.

"Three strikes, you're out," Karen thought as she walked briskly to Jeff's desk in the back of the room. Standing beside him, she tore a piece of paper from his hand and ordered him out of the class. It was the third time in three weeks that she had found Jeff—an A student who was easily capable of doing the work—cheating on a test.

"I wasn't cheating! Read what it says!" Jeff said as he willingly surrendered the paper. Karen felt the rest of the class looking on almost conspiratorially, gleeful that another confrontation was developing between the two.

"Out! Out! Now!" Karen shouted, incredulous that Jeff could plead his innocence even as she held prima facie evidence of his cheating in her hand. "Get down to the guidance office. I'll see you there after class."

"I wasn't cheating! Read it!"

"Out!"

"I wasn't cheating, you bitch!"

"What?"

"You want me to say it again? I wasn't cheating, you bitch!" Shoving his books from his desk and flinging his test paper in Karen's direction, Jeff stormed from the room, slamming the door behind him.

Karen, just four months into her first teaching job, fought to contain her rage and hold back her tears as she returned to her desk. As she gazed at her grinning students, she wondered who they thought had won this latest struggle for control of the class.

"Back to work," she said. While the students spent the remaining twenty minutes finishing their tests, Karen sat at her desk wondering why this class had gone so wrong.

Although it was only December and the school year was just fourteen weeks old, Karen Lee was the fifth teacher for this tenth-grade, above-average-track Spanish III class. Three substitutes had been hired after the regular teacher went on a leave to receive treatment for cancer just before classes started in September. The teacher returned to school in mid-November, but she left again after only a few days when she found the treatments had left her too weak to resume her work.

The principal was reluctant to return Spanish III, a language and culture class, to another string of substitutes. Karen had been teaching part-time and eagerly accepted the class when she was asked to take it, even though her entire schedule had to be shuffled to accommodate it. Nevertheless, the new assignment brought Karen up to a full class load at Littleton High School, and although it wasn't a permanent appointment, Karen was pleased that she now would be working full-time as a teacher after being out of college only a few months. Both of her parents were teachers, and she had held the hope all through high school and college that she would be a teacher also. At just 24, Karen felt she had reached her career goal.

Spanish was a passion for Karen. She began studying the language in ninth grade at a public high school not far from Littleton. She spent her senior year as an exchange student at La Escuela Superior de Cardinal Cushing, a private school for Catholic girls in Bolivia. After a year in Bolivia, Karen returned home and enrolled at a college near Littleton, where she received a bachelor's degree with a major in Spanish and a minor in education. After graduation, she rewarded herself with a summer of traveling in Mexico. In the fall, she returned to the United States to accept the part-time position at Littleton High School.

Karen started with three classes in September and picked up a fourth when another teacher was named an assistant principal and had to give up his classes. She added the Spanish III class to her schedule the Monday after Thanksgiving.

There had been no warning that the new class might be a problem. The principal told her only that it was an above-average-track class of twenty college-bound students, all sophomores. Her other classes were going well, and Karen had no reason to suspect that this one would be any different. She expected that she would simply open the text to chapter 4, where the state curriculum indicated the class should be, and pick up where the other teachers had left off.

But Karen discovered on the first day that the substitutes had made little progress. The students were far behind the course outline and would have to do nine months' work in six months' time if they were to complete the Spanish III curriculum and be ready for Spanish IV in the fall.

Karen's second discovery was that the different-teacher-every-three-weeks syndrome had left the class in near anarchy, with little respect for the teachers and with no expectation that any real learning would take place.

The sense of lawlessness was heightened by the fact that there seemed to be no real cohesion among the twenty students. Although there were two distinct groups of students in the class—Karen had categorized them in her mind as "greasers" (those who wore leather motorcycle jackets and boots and seemed indifferent to school) and "jocks" (the clean-cut students dressed in the latest fashion)—there was little unity even within those groups. It was difficult to get any of the students to work together. The only thing that united them, Karen thought, was their ability to sabotage her lessons and frustrate her teaching efforts. They would rally around that and nothing else.

The class had only one leader: Jeff Cole, a 16-year-old fullback on Littleton's football team, who was one of the brightest students in the class as well as the most disruptive. He seemed to have a constant need to retain his role as leader, or at least as chief instigator. Jeff never missed an opportunity to disrupt the class or to obstruct any momentum Karen tried to build. Most of the others would follow Jeff's lead without much hesitation.

To try to contain their disruptiveness, Karen organized the students into five neat rows of four, with as much space between rows as possible. Her strategy was to divide and conquer and to try to keep the students focused on her as she introduced new nouns, verbs, and sentence constructions from the front of the room. The students needed a great deal of drill work to bring them up to date, so Karen emphasized repetitive grammar exercises. Most days, she reviewed the material, had the students repeat it, and then assigned related written exercises in their books.

From the outset, however, Karen felt that they regarded her as only another substitute, and she constantly struggled for control. At first, the problems seemed relatively minor: side-bar conversations, off-task activities, minor disruptions. But gradually the students' inattention increased, and whenever she demanded their focus, they would chatter about a football or basketball game or about the upcoming ski season or anything else that was unrelated to the material.

Gradually the problems escalated. During the first day of her second week, Karen was caught in a crossfire of coins being flung around the room behind her as she tried to conjugate a verb on the chalkboard.

"This is craziness, absolute craziness," Karen thought as she listened to the ping of coins bouncing off the walls. She held the brief hope that the disruption would subside on its own if she ignored it. She continued writing on the board, reciting the verb as she conjugated it and pushing dutifully ahead with the lesson plan. "Comi, comiste, comio," she said. "I ate, you ate, he-she-it ate."

A sudden loud CRACK! shattered Karen's concentration and her sense of safety. Instinctively, she jumped back from the board and swerved to face the class. A Kennedy half-dollar, which had ricocheted off the chalkboard only a few inches from her ear, fell to the floor and rolled to the back of the room, accompanied by a chorus of chuckles from her students.

That was the last time Karen turned her back on the students. From then on, she used the overhead projector rather than the chalkboard whenever she needed to illustrate something to the whole class.

After the coin-tossing incident, Karen tried a variety of the assertive discipline techniques she had learned in her college education courses, but few seemed to have any effect. For example, each time a student acted up, she placed a check next to his or her name on the chalkboard. If a student received five checks, he or she was assigned an hour of detention. But it became a game before long as students competed for the checks and ignored the detention assignments.

That illustrated another problem. The school's policy concerning after-school detention undercut her efforts to run the class. At Littleton High School, only an administrator could authorize after-school detention, and school officials would not back up Karen's detention assignments. They said that the district's inflexible bus schedule made it awkward to detain students who lived far from the school.

Another school policy, one which allowed students to have class schedules without a lunch period, gave Jeff and six or seven others a daily opportunity to disrupt the class. According to the policy, students who did not have a regularly scheduled lunch period could take five minutes from their sixth-period class and ten minutes from their seventh-period class to eat. Jeff and several others had no scheduled lunch. Invariably, they would arrive fifteen minutes late for the forty-minute class and would require another five minutes to settle down. Once seated, with their notebooks open, they would complain that the lesson was difficult to follow, forcing Karen to start over again.

Karen worried that the abbreviated classes might be an insurmountable handicap to a class that already was several months behind. She offered the students a compromise: Come to class on time, and you may eat at your desks. Jeff and the others seemed to appreciate the compromise at first, and they regularly brought their lunches to class. But within a week, they slipped back to their routine of showing up ten to fifteen minutes late, and they brought their lunches to class as well.

For Jeff, the potential for disruption was doubled by his luncheon selections: carrots, potato chips, hot peppers, sardine and onion sandwiches, carbonated sodas—anything that made a loud crunch or sprayed into the air or that was exotic enough to provoke some reaction from the others. After the first few days of Jeff's in-class luncheons, the students would sit each day in breathless anticipation of what Jeff would have in his lunch bag. Almost always, it drew a reaction, which only encouraged Jeff to be even more outrageous the next day. Karen felt that the lunch fiasco was typical of the way Jeff turned her peace gestures against her.

The cheating incidents also were typical. Karen could tell from Jeff's transcripts and test scores and from the brief moments when he did participate in her class that he didn't need to cheat to get good grades. Instead, Karen believed, Jeff's cheating was only an attempt to entertain himself and to prove to the other students that he could outwit her.

Jeff cheated on the first two tests, and both times she caught him. Because Jeff was a leader and an instigator for the rest of the class, Karen feared that his cheating would spread unless she made an example of him. She responded harshly; each time, she gave him a zero on the test, plus two days' detention, and she sent notes to the guidance office and to his parents.

But now, sitting at her desk after ordering Jeff from the class for his third cheating episode, Karen thought that this incident was different from the earlier two. In the other two, Jeff clearly wanted to get away with it and was embarrassed at being discovered. This time, his cheating was blatant. He had nearly waved his crib sheet in the air. Karen felt sure that he wanted to get caught.

The period ended, and the other students turned in their tests and shuffled from the room. Karen's mind turned back to the paper she had taken from Jeff before sending him to the guidance office. When the last student left the room,

Karen took the paper from Jeff's test, where she had stapled it. She unfolded it to see what he had written.

In bold red letters, it read: "¡No estoy haciendo trampa, Tonta!"

Karen mentally translated—"I'm not cheating, you idiot"—and sank into her chair, thinking that Jeff had won again.

Maggie Lindberg

A first-year teacher is afraid to take her third-grade class on a nature walk because the children's behavior is so poor that she does not believe they can be controlled outside the classroom.

It was already the third week of October, and Maggie Lindberg knew she couldn't put off taking her students on a nature walk much longer. All the other third-grade classes had ventured out and returned with the materials they would study as part of a science lesson. Her students were asking when they were going, and Maggie knew she was running out of time; in another two weeks there would be no more brightly colored leaves to study.

Walking past a bulletin-board display entitled "The Splendor of the Changing Seasons," the result of a nature walk taken by the third-grade class next to hers, Maggie couldn't help smiling to herself. "I guess it would be irresponsible of me to just ignore this annual phenomenon of nature," she thought. But she wished that she could.

This was Maggie's first year as a full-time teacher. She had graduated from college midyear and then substituted in several nearby school districts for the rest of the school year. Littleton had offered her a full-time position starting in September, and she was assigned a third-grade class of twenty-six students. Maggie had been excited by the prospect of teaching her own class. She spent much of the summer defining her objectives for the year and planning activities and curriculum materials to achieve them. Maggie had wanted to be a teacher for as long as she could remember, and now her goal was a reality.

Maggie's experiences as a substitute teacher had shaped her opinions about teaching almost as much as had student teaching. Maggie knew that substitute teaching was often just an exercise in crowd control, and she had "baby-sat" many classrooms full of unruly children with grace and patience. But she vowed to herself that her own classroom would be orderly and her students better behaved. Unfortunately, that goal was proving elusive.

Maggie also had a specific experience while she was substitute teaching that really frightened her. The incident involved a fourth-grade class scheduled to take a field trip to a local fire station. She vividly recalled the feeling of panic that overtook her when one of the students bolted from the group and ran off the school grounds into a nearby wooded area. Maggie had the parent

13

volunteer who was accompanying the class on the field trip take the rest of the students back to their classroom. Maggie then went after the runaway student, eventually located her, and brought her back to the classroom. When she returned, she found the principal with her class. While the principal did not rebuke her, the memory was a constant reminder of what could happen when the students were not in the teacher's control.

At the moment, Maggie was headed for the art room to pick up her class. As she stood in the doorway, she couldn't believe how intent her students seemed to be on their projects. "These kids must love art," she thought. "They never act like this in my class."

Maggie reflected on the reading lessons she had taught earlier that morning. Because the students had art on Tuesdays, Maggie felt real pressure to have the reading groups stay on schedule so that she could meet with all three groups between 9:15 and 10:30, when art was scheduled. But the students seemed to be even less cooperative when Maggie most needed them to stay on task.

She had begun the lesson by reminding the students of the morning schedule. "Since today is Tuesday, we really need to get everything done on time so that we can go to the art room with all our reading work finished."

Some of the children began to clap. Several commented to each other about going to art. Maggie ignored the interruptions and continued, "Look up at the board, and you'll see the assignments for each group. I want the Chocolate Chips with me first today. Twinkies should be reading the story that starts on page 49 of your reading books and then doing the workbook pages on the board. Oreos have to complete the workbook pages left from yesterday and then start a new story, beginning on page 141 of your reading books." Maggie pointed to each group's assignment, which she had written on the chalkboard.

As Maggie was giving the students their directions, many of them were occupied with other activities. Several were walking around the room—some to the pencil sharpener, others to the cubbies to retrieve books or supplies—and a few were gathered at the reading center in the back of the room.

Maggie spoke sharply. "You're not listening to me! I want the Chocolate Chips at the reading table *now*. Everyone else, in your seat and doing the work that's on the board."

The children began moving toward their places. Four children gathered at the reading table, while others went for their books and then headed to the table. Two children, sitting at their desks, had their hands up. Maggie noticed and said, "Yes, Melody, what is it?"

"Why do we have to do yesterday's pages? I'm tired of them."

Other children immediately joined in.

"Yeah, don't make us do the old stuff."

"I already did that stuff."

"All we do is the same stuff all the time."

Maggie again raised her voice to be heard over the din. "That 'stuff,' as you all refer to it, is our work. And you will do it, *now*. I don't want to hear any more complaints, and I want to see everyone hard at work or the whole class will stay in and do the work during recess. Chocolate Chips, you should all be at the reading table. Let's move it."

Maggie's frustration was evident in her voice and the set of her shoulders. Ten minutes of an already shortened reading period had been lost getting the children to settle down to their tasks. She sat down with the Chocolate Chips and, trying to lighten her tone, said, "Okay, Chippers, we're reading on page 76. Emanual, why don't you begin."

Emanual was quiet. John said, "He don't got his book."

"Where's your book, Emanual?" Maggie tried to keep the impatience from her voice.

"In my cubby."

"What good will it do you in your cubby? What have you been doing all this time? Emanual, you know that one of our class rules is 'Be prepared,' but you're not, are you?" Maggie's voice again began to reflect her tension. She turned to the rest of the Chocolate Chips. "Does everyone else have a book?"

Of the nine children in the group, three had come to the reading table without their books. Maggie sent them to get their books and tried to keep the other children quiet while they waited to get started. It was taking all her control to remain calm. She was tempted to banish the three children who had not brought their books, to make a point about being prepared, but she knew that they needed the reading time too much. However, as a result of all the confusion and interruptions, all the reading groups spent far less time reading on Tuesday than they should have. That was one of the things that bothered Maggie the most.

Of the twenty-six children in her class, more than half had come into third grade below grade level in reading. Maggie wanted them to leave her class reading far better than they did when they came in, and she needed maximum reading time to accomplish her goal. She also knew that third grade was a crucial time for these children. In order to succeed in the upper grades, where there was more emphasis on reading content than on reading skills, they would have to "break the code" and learn to be efficient readers this year. Maggie wanted to be the teacher who enabled them to meet that goal. But, so far, she had not been very successful.

Maggie's reverie about the morning was interrupted when the art teacher noticed her in the doorway. She called to Maggie and waved her into the room. The art teacher directed the children to put away their work. As Maggie watched the children clean up the art room, she was fascinated by what she observed. When the art teacher was satisfied with the cleanup, she had the children line up at the door. Maggie found it hard to believe these were the same children who, forty minutes earlier, had been causing her such consternation. However, as soon as the class stepped into the hall, Maggie remembered why the children frustrated her. She walked down the hall trying to keep order.

"Tommy, don't run ahead of the class. You know the rules."

"Maria, please try to keep up. Don't dawdle."

"Matt, come walk next to me. I've told you not to bother the girls. Could we all please keep the noise down?"

Maggie looked at the children straggling into the classroom and thought, "What's the matter with these kids? Why don't they listen to me? Is it because I'm so young?"

Eventually Maggie was able to herd the last of the students into the classroom. She looked at the clock and saw that it was 11:25; her social studies lesson was beginning late.

"Okay, everyone in your seats now and take out your social studies books."

The students continued talking to each other as they made their way to their desks.

"Please quiet down. I want to see all of you in your seats, because we have a lot of work to do."

Looking out over her class, Maggie saw that most of the students were ignoring her. Two students were in the library corner; a group of boys had their heads together over a comic book; and one little girl, looking for a pencil, had emptied the contents of her desk onto the floor.

Maggie went over to the boys, took the comic book, and told them to take their seats. The boys complied but continued to talk above the noise of the rest of the class.

As Maggie walked toward the girls in the library corner, she heard a loud crash from the front of the room.

"Miss Lindberg, it wasn't my fault. Tony was pulling it down too hard."

Maggie saw the world map crumpled in a heap on the floor in front of the chalkboard.

"Well, why were you pulling the map down? Please sit down, and I will take care of the map."

The sound of the map crashing to the floor had captured everyone's attention, and the students listened to hear what would happen next. Maggie was angry enough to raise her voice.

"I mean it. I want all of you in your seats *now*. Let's get out those social studies notebooks, and if I hear one more word from anyone, there will be no free time this afternoon."

As Maggie walked briskly to the front of the classroom, she looked at the clock. It was 11:35. She would barely have time to introduce the social studies lesson before the lunch bell at 11:45.

The classroom was filled with the sound of rustling papers as the children searched for their books. As Maggie watched them, she tried through sheer force of will to repress her dismay and replace it with the excitement and anticipation she had felt on the first day of class. Maggie did not want to let herself become discouraged; she wanted to teach these children something! But too often they wouldn't even listen to her, and the idea of organizing the group for a field trip seemed like a nightmare.

Looking out the window, she again noticed how brilliant the leaves had become. She knew she had to take the students on a nature walk, and she had to do it soon. She was sure that they would enjoy some time outside and that a science lesson based on materials they had gathered themselves would be a good learning experience for them. "But," she thought, "I can't even control them in here!"

Barbara Parker

An experienced high school teacher meets "the class from hell" and handles it by becoming extremely firm and autocratic. She comes to hate the class and is sure that the students hate her.

Barbara Parker walked toward the room assigned for her seventh-period social studies class feeling the rush of adrenalin that always greeted the first day of school. In spite of the fact that she was beginning her fifth year of teaching, Barbara felt excitement and anticipation at meeting each new class of students and getting the year under way.

Barbara's morning classes went well, and she enjoyed visiting with some of her former students during lunch. Her next class was an average-level ninth-grade class in Afro-Asian studies. While the title of the course implied a focus on cultures not normally studied in suburban high schools, the course essentially covered typical world history content, except for European history, which comprised the sophomore social studies curriculum. Even with that major omission, Barbara found the breadth of content a challenge; the course covered the Middle East, Africa, India, China, and Japan, spanning history from the dawn of civilization to present-day culture and politics. But the planning and review that Barbara began over the summer renewed her interest in the subject and the possibilities she could explore to teach it. In the morning she had taught this same course to honors classes, and she was encouraged by their reaction to her introduction.

Barbara entered room 303 a few minutes before the bell and walked to the front to check that textbooks had been delivered to the room. As she pulled the class roster and her introductory notes from her book bag, students began to drift in from lunch.

"Hey, watch it!" snarled a girl standing in the classroom doorway as she turned and confronted the student behind her.

"Well, move your feet, girl!" replied the perpetrator, a pretty girl with long dark hair. She sauntered past the girl she had pushed and came into the room. Calling over the heads of several students, the dark-haired girl addressed her friend in the back of the room: "Hey, Angela, how was math? Was Alan there?" Angela's reply was lost in the general din, which escalated as more students spilled into the room.

Barbara stood up at the sound of the bell—a harsh, discordant note guaranteed to command attention—and walked toward the classroom door. She expected a certain amount of dawdling right after lunch and was prepared to usher the few students who remained in the hallway into the room and to their seats. But there were fifteen or more students milling around in the hall, and Barbara wasn't sure which ones belonged in her class.

"Would those of you enrolled in ninth-grade social studies please come in?" Barbara asked the throng in the hall.

"Yo, Miss. Name's Jackson," replied a skinny, wiry black student who slid past Barbara into the room. "Hey, Marcus, how's my man?" Jackson spied a compatriot standing at the back of the room and made his way into the classroom.

"Excuse me, class has begun," repeated Barbara to the students in the hall. It was apparent that she was not capturing anyone's attention, so she backed into the room and began to close the door.

"Hey, what are ya doin'!" A few students bolted toward the closing door and muscled their way past their teacher.

"Class begins with the bell, and I expect you to be in your seats," Barbara said to their retreating backs. Not one of them seemed to hear her, and no one made a move to sit down. Barbara closed the door the rest of the way and walked to the front of the classroom to address her class.

"Please take your seats," she called, thinking to herself that the typical first-day excitement was extreme with these kids. "This is Afro-Asian studies, and anyone who doesn't belong . . . " Barbara let her voice trail off as she realized that no one was listening to her. Students were grouped in pairs and threes, mostly standing, but some had turned their desks to face each other and converse more comfortably. The door opened and two girls entered, deep in conversation. After surveying the commotion in the room, the girls resumed their discussion and walked toward the windows on the other side of the room.

Barbara had always found ninth-graders to be somewhat shy and intimidated on their first day of high school. The possibility that opening day would be a disciplinary challenge hadn't occurred to her. She raised her voice slightly. "Would you please choose a desk so that I can take attendance and distribute your texts?" Barbara felt as though there was an invisible partition between herself and the students, so totally did they ignore her request. With exasperation she reached for the pointer lying in the chalkboard tray and banged it on her desk. "Take your seats!"

"Oooohhh . . . " The sound floated tauntingly toward Barbara as most of the students turned to look at her appraisingly. A few groups arranged themselves at desks near where they had been standing, but at least ten of the thirty or so students in the room assumed "make me" postures and continued to speak to each other. The conversation in the room subsided but did not disappear.

Barbara immediately regretted her act but at least tried to seize the opportunity to be heard. "This is ninth-grade Afro-Asian studies. In this class you can study some interesting and exciting things. I want to get to know you and tell you about the class. Would the rest of you please sit down so that I can call your names?" By the end of her speech, Barbara realized that the noise in the room was increasing rather than diminishing in response to her message; unbelievably, two students who had sat down when she banged the pointer now left their desks to call to someone out the open window. None of those standing made any move to sit.

Barbara looked at the unruly group for a moment and then picked up her roster and walked to the nearest boy. "Who are you?" she tapped him on the shoulder to interrupt his conversation with the boy at the desk behind him.

"Mason Dixon," replied the boy with a respectful smile. Barbara instinctively looked down her roster to the *D*'s, prompting uproarious laughter from the student who had spoken and three others within earshot. As she searched in vain for "Dixon" on her printout, Barbara thought about his reply and realized she had been had. She couldn't resist a smile, though, as she reflected that at least this boy had learned something from eighth-grade American history.

"Very funny, Mason. What else do they call you?" Barbara's easy response was natural; she could usually take and even enjoy a little teasing from her students. She had found that this approach tended to minimize the us-her attitude that could fester in classrooms. But the quartet's reaction to Barbara's friendly response was anything but appreciative. Her failure to be punitive or angry was apparently taken as license to act out. The boy sitting behind "Mason" pushed him roughly, and the two boys sitting across the aisle laughed so hard—or pretended to—that they rolled out of their seats and into the aisle. Once away from their desks, they simply stood up and moved off in search of more interesting pursuits out of Barbara's range.

Barbara couldn't believe what had just happened, and when she looked up, she saw that the brief tempering effect achieved with the pointer had evaporated while she focused on Mason Dixon. She turned to him angrily. "What is your *name?*"

"Lincoln Maxwell," replied Mason Dixon. His tone was now matter-of-fact, and a small smile played at the corner of his mouth. His expression was so soft that Barbara almost read pity in his eyes.

"Thank you." She glanced down the roster, found his name, and checked it off. She consulted the seating chart she had tucked under the roster on her clipboard. "You will sit at the second desk in the third row." Glancing at the thirty other students milling around the room, Barbara turned to the boy behind Lincoln with a growing sense of futility. "What is your name?"

"George," replied the tall student who lounged easily at the tiny tablet desk.

"George what?" asked Barbara as patiently as possible.

"George Washington, nice to meet you. What's your name?"

Barbara looked at the student's irritating grin and turned away without reply. She marched to the front of the room and over to the metal filing cabinet that abutted the teacher's desk. Retrieving the pointer, Barbara called as loudly as she could without yelling, "Class, enough. *Take a seat!*" With that, she slammed the pointer into the side of the metal cabinet and felt the impact travel through her wrist and up her arm.

The crack commanded the students' attention, at least, and Barbara moved swiftly to seize what might be her only chance. "You, in the back. Sit down. Here, take a seat." As she spoke, Barbara moved toward the windows and the few students who remained standing. As they sat in nearby desks, she quickly filled the silence. "I will read your names. When your name is called, come to the front and sign out a book. Then go sit at the desk I assign."

"What, assigned seats?" The long-haired girl who had pushed her way into the room complained loudly from the rear.

"What is this, middle school again?" Angela took up her friend's cause.

"I don' wanna move!" Another student joined the fray.

Barbara ignored them and walked to the front desk in the row by the windows. "Andersen, Christine." Barbara scanned the faces now watching her sullenly. "Is Christine here?"

A tall blonde who looked at least 16 rose gracefully—and provocatively, Barbara thought. "Ooohh . . . " A soft sound of appreciation arose from the back of the room, but the rest of the class remained mercifully quiet.

"Hello, Christine. Please sign this card, take a book, and sit at this desk. Baxter, Manuel? Is Manuel here?"

"What—I gotta sit in the front just because my name starts with *B?* Forget it!"

"Manuel, I am assigning seats alphabetically, and yours is here behind Christine. We will change seating periodically throughout the year. Now go get a book."

Barbara proceeded as quickly as she could down her roster, tolerating the soft conversation that recurred among those students not getting a book or moving to a new seat. She had twelve of them seated when she got to Jared Jackson.

"Jackson, Jared? Come on, Marsha, hurry now." As she looked for a response to her call for Jared, she encouraged a girl in the book line to move along. Barbara glanced at her watch and realized she had ten minutes left in the period in which to finish assigning seats and signing out texts, explain class rules, introduce the course, and make tomorrow's assignment. She tried not to let impatience show in her voice.

"Is Jared here?" Suddenly the small boy who had introduced himself as he entered the classroom a half hour ago popped up from a seat at the back of the room. He glanced at the desk Barbara now stood beside.

"Call me Jackson. I don' wanna sit there."

"I'm assigning seats alphabetically for now, Jackson. Please get your book and then sit here."

"No. I don' wanna sit there." Jackson glanced furtively at two boys Barbara had already placed at desks nearby.

"Well, little man, come sit by us!" Sasha Campeau grinned innocently.

"Yea, wassa matter? Hey, lady, he's in the wrong class anyway. Jackson, din' you know ya gotta be as tall as this line to go on this ride? Get back to grade school." Joe Denton held out his hand about 4 feet above the floor and looked around the room for a response to his witticism. As Sasha complied with loud and affected laughter, Barbara felt her irritation rise again.

"Sasha and Joe, quiet down. Jackson, you sit up there, in the first seat of the next row." Jackson swaggered past Barbara and his enemies, and Barbara glanced again at her watch. She realized that she was never going to get everyone rearranged before the bell rang.

As she looked up from her watch, Barbara spotted Lincoln, the student who had relented by giving her his real name twenty minutes ago. Sitting at a desk she had not yet reassigned, he was speaking softly to "George Washington," whose real identity she still did not know. "Lincoln, will you and George Washington go get the rest of the books and put one on each of the rest of the desks? Everyone else, stay where you are and raise your hand when I call your name. We have better things to do than play musical chairs for the rest of this period."

Grumbling and the hum of elevated conversation greeted this pronouncement. "Hey, lady, this was your idea!"

"Gee, she's testy!"

"Make up your mind!"

"Does that mean you're not assigning seats? Can I go sit by Angela?" Marie Firabello, the long-haired girl who had shoved her way into the room an eternity ago, called from her assigned seat in the second row and indicated her friend across the room.

"No, uh . . . " Barbara consulted her seating chart. "No, Marie, stay where you are. Sarah Larsen? Is Sarah here?"

"What a bitch!" Marie's reply to Barbara's refusal was clearly audible, but Barbara decided to let it go. By now the seven minutes left in the period seemed like forever.

Sarah Larsen raised her hand, and Barbara checked off her name. "Edward Minot?" Barbara looked around in vain and was about to pencil an X by that name when George Washington came around from behind her with his arms full of textbooks. "Yo!"

Barbara smiled and mustered the little good humor she felt she had left. "Nice to meet ya. Name's Mrs. Parker." Barbara checked off Edward's name and called out the next; with four minutes to go she had identified every student and taken attendance. She put the clipboard down on the desk and stood straight, facing the class.

"This is ninth-grade Afro-Asian studies. I am Mrs. Parker, and I am looking forward to a fruitful year. Tomorrow when you come into class, I want each of you to take the seat you are now sitting in, and I want you in your seats by the bell. I do not have many rules, but promptness is one of them." As she spoke, Barbara realized that she was again competing with the sounds of student conversations in the room. She reached for the pointer and whacked the desk. Heads turned; some students laughed, but most became quiet.

"This course will begin with the study of countries in the Middle East. If you look at the table of contents in your books, you will see that we are also going to study Africa, Asia, China, and Japan before the year is over. I think you will find these cultures . . . "

A scuffle and muted laughter distracted Barbara and captured the attention of the class, which turned en masse to look toward the sounds at the back of the room. Lincoln had apparently grabbed Edward's book when Edward tried to open it, and a page was ripped halfway out of the book.

"Lincoln, sit back in your seat. Keep your hands to yourself." Barbara refocused on the rest of the class. "I do not usually go over class rules explicitly with my high school students; most of my classes are old enough to behave. But I see that I must start by teaching you all how to act in high school. Tomorrow we will begin with a review of my class rules and what you can expect if you do not follow . . . "

The harsh air-horn sound of the bell drowned out Barbara's words, and the students rose as a unit to make their escape. Desks scraped linoleum, papers shuffled and books banged, and thirty-one students began uninhibited and unrestrained conversation. Barbara just watched them go.

• • •

Barbara heard the bell signaling the beginning of the seventh period and looked up from her preparations. About half of her twenty-eight students (she had mercifully lost two to transfers and one to the American Beauty Academy) were seated. Others cruised the room or hovered, talking and laughing, just outside the room.

Barbara marched purposefully toward the open door and waved the students into the room. "All right, inside. Names will go on the board. Let's move!" To herself, she thought, "Lord, I hate this class." With a sigh, she donned the mental armor she would need to face another day with these students.

After her dreadful first day, Barbara had spoken to friends who taught at the Littleton Middle School. They were astounded that so many difficult students had been placed in a single class. Barbara had to contend with several distinct groups of troublemakers, and since none of these groups looked to the others for leadership or direction, what worked to quiet one group seldom worked with the others.

In the two months that had passed since the first day of class, Barbara tightened control and established a routine. Rules were explained and posted: Come to class on time; come prepared; speak and listen respectfully. Barbara also introduced a luncheon detention system as a lever to enforce the rules, since school policy required an administrator's decision to impose after-school detention. Lunch detention was not nearly the deterrent for these kids that after-school detention would be, especially since many of the boys were now trying out for junior varsity teams and had practice after school. But it was the best she could do.

Barbara returned to the teacher's desk and stood behind it. "Good afternoon. I see notebooks out and open on only a few desks, and you know that being prepared in this class means being ready to take notes." Barbara was tempted to chastise the class further; it was early November, yet the students were still acting as if it were the first week of school. But she had discovered that nagging often backfired, and she tried to remain as businesslike as possible.

She glanced down at the notes she had spread on the desk in front of her. During this pause, students shuffled papers, retrieved notebooks, and whispered and giggled. Barbara began speaking loudly enough to be heard above this rustle. "This week we are going to begin our study of Iraq and Iran. Last week we completed our study of the history of this region, and you know that the Tigris and Euphrates rivers, which flow through modern-day Iraq, formed the cradle of civilization, which was . . . "

"Miz Parker, I don' got no pen." Lincoln Maxwell waved his hand wildly from his seat smack in the center of the room.

"Oh, Lincoln, again? All right, get up here." Lincoln uncoiled his long legs from underneath the tablet desk and strolled forward. When he reached her desk, Barbara handed him a pen from the top drawer and asked, "Where's your collateral?" She had begun "selling" supplies in this class as a relatively efficient way to minimize the delay caused by unprepared students. Students could use her supplies as long as they gave her something to hold as collateral; they would get their collateral back when they returned the borrowed item.

"Uh, like what?"

"Come on, Lincoln, you know the drill. You are wasting time." Barbara thought there might be some hope for Lincoln, but he was so often a source of delay and distraction in the class that she had little time to encourage the possibility. Lincoln came from a single-parent family, and when Barbara telephoned his mother, the woman mumbled something about her job and Lincoln's job and said that class matters were Barbara's job. Lincoln wasn't as blatant as some of the other characters in the class, but he was frequently a cause of disruption.

Behind Lincoln's back the class was getting more and more restless. "While we're at this, does anyone else need a pen?" Barbara had been interrupted more than once on many days, and she decided to get it over with. Two more students raised their hands, and she waved them forward.

"Here's a Whitney Houston tape," volunteered Angela as she tossed the cassette onto Barbara's desk.

"God, that's mine. Don't give her that!" Marie Firabello, whom Barbara had placed at the front desk in the center row, could clearly see the transactions going on at the teacher's desk.

Barbara ignored Marie and smiled at Angela. The two girls were friends, and Barbara thought Marie was a terrible influence on Angela's behavior in class. Barbara had decided on a divide-and-conquer strategy with the pair.

"Don't worry, Angela, you'll get it back," Barbara said as she met Angela's gaze with a genuine smile. "I already have that tape." Angela looked both surprised and impressed and smiled back at Barbara hesitatingly. "I'm not so bad after all, sweetheart," Barbara thought to herself as she watched Angela return to her seat.

When the other students had returned to their seats, Barbara tried to pick up the thread of her introduction. "All right. What was the name of the ancient civilization we first studied, which was located here?" As she spoke, Barbara pointed to Iraq on the map of the world that hung in front of the chalkboard. The class stared back at her in stony silence, except for two boys who were passing notes in the back of the room.

"Come on, people. We just had a test on this last week. Edward, what civilization was located at the Euphrates River?" Barbara addressed the question this time to George Washington, who was half of the pair passing notes in the back. She walked down the aisle toward him as she spoke.

Edward looked up blankly. "Uh, could you repeat the question?"

"Never mind, Edward. Give me the note." Barbara held out her hand, and the boy surrendered the torn slip of paper he had crumpled in his fist. She walked back to the front of the room and wrote Edward's and Robert's names in the leftmost corner of the board, beginning her lunch-detention list for the day. Then she turned to the class.

"Mesopotamia, class. Mesopotamia was the civilization we studied three weeks ago that was located where Iraq is today. Present-day Iraq is governed by . . ." Barbara began her introductory lecture, discouraged as usual by the class's lack of interest in participation. In other classes, Barbara sometimes used grouping, creative assignments, and projects in addition to lecturing to communicate content, but with this class any deviation invited bedlam. The students seemed to think that if she wasn't "telling," she wasn't really teaching, and they would take advantage of what they thought was an "easy" day.

So she told them about Iraq, making notes on the board as she spoke. The students were to copy the notes into their notebooks, and Barbara periodically spot-checked and graded their notebooks for neatness, thoroughness, and accuracy.

Barbara was discussing the hostilities between Iraq and Iran when Lincoln interrupted again.

"Miz Parker, Miz Parker?"

"Lincoln, raise your hand to speak in this class. I can see I'm going to have lots of company tomorrow." Barbara wrote Lincoln's name on the board alongside Edward, Robert, and the three others she had added to the list during her lecture.

"Oh, Jeez, Miz Parker, why you always pickin' on me? People's talkin' all the time in this class."

Barbara ignored Lincoln's complaint and tried to steer the class back to the topic. "Did you have a question about Iraq, Lincoln?"

"Well, yeah. Who was that Ayatollah guy, anyway?" Lincoln looked genuinely curious but a little embarrassed to be asking a "real" question.

Barbara was delighted. "You know who the Ayatollah was?" she asked with a sincere smile.

"Yeah—that religious nut. Who was he anyway?"

"The Ayatollah Khomeini was the religious and political leader of Iran until his death in 1989," replied Barbara. "That was a good question, Lincoln, and we will talk more about the Ayatollah starting on Wednesday, when we'll talk about Iran in more detail. Let's get back now to where we were in chapter 9 so that we can finish the introduction and do the worksheet on Iraq today."

After five more minutes, Barbara completed her comments and reached for the pile of worksheets in her book bag. "I want you to complete these individually while I walk around the room to look at your notebooks." A collective groan greeted this announcement, since several of the students hadn't opened a notebook during her overview (which was precisely why Barbara had decided to grade them today). She began handing papers to the students at the front desk of each row.

Marie Firabello, the student at the front of the middle row, was Barbara's biggest problem. Marie came from a large and extended Italian family; most of her relatives lived in North Littleton, and she had many cousins in the school. Barbara had spoken to Mrs. Firabello, who was timid and resigned and no help at all: "Oh, I know, Mrs. Parker. I'm having so much trouble with her—it's the age." Barbara suspected that Marie led a wild social life and was experimenting at least with liquor if not drugs.

Marie's challenges to Barbara's authority were so frequent and so brash that Barbara bluntly encouraged the girl to transfer out of the class. But Marie elected to stay and harass her.

Characteristically, Marie was ready when Barbara approached. "I don't want to do no dumb worksheet again. My boyfriend Rick is in your morning class, and he said they did some deal where they wrote a letter home from visiting some shrine or something?"

Marie was referring, Barbara knew, to her honors Afro-Asian studies class, which was as different from this class as night from day. There were only fourteen students in the class, and they were lively, interested, and motivated. They were a chapter ahead of the seventh-period class, studying the tenets of Islam, partly because they moved through material more quickly and partly because Barbara had abbreviated her coverage of ancient history with them in order to focus on current events in the Middle East. Rick had told Marie about the assignment in which the students pretended they were visiting Mecca and wrote home about their experiences.

"Marie, I'm glad Rick liked that assignment. Maybe we'll do that or something similar when we get to our study of the Moslem religion." Barbara smiled, handed Marie the worksheets for her row, and turned to move on.

"You think you're hot shit, don't you?" Marie snarled to Barbara's back. The ten or so students within earshot hooted and laughed, and Barbara began to feel real anger. "I hate that girl, and she hates me—period," she thought. Aloud, she said, "All right, Marie, that's it. Not another minute in my class."

"What'ya mean?" asked Marie indignantly.

"You may not stay in this class after that outburst. Stand in the hall, right now." Barbara indicated the door to Marie and crossed to the telephone, which hung on the wall by the door. Barbara waved Marie toward the hall as she lifted the receiver to call the office.

Marie slammed her books together in a show of bravado designed to mask her embarrassment and flounced out of the room. Barbara completed her conversation with the school secretary and then followed Marie outside to ensure that she stood where Barbara could see her through the open door until a staff member arrived.

After Marie was settled, Barbara returned to the classroom, resigned to the inevitable disruption that this episode had caused. As she reentered the room, a paper airplane made of the Iraq worksheet sailed by her head. Conversation and laughter swirled throughout the room. Several students were standing by the open windows, sailing airplanes outside and calling to friends.

"All right, ladies and gentlemen, quiet down." Barbara no longer hesitated to raise her voice to the level required to compete with this group. "We've had enough excitement for one day." Barbara crossed purposefully to the other side of the classroom and shooed the standing students to their seats, closing the windows as she did so. "Back to work. These worksheets will be collected in ten minutes so you'd better get busy."

"Hey, Babs, I ain't got no book. How'm I gonna do a worksheet?" cried Jackson loudly. Barbara sighed as she turned to the board and wrote Jackson's name in the detention space; then she retrieved her own book on her way back to his desk. Barbara really liked this•kid, but she couldn't tolerate disrespect. "My name is Mrs. Parker, and next time remember your book!" she said as she handed Jackson hers.

Barbara gradually got the students settled. As they worked on their task, she managed to review notebooks—or annotate the absence of same—for seven students. Soft conversation permeated the room, but that was all right. When completing worksheets, students were allowed to ask each other for help, as long as the answering student gave only the number of the page where the answer could be found rather than the answer itself. Barbara assumed that the hum of conversation out of her direct hearing was productive, for she hadn't the energy to mount a challenge now. She kept one eye on Marie, sulking in the hallway, at all times; it took about five minutes for Sandy, a school secretary, to come for the girl.

Barbara completed marking a notebook grade in her grade book and scanned the room. Lincoln, she saw, had fallen asleep. Barbara generally left Lincoln alone when he dozed off in class; the periods when he slept were among the class's more productive ones. "Probably drugs," Barbara thought sadly, remembering his expression of shy curiosity when he'd asked about Khomeini.

Without warning the bell rang and the students scrambled for the door. Lincoln lazily stretched and sat up, closed his book, and rose to go. Several incomplete worksheets littered desks and the floor, and two texts had been left in the classroom.

Barbara walked slowly to the front of the room and began to erase the board. Angela came to reclaim her tape; the others either forgot or didn't care about whatever they'd left in exchange. As Barbara watched Angela go and gazed at the empty room, a feeling of malaise crept upon her. She wondered unhappily what she might do to break this class "or when this class will break me."

Christie Raymond

*A mature woman in the first month of her first full-time position teaching mu-
sic in an elementary school loves the work as long as the children are singing,
but dislikes the school's emphasis on and her part in disciplining the students.
The case describes Christie's classroom teaching in detail as well as her after-
school bus duty.*

Christie Raymond liked to tell people she was a permanent substitute. "And
that," she thought, "is the least of the contradictions in my life."

Christie was two weeks into her first teaching assignment, as the music
teacher at Roosevelt Elementary School in Littleton. Since competition for jobs
in the area was fierce, she considered herself lucky to have stepped into this position mid-March, as the replacement for the regular teacher who was on ma-
ternity leave until the end of the school year. Christie fully intended to perform
well enough to secure a permanent position in the district the following fall.

But that meant resolving the basic dilemma that was slowly crystallizing as
an almost insurmountable roadblock. Christie was the product of a teacher-
preparation program that used case method and discussion teaching almost exclusively to train its enrollees. The legacy of that education, for Christie, was
an overriding conviction that all classroom events—particularly problems—
were her responsibility. Misbehavior, she believed, did not mean that the kids
were bad.

"So maybe that means I'm a bad teacher," Christie reflected ruefully as she
unlocked the music room door and shrugged off her coat. The room was in a
new wing of the school and was pleasant although small. Rooms for music, art,
remedial reading, counseling, and other special classes were about half the normal classroom size. Christie's room was not specifically designed for music; it
was simply a narrow space with closets and shelves at one end and windows
at the other. A chalkboard spanned one of the long walls and cement blocks the
other. A small bulletin board sporting singing spring flowers broke that wall's
monotony.

Christie shoved a plastic student chair out of the way with her knee in order to open the closet where she hung her coat and kept her personal things.
Mrs. Blatner, her predecessor, had arranged the thirty chairs around the perime-
ter of the room so that students sat in an oval; she had used this configuration
for all but the first and second graders, who sat in rows on the floor facing the

27

chalkboard. Christie had decided not to change this, at least initially, in order to minimize the transition when she arrived.

Christie reflexively glanced at her reflection in the small mirror inside her closet door—it seemed more and more like a gym locker—and wove around student chairs to get to her desk, which was tucked in a corner behind the oval. She withdrew her lesson plans for the day and her weekly schedule; she still had not memorized which classes she saw during which time slots on which days. She drew a deep breath. Fridays meant two groups of fifth graders followed by two classes of sixth graders and one fourth-grade class, each at half-hour intervals, and all before lunch. The afternoon meant switching gears for two second-grade and then two first-grade classes.

As she opened her lesson folder Christie also unfolded a note she'd picked up in the office on her way in. It was from one of the second-grade teachers: "Christie—We're going to the natural history museum on a field trip today, and I don't think we'll be back by 1:00. Enjoy the break!" Christie's first thought was that she'd get an hour for lunch. Her second thought was to feel guilty for her first.

The sound of shuffling feet signalled the approach of her first class, and Christie hurried across the room to meet them at the door. She smiled a greeting at the classroom teacher with the fleeting wish that she knew her new colleagues better, and she spoke to the students as they filed in. Christie was desperately trying to learn names, but since she saw 200 students each day it was a slow process. Mrs. Blatner had assigned seats around the oval in each class, and Christie hadn't tampered with the seating. She could have referred to her seating charts for names, but that felt awkward. So did asking students their names after two weeks on the job. It had occurred to Christie that the students might not even be sitting in their assigned seats; she had not specifically checked or taken attendance against the seating chart since her first meeting with each class. But half an hour seemed like so little time with each group, she hated to waste a third of it just to be sure they sat where assigned, particularly since she was ambivalent about assigned seating anyway. One example of her child-centered philosophy incubated by her teacher-preparation program was a desire to respect her students' individuality enough to let them sit where they chose. She hoped that her teaching would be so engaging that she would command their attention whether they sat by their friends or not.

This conflict aside, Christie was grateful that so far this particular class, which she also saw for a half hour on Wednesdays, had been fairly cooperative. She ushered in the last of the line and closed the classroom door. "Good morning," she said to the ring of faces around her. She crossed from the door to the center of the room, turned full circle to scan the settling children, and then walked back to the shelves. "Excuse me," she murmured to the several students whose chairs were in front of the shelves, reaching over them for the textbooks stacked above their heads. "Will you help me pass these out?" she asked the two students seated directly beneath her, as she pulled several books from the stack and then stepped back to permit them to stand. The pair, a boy named Josef and a girl whose name Christie couldn't remember, rose eagerly and began haphazardly distributing books around the oval.

Christie returned to "center circle" and spoke loudly in order to compete with the chatter and activity. "We're going to learn a new song this morning and then sing some old favorites. When you have a book, turn to page 2."

During the few minutes it took the two students to distribute texts and for the rest of the children to shuffle pages, Christie retrieved a xylophone from among the instruments on the shelves and placed it on the floor in the center of the circle. She wished that the room were large enough to keep the piano in it permanently; it was outside along the wall in the hallway, and she had wheeled it in only once. She tapped out the tune of the new song—"Hey, Diddle de Dum"—on the xylophone even though the group was not ready.

The music helped arrest their attention, and Christie spoke into the lull. "All right, people, listen to the melody of the first two lines, and then we'll sing them together." As she spoke she lifted her eyes from the score and promptly hit a wrong note; the dissonance was obvious. She grinned and added, "And if you hear me make what sounds like a goof, raise your hand!"

The class agreeably listened and then sang, and they repeated the song several times until Christie felt they might hum it in the halls. Christie was very grateful for one characteristic of Roosevelt students: they liked to sing. She remembered from her own school experience that it had been "uncool" to sing in music class, and she had dreaded the cajoling and threatening her teachers long ago had employed to get their students to participate. "I guess that starts in junior high," Christie thought as she sang with the class and paced the circle directing them. She did love to sing with children, and she loved to smile right into their eyes as they sang and smiled back.

The problem was when they were not singing. As they gave themselves a round of applause for "Hey, Diddle de Dum" and turned to page 60 for the next number, the inevitable talking and laughter began. Christie had to raise her voice to be heard above it. "That was terrific—you guys sound wonderful." The din quieted somewhat and she continued. "That's one point for sounding terrific!" A boy seated in front of the chalkboard turned without Christie's permission and marked a "1" on the board, circling it with a flourish. "Thank you, Jamal," Christie said. "You may be the scorekeeper today. Please turn around now and join us on page 60." Jamal bent to retrieve the book that had slid off his lap to the floor when he pivoted; several other students had let their books drop to the floor, and a few of them did not bother to retrieve them. "If I could only keep them singing continuously for thirty minutes," Christie mused. "They only behave when their mouths are busy singing."

That thought motivated her to cross to the record player and cue the recording of "The Eagle," a favorite song she was about to let them sing, rather than stop to chastise them for their chatter. As she walked she put a finger to her lips and raised the other hand in a "peace sign," the universal signal at this school for quiet. A few students responded as they had been taught, by quieting down and mimicking the gesture, but more ignored it. Every time Christie used this gesture, which she thought vaguely silly, she remembered her first day on the job, when students had been raising their hands right and left, and she had thought they wanted to speak. She would call on them and they would shake their heads, lower their arms, and look at her with indulgent disdain. It had been third period before a kind group of fourth graders had clued her in.

The sound of the prelude to "The Eagle" quieted the group—Christie had the volume up high—and as the first stanza began the class sang loudly in unison. This was indeed a lovely and well-loved song that Mrs. Blatner had taught them early in the year.

As they sang, Christie glanced at the list of class rules written in Mrs. Blatner's handwriting and posted on one side of the bulletin board:

1. Participate attentively.
2. Raise your hand to speak.
3. Follow directions carefully.
4. Play instruments only when instructed.
5. Show respect.
6. Keep your hands, feet, and materials to yourself.

Below this chart, another described the rewards and penalties agreed upon by all of the teachers who saw children for limited blocks on a rotation basis:

PROCEDURE

1. Warning
2. Time out—chair or hall
3. Office

REWARDS

1. Special helper award
2. 5 points/day
3. 100 points—class party

One of Christie's recurring uncertainties, which occupied a corner of her mind even as she directed and sang, was whether or not she should enforce these rules more stringently. Her decision of a split second earlier, for example, troubled her. She had chosen to quiet the class using music rather than insist upon silence by reminding them of Rules 1, 2, and 3. "Maybe I should have tried to single out egregious chatterboxes for the time-out chair," she thought. She knew that her classes were gradually getting the idea that she wouldn't ride them too hard, but becoming stern did not feel natural to her. Christie did not want the reputation of a pushover, but she truly believed that if she taught well enough—if her lessons were imaginative and engaging and if she respected her students and expected the best of them—they would be motivated to cooperate and to learn.

The class launched into the third verse, although about half the group had to scramble to find the right place. Following the repeats and *D.S. al Coda* directions in the score was a challenge complicated by the fact that this recording sometimes skipped at inopportune places. As everyone found their place and the song went on, Christie became aware of drumming behind her. She turned to see Robert tapping an accompanying rhythm on his plastic seat. Many students immediately looked at him and then glanced at Christie for a reaction even as they continued to sing. Christie walked toward him but did not admonish him. Rather, she smiled and nodded, matching his rhythm with her conducting hand as she neared his end of the oval.

When the song was complete, Christie congratulated the class on their performance. "You know, I have the best spot in the house. I get to stand here in the middle and hear you singing all around me. It's like the best stereo system in the world!" Christie turned to Robert. "And you sounded great! You beat out a nice rhythm, Robert." She saw surprise and then pleasure dance across Robert's face, and Christie privately congratulated herself. She'd guessed that he just wanted her attention, and she was glad she'd decided to give it to him positively.

Christie turned to the class. "Do you think we should have him do that on a drum this time?" She shared a smile with Robert as several of his classmates called out, "Sure!" "Yeah!" "Great!" Christie let the noise escalate as she motioned to the students sitting in front of the closet to move and reached in for a small tom-tom. She handed it to Robert with silent gratitude that her improvisation hadn't led to universal pleas for percussion instruments. She had only mustered the nerve to pass out the bells, drums, and tambourines once, and she had regretted it.

Robert immediately began tapping his instrument, and Christie put a gentle restraining hand on his forearm. "Only when we sing," she said softly. She then leaned over for her book, which she had laid on the floor when she bent to get the drum. "People, listen, please." She awkwardly held the book under her elbow as she used both hands for the Roosevelt sign for silence. "Sshh . . . I need to speak . . . I am waiting . . . " Gradually the class settled, and Christie paced from one hot spot of conversation to another with one hand in the air and the other to her lips, trying to use the physical proximity of her body to achieve attention. She hated this long ritual wait for attention. "I feel like a damn pinball ricocheting around this room," she thought as she crossed and recrossed the small room. Finally the group was quiet enough for her to be heard. She silenced a lone beat from Robert with as mean a glance as she'd mustered today, and she resumed the lesson. "Look at the score, people. Let's review the organization of this song before we sing it again. Who can tell the class how to follow the repeats and signs in this song?" Several hands went up, and a few eager students leaned half out of their chairs. Popping up from their chairs was an increasing phenomenon in this and all her classes. "Yes, Martha?" The chosen girl explained haltingly the order of verses and repeats, speaking so softly and hesitantly that it was difficult for Christie, let alone the other children, to hear. Christie tried not to let herself feel impatience as she waited for Martha to finish, but once Martha was halfway through her explanation and looked up inquiringly, Christie took over. "Good, right." Christie held her book open in front of her chest and paced around the room, pointing to the repeats and the coda so students could see. She reiterated and clarified what Martha had tried to explain. "OK? Everyone with the program?" Her sweeping glance caught several nods so she cued the recording again.

Robert's accompaniment on the drum was actually more pedestrian than his improvised tapping on the seat had been. He beat a loud, steady four/four time rather than the more intricate but appropriate rhythm he'd achieved with his fingertips. But Christie had liked the look on his face when she'd recognized his contribution as constructive, and when the song was over she praised his effort. She awarded the class another point of their possible five for their rendition and moved to her desk.

"Now we're going to play a game to review some of the musical symbols we've discussed this year." Christie had devised this game as a review and in order to determine how much music these ten-year-olds could read. She explained the rules over a low hum. The students were divided into two teams, and each team took turns identifying each musical symbol Christie displayed. If they got it right they got to make their mark on a tic-tac-toe game she drew on the board.

The game went well enough, in that the class did not become too disruptive even though they were not singing. Christie could tolerate a fairly high level of noise and even the jumping up from chairs, which she took for enthusiasm rather than misbehavior, did not bother her. Her patience was tried at one point, though, when one team erupted into loud argument not over the identification of a half-rest, which they recognized correctly, but over where to put their "X." After the student who had answered the question correctly and marked the first "X" sat down, another rushed from his seat, erased the mark, and moved it to a position blocking the "O" team from victory. The "Os," of course, erupted in objection.

Christie gratefully replaced her symbol sheets on her desk when the tic-tac-toe game ended in a draw and glanced at the wall clock to see that thirty seconds were left in the half hour. Without preamble she depressed "Play" on the tape recorder on her desk, and strains of "Lean on Me," which she'd cued earlier, filled the room. Christie's classroom management strategy was quickly evolving into constant singing. She intended to keep them warbling until she saw their teacher in the hall.

The rest of the morning went fairly smoothly, with each class of upper-grade children following basically the same lesson plan. Christie did deviate for her third group to let them sing a few requests; she firmly believed that music was to be enjoyed, and she loved it that students had favorite songs.

Her last class before lunch, though, was a particularly troublesome sixth-grade group with whom she constantly struggled for control. While the antics of other classes were generally limited to good-natured chatter and manageable infractions like Robert's drumming, this class had a tendency toward meanness. Christie often realized, for instance, from the smirks on the faces of children she faced that children on the other side of the circle, behind her back, were mimicking or otherwise making fun of her. She would swivel quickly, but usually they were too fast to get caught.

Today's rudeness was supplied by Roy, who inspired raucous laughter when Christie reached over his head to retrieve another record from the shelf. A girl to his left explained indignantly, "He plugged his nose when you reached over his head!" Christie didn't know if she was more offended by the girl's tattle-tale whine or the boy's rudeness, but she resorted to the time-out chair where Roy remained for the rest of the period. Christie was beginning to realize that she might soon have to put Roy and the other worst offenders in the hall chair to give them a chance to gain control by themselves or even to start sending kids to the office. But she worried that once in the hall they'd continue their misbehavior in public, and she thought the principal would think her ineffective if she had to rely on him for discipline. And, usually, by the time a class's naughtiness escalated beyond her tolerance, a glance at the clock told her only five more minutes, and she knew she could last. She'd just start them singing.

When Mrs. Peabody, this class's regular teacher, arrived to escort them, Christie had them complete their song and then motioned for them to move into a line. This was accomplished with noise, shoving, and commotion which Mrs. Peabody could clearly see through the window on the music room door. She opened it and hurried through the milling students without waiting for Christie's invitation.

"Boys and girls!" She spoke sharply and loudly, although it still took several seconds for the class to hear her over the din they'd created. She repeated herself several times, moving all the way into the room and walking up and down the ragged line. "Roy, quiet down. Betsy, that's enough. Jared, I still hear you," she called to a boy at the other end. "Boys and girls, this is not how we behave in line. This is not how Roosevelt sixth graders behave. Clarence, stop it now!" Mrs. Peabody kept up these constant remonstrations without even looking at Christie, who also began pacing the line and calling for quiet, somewhat meekly. When the line was almost silent, Mrs. Peabody stood back a step or two and scanned the group. Christie hadn't heard it, but apparently Mrs. Peabody detected a glance or a whisper from somewhere. "Macon, over there!" Mrs. Peabody gestured harshly with her thumb over her shoulder, indicating that he should leave the line and sit in a chair on the other side of the room. "Yes, you. Move!" To Christie, the group seemed quiet now, but Mrs. Peabody gestured or called to three other students and sat them across the room. The remaining twenty-two students were now silent and their line was straight. "All right, the rest of you may file directly out the doors to the playground." Christie knew that this group left her class for recess. "I want to speak to you four," Mrs. Peabody explained, rather unnecessarily, over her shoulder. "I want the rest of you straight outside and behave as you know how until you are outside!"

When the door had swung shut behind the silent marchers, Mrs. Peabody turned to face the seated Gang of Four. Christie sat in a student chair across the room—a spectator in her own classroom.

"Now, you people seem to have forgotten how we behave in line. I can't imagine why you have forgotten this since it is March and you have been at this school for seven years, but your behavior here was unacceptable." Christie marveled at how pinched and acerbic Mrs. Peabody could make that word. "Macon, do you know how to behave in line?" Macon nodded sullenly without looking at anyone. "Tell us how you behave in line."

"Face front, no talking, hands to yourself," he mumbled in a monotone. Christie observed that Macon seemed subservient on the surface. He was acting as humbled as Mrs. Peabody wanted. But she sensed subtle rebellion underneath. This eleven-year-old, Christie thought, would not learn self-control from this treatment. He just knew how to act self-effacing and cowed until he was out from under the direct gaze of insistent authority. Christie could just imagine his bravado once he reached the playground. She could also imagine his hostility eventually surfacing as adolescence erased his desire to even pretend compliance. Christie wanted to reach students like Macon, not harangue them.

Mrs. Peabody harbored no such apprehensions. "That's right, Macon," she responded. "Do the rest of you have any disagreement with what Macon said?" Silence, of course, was her response. "Do you all know how to behave in line?" Four heads bobbed. "All right, let's line up the way you know how." The four students seemed to tiptoe as they headed for the doorway and stood in line. Macon brought up the rear. "All right, you may proceed to the playground."

When the students were out the door, Mrs. Peabody, a young woman who had been teaching only a few years herself, turned to Christie almost as an afterthought. Christie still sat in a student chair near the door. Mrs. Peabody smiled graciously. "Gosh, I know they're tough," she said with a sincere warmth. "I have them all day and I know, they're tough!"

"Well, I learned something from watching you," Christie replied, hoping she didn't sound obsequious. In fact, she wasn't sure what she'd learned, but she filed it away for later analysis. "Thank you."

Mrs. Peabody flashed a smile, which bespoke a warmth as genuine as her earlier icy strictness, and marched out the door. Christie sat in the empty room and tried to muster some energy for her mercifully long lunch.

The afternoon was a relative pleasure. Christie had reflected more than once that the schedulers knew what they were doing when they put the compliant, cooperative, grateful little kids at the end of the day. One class of second graders was a bit disruptive, but nothing compared to the older classes. The first-graders who peopled Christie's final two periods were a particular pleasure—almost a balm to soften the memory of earlier cacophony. When the last teacher came to pick up her brood Christie felt fulfilled and purposeful; her sense of accomplishment and control had returned and she wanted to sweep the whole line of children up in a hug. She settled for whispering to one especially cute little boy, "You sang great today!" She was rewarded with a bright grin of pride.

As this class of six-year-old allies marched out, Christie grabbed her room key from her purse in the locker, locked the door, and headed up the hall. She smiled a warm hello to the principal, who happened to be coming her way with two boys in tow, and replied, "Terrific!" to his passing inquiry about the job. She made it to the gym five minutes before the final bell. Her Fridays ended with bus duty.

Christie waited in the cavernous room as students trickled, and then poured, in. She was grateful that the gym was carpeted, with grey, industrial carpeting painted over with court demarcations, for it muffled the noise of the arriving stampede. The other teacher assigned to Friday bus duty arrived shortly, and both women circulated among the students. "Sit down facing front!" Christie's counterpart intoned. "No talking! Face front! Quiet! You may do homework! Only look at your own things! Quiet! No talking!" This other teacher—Christie had met her last Friday for the first time and they had not exchanged names—kept up a constant stream of admonition. By unspoken agreement, she patrolled one end of the gym and Christie the other, pacing the rows of seated children rapidly forming behind large posted bus numbers affixed to the wall. Christie was silent and simply paced the rows, letting the other teacher's words speak for her and actually thinking that the woman was becoming annoying. Christie was careful not to trip over the lunch pails, backpacks, jackets, and opened notebooks which began to spill from the lines of cross-legged students. Within ten minutes there were at least two hundred children in the gym.

Patrolling her lines, Christie saw two students standing on the other side of the gym. While her fellow police-teacher castigated a third child, a young one, this time, Christie realized that Mrs. Whoever was making miscreants stand in place among the seated children. The last youngster singled out shifted with embarrassment and looked at her feet to avoid the weight of 400 eyes.

Christie had made it to the front of the bus lines at her end of the room and gazed out over the crowd. She was aware of the quietest of whispers between a few pairs of children, but those few conversations seemed purposeful. One within her direct line of sight was clearly consultation over schoolwork. Three boys way in the back had a three-ring binder full of baseball cards open, and all three were looking through it. While she did not see them talking Christie assumed that they were, but she did not mind. She thought these kids were showing remarkable patience as they waited to go home, especially since it was Friday.

"Max! Stand up!" Christie's satisfaction with this sea of cooperation was sundered by the sharp voice of Mrs. Other Teacher, who addressed a six-year-old sitting at the head of a line exactly in front of Christie's feet. Christie had not seen her fellow guard approach her side of the room, but now that she looked left she saw the woman within five feet of her. Ten or so lone standing students waved among the seated throng on the other woman's side of the room. "Maxwell, you cannot be quiet! Stand up! Come here!"

Christie knew the little boy seated at her feet; he was one of her treasured first graders. He looked fearfully around him to see if Mrs. Teacher was really addressing him and then stood slowly. Although Christie's focus had been over Max's head at the students in the back, she had not heard a sound from his position near her feet. Now she was sorry for his look of confusion, mingled with false bravado, and simultaneously embarrassed that Mrs. Other Teacher had felt the need to discipline a child right under Christie's nose.

"Maxwell, come here," Mrs. Mean Teacher commanded. The boy complied. "Get your things." Mrs. Teacher led the boy to one of two doorways, and Christie heard her instruct another adult at the threshold. "Will you take Maxwell . . . " The woman's voice faded and Christie lost the words. " . . . he CANNOT keep his mouth shut."

Christie resumed her pacing, now increasing her vigilance and gently reminding even the seemingly innocuous conversationalists that absolutely no talking was allowed. Eventually all but two bus loads of children had been called and Mrs. Other Teacher walked toward the remaining two lines. "City bus, what time does your bus arrive?"

"Five after four," several students replied.

The woman looked at the wall clock. "All right, you remaining lines may talk in a LOW whisper." She returned to the door to await the safety patrol which would escort the next line to the bus, and Christie smiled at the remaining children. As the final group left for the day, Christie stood at the door and quietly spoke to as many as she could, "Have a good weekend. . . . See you Monday. . . . So long."

It didn't take her long to straighten the room, cue a tape she planned to use

Monday, and gather her things. Christie was worn out by Friday and made it a short after-school stay. But as she locked the door and headed for her car, she knew that the events of the day would trouble her all weekend. She had to find the balance between the acrimonious, autocratic mien of Mrs. Other Teacher the Witch and her own good nature which was about to unleash a tidal wave of obstreperousness. Christie knew that a room full of 200 children was different from a classroom of twenty-five and that the least discussion in such a setting could quickly escalate out of control. She knew the parallels to her own teaching and classroom management strategies were limited. But still she could not help make some connections, particularly considering her varied and exhausting day. She kept seeing the expressions on Maxwell's and Macon's faces.

"Is the price of peace the dignity of my students?" Christie still believed, deep in her heart, that the reason she had behavior problems was that her teaching was not right, that she hadn't consistently captured her students' innate desire to learn and to make music. She wanted to treat them like individual, valuable human beings, not like interchangeable cogs in the school wheel who could be humbled and humiliated. But the need for control was gradually eclipsing her commitment to creativity and was sapping her energy and drive. "What my teaching program omitted," she thought, "was a course in being mean."

Melissa Reid

An enthusiastic young student teacher struggles to gain the respect and improve the behavior of her senior-level composition class and is devastated by one of her student's papers.

Melissa Reid, a student teacher in the English Department at Littleton High School, sat in the empty classroom working over and over in her mind a story one of her students had just turned in to her. The story, full of vindictiveness and hatred toward a young man's "unfair, worthless, nobody of a student teacher," shook Melissa to her core. She had never read a student's story so mean-spirited. Her student-teaching experience was turning into a nightmare.

Melissa was a twenty-three-year-old senior at Metropolitan University majoring in English Education. For as long as she could remember she had wanted to be a high school teacher, and during her last semester in college she was finally getting her chance in the classroom as a student teacher at Littleton High School. When she began, two months before, everything had gone well. Her cooperating teacher, Jane Maddox, had turned out to be someone to model—organized, creative, fair, intelligent, respected by her colleagues and students, and tolerant of and helpful to Melissa.

Melissa was responsible for student teaching in two tenth-grade American literature classes and three twelfth-grade composition courses taught by Jane Maddox. Jane had given Melissa her opening lesson plans to review at their first meeting, saying, "I want you to become familiar with the course, the students, and the curriculum. I want you to begin to teach classes yourself as soon as you feel you are ready."

Jane seemed open to Melissa's ideas and regularly sought Melissa's input on her lesson plans and encouraged her to implement new cooperative learning teaching strategies. By the end of the third week of school, Melissa had assumed classroom teaching responsibilities in two of the twelfth-grade composition classes.

The second-period average-level section of composition intrigued Melissa the most. Of the second-period twenty-six students, only two were girls and nineteen of the boys were Latino. This composition allowed Melissa to come to know the students more quickly. First, there were the two girls. Maria, a sweet, determined young woman, worked as hard as she could although she never earned more than a B in any work she turned in. Toni was her opposite. She constantly flirted, talked and generally disrupted class. Melissa had met privately with Toni, suggesting to her that her behavior seemed to be most disruptive when Toni didn't understand the material and offering to work with her on the more confusing assignments. Rather than accepting her offer, Toni seemed to resent Melissa's suggestions and continued to disrupt the class.

The five Anglo boys also had their unique characteristics. Brandon and Ted proved frustrating to her. Ted was a capable student but put in minimal effort. His friend, Brandon, frequently copied Ted's work and handed it in as his own. Michael, James, and Gregory were the class clowns. Michael was the most capable of the three, but didn't want his friends to know he could be an A student. James was reasonably bright, as well, but put in only enough effort to pass. Gregory didn't even try to succeed academically. He entertained the class by trying to flirt with Melissa and sidetracking his friends with endless attempts at humor.

Many of the remaining nineteen Latino students were Melissa's favorites. The two informal leaders, José and Eddie, were always respectful of Melissa and often kept their classmates in line during class. Jane Maddox had failed José in her class last year, and she commented regularly on the change in his behavior since Melissa had taken over the class. Jane attributed this to a conference Melissa had with José after the first journal assignment. From the journal Melissa learned that José had been devastated the previous semester by his grandfather's death. She had a discussion with José the next day and shared with him her own experience and sense of loss at her grandfather's death the year before. After that, José began to volunteer in class discussions, complete every homework assignment, and hand in extra-credit assignments.

Other students followed José's lead and began to accept Melissa. While Melissa was stern and firm in the classroom, she seemed able to establish a comfortable rapport with the students. Several began to confide their personal problems to her and to seek her advice about career and college plans.

By the eighth week of the semester, things seemed to be going really well. While students still challenged her and their behavior was not always close to what she would have liked, she felt more in control. Jane began to allow Melissa to teach entirely on her own. She started by leaving the room for ten-minute intervals, during which her absence was barely noticed. After a few days, she remained out of the room for the entire period. However, as Jane's regular absences became noticed, the second-period class would sometimes become disruptive.

For the last week of October, Melissa had planned a unit using horror and suspense stories, hoping the relation to Halloween would provide some interest. For the final project of the unit, each student was to write a suspense story. When Melissa introduced that particular requirement the day before the class was to begin writing, the students' reactions surprised her.

"Oh, man, I can't do this!" complained Brandon loudly.

"Yo, Miss Reid, you're making this way too hard," agreed José.

Other students chimed in with their responses, all of them negative.

Melissa waited for the grumbling to subside and responded. "Listen up.

You people are always selling yourselves short and always being surprised when you do well. It's time you have some confidence in your writing. All of you are doing very well, and if you stop complaining and start working we can get this completed a lot faster!"

"Well, I can't think of a story, Miss R. I don't even like horror stories," Toni griped.

"This is such a dumb assignment," muttered Brandon.

Melissa gave them an exasperated look. "OK, that's enough! We still have a lot to do today. If you quiet down and finish today's work, we can start generating some ideas to help you get started tomorrow."

Later, during lunch, she met with Jane to discuss her morning troubles. "If it's not the lesson, it's got to be me. I really haven't figured out how to manage this class. All they do is gripe about the lessons when you're not in the room."

"They do that, regardless. You know these kids," Jane responded. "Maybe you need to assert yourself. Remind them that you're in charge. Use some of those behavior modification ideas you talked to me about."

Melissa agreed and asked Jane to sit in on the first few minutes of class the following day. "I'd like you to be there to make sure I handle this well."

Melissa came to the class earlier the next day and used the time to write in large letters on the board:

GROUNDS FOR DETENTION

1. LEAVING YOUR SEAT WITHOUT PERMISSION
2. DISTRACTING YOUR NEIGHBORS
3. TALKING TO FRIENDS
4. CHEATING
5. USING INAPPROPRIATE LANGUAGE

After the class was seated, Melissa began. "I've noticed that many of you have forgotten the class rules Mrs. Maddox outlined on the first day of school. I've decided to refresh your memory of what they are, as well as what the punishment is for any infractions. If you do not understand what we are doing in class, that's OK. You can ask me. However, I will not hesitate to recommend you for detention if you cannot conduct yourselves properly. Does anyone have any questions?" Absolute quiet. No one responded. Mrs. Maddox gave a thumbs-up sign and a smile and quietly left the room.

For a half-hour, Melissa enjoyed an attentive classroom. Everyone participated in the brainstorming activity, even Toni.

"OK, we've come up with some great ideas for plots. Now let's discuss where these can be set. Where could our horror story take place?"

"A haunted house?" Toni volunteered.

"Good," said Melissa. "Let's start with that. Who can think of some adjectives to describe the house?"

"Creepy," "dark," "mysterious," "looming," answered a chorus of voices.

"Cheesy!" It was Gregory's voice.

Melissa turned toward him. "How does that fit, Greg?"

"Actually, that describes that restaurant I saw you working at, Miss R."

"You work in a restaurant, Miss Reid?" Carlos asked. "Which one? I'll come visit."

"*Peppe's Italiano*," yelled James.

"That's enough, guys. We're discussing setting, not my night job."

"I thought this was your job, Miss Reid. How come you work in a restaurant?" asked Maria.

"Teaching will be my entire career when I get a job," Melissa tried to explain. "Student teaching isn't a full-fledged job. It's like an internship."

"Like my beautician classes at the Hair Palace?" asked Toni.

"Right. Now can we get back to the lesson?"

"You mean you're not a real teacher?" asked Michael, almost too innocently.

Melissa took a deep breath. "Yes and no. I'm not officially on staff, but I am responsible for teaching you, and I can determine your grades. So, let's get back to work."

"Why? You just said you're not a real teacher. You can't do anything to us!" Gregory taunted.

"Yo, Miss R., that's diss! I'd give him detention if I were you," exclaimed Luis.

That's about enough! Do I have to go through that list again? I don't want to hear another word about waitressing or my status as a teacher. If you're really interested in how one becomes a teacher, I'll be happy to explain after school. For now, we're concentrating on writing a short story."

A paper airplane sailed across the room.

"You're testing my patience."

"What are you going to do to us?" yelled Michael. "You're only a dumb student teacher. You can't give us detention."

"Would you like to test me on that, Mr. O'Connell?" Melissa glared at him.

Michael responded by punching James in the arm and both laughed hysterically.

"This is your last chance. The two of you have been distracting this class all week. I advise you to knock it off right now!"

"What's the big deal? What's she getting so pissed off about?" Toni added.

"She's trying to be tough with us," sneered James.

"You don't know when to lay off, do you," José snarled at James. "I hope she gives your ass detention."

"Bullshit!" yelled James and Michael almost simultaneously.

"Well, two rules have been violated. I'm recommending both of you for detention by tomorrow," Melissa announced just as the bell rang. She watched Michael and James saunter out the door, laughing.

During lunch, she described the class to Jane as best she could. "This doesn't seem to be working. The kids will work for me only if you are in the room. I appreciate your confidence in me, letting me fly solo, but I think it would be better if you sat in during second period from now on."

Jane was quick to respond. "I disagree. The students have to learn that you're the teacher. If I come back now, they'll think they were right and you don't deserve the respect you're trying to achieve. I'd be doing you a disservice by returning. Now, come on. Let's file these detention referral forms at the dean's office before next period."

The next morning Melissa called the mothers of the two boys. Jane was at her side. Michael's mother was apologetic and offered to help in any way she could. James's mother, however, began to cry as soon as she heard the story. "This is the second call I've gotten about him this week. I know something is wrong with him, but I'm just at my wit's end. My husband thinks we ought to call a psychologist. What do you think?"

The call upset Melissa. "Do you think I was too hasty with the detention?" she asked Jane.

"Not at all." Jane was emphatic. "If you didn't do it now, they'd never believe you would do it."

Later, Melissa screwed up her courage and walked into the second-period classroom. Michael and James were already playfully roughing each other up.

"Didn't you guys learn your lesson yesterday? I hope your meeting with Dean Weiss will help you remember the rules of conduct for this class."

"You didn't really give us detention, did you?" asked James.

Standing in the doorway, Jane interrupted. "Yes, boys, we did. And we also spoke to your mothers this morning. So I would advise you to cut the nonsense and get to work." She turned and walked from the room.

James's face reddened. "You called my mother?"

"Yes. She'll talk to you when you get home." Melissa turned from James to address the rest of the class. "Now, let's start on your stories. I'm distributing a blank outline to help you get started. We've wasted enough time."

Melissa watched James with concern and confusion. He sat rigid in his desk, staring angrily at his papers. His jaw was set, his neck and face red. "He's a good kid." Melissa thought, trying to reassure herself. "He's a joker, no question, but not malicious." She remembered having spoken to him several weeks before about his laziness, and he had expressed an insecurity about his intelligence to her. He always finished his assignments quickly, without much effort. She tried to encourage him to spend more time, but he resisted. She wondered then about him, but now she was really concerned at his overreaction to this situation.

Walking over to him, Melissa pulled a chair next to his desk. "What's the matter, James? Did you think I was going to let yesterday slide by?"

He didn't respond. He just looked at her with disgust and turned away.

"Don't you want to talk about it?"

He remained silent.

"OK, have it your way. But you still owe me a rough draft of your story by the end of the period."

As the bell rang, the students gathered their things and left quickly, stopping only to place their stories on the front desk. James was the last to approach. Handing Melissa his story, he said, "I hope you enjoy reading this."

After he left, Melissa began to read the story. It was about the detention incident of the day before. Her character was described as an "unfair, worthless, nobody of a student teacher." The story described his friend as not minding the punishment, but himself as unforgiving and vowing revenge. His last words were, "When I go home tonight, I'm going to get my father's shotgun. I know just where he hides it. Then, tomorrow, I'll come into school real early, hide, and blow the bitch away."

Melissa's body went tense as she read his words. She felt an adrenaline rush of fear. Should she treat James's threat seriously? Could she just ignore it? She wasn't sure how to respond, but her instinctive feeling was to be frightened, really frightened.

PART TWO

Teaching and Learning

Therese Carmen

A first-grade teacher in her second year of teaching is presented with a new districtwide science curriculum that she finds unteachable.

Therese Carmen looked out over her class of seventeen first-graders and smiled as she watched them prepare for the science lesson.

"Maybe I love first-graders so much," she thought, "because they are so defenseless, so needy." Therese walked up one aisle and down the next, helping one child make a place for his math book in his desk and another fit her crayons back into their box. The children, while fidgety and noisy, were responsive to Therese's attention, and their immature behavior and dependence did not bother her.

Once all the desks were clear, Therese began her introduction to the lesson. She perched at the edge of her desk and held up several circles of different colors and sizes. "What are these?" she asked.

Some children responded. "Balls, dots. . . . "

"Yes, these look like balls and dots. What *shape* are they?" Therese emphasized the word *shape* and pointed to a bulletin board that showed circles, squares, and triangles.

"Circles." Most of the children called out the answer.

"Good. These are circles. Are all the circles the same?"

The children were quiet. Some were no longer watching Therese. William called out, "Some are different."

"How are they different, William?"

"Some are red."

"Yes, some are red. Let's put the red ones here." Therese put the red circles on the flannel board and looked out at her students. Three or four had opened their desks and were looking inside. Other students were bouncing in their seats or talking to the children next to them. Fewer than half of the students were watching Therese.

"It's this damn science curriculum," Therese thought as she observed her students. The curriculum seemed poorly matched to the needs of her students and to their maturity levels. It was written by a new science coordinator, Carol Miller, who had been appointed two years earlier. The elementary level of the

45

new science curriculum evolved from her work with a committee of elementary school teachers. It took them a year and two summers to produce the curriculum that Therese was now trying, unsuccessfully, to use. She wondered which of the teachers on the committee had decided that first-graders would be ready, in October, to begin a two-week unit on classification. Regardless, she plunged ahead.

"OK, everybody. Eyes front. Look at Miss Carmen. Rosa, Anthony, Jacob." As she called the names of several students, all the children turned toward her.

"William told us that some circles are different because they are red. Kelly, how are some other circles different?"

Kelly shook her head but didn't answer.

"Tiffany, do you know?"

"Some are round."

"Yes, all circles are round. How are they *different?*"

When none of the students responded, Therese answered her own question. "Some of the circles are yellow," she said as she placed the yellow circles underneath the red ones on the flannel board.

"What color do I have left?"

"Blue," several students responded.

"Good," Therese said enthusiastically as she put the blue circles on the flannel board. "We have circles that are different *colors*. What colors are they, class?"

A few children answered, but most were no longer looking at the teacher or the flannel board. Again, Therese thought about what a poor idea it was to teach classification in this way to first-grade children. It occurred to her that tomorrow might be better because the lesson involved animals, and she knew that the children would be more interested in animals than in circles.

But she had to get through today's lesson before she could introduce tomorrow's, so she again sought the children's attention to continue the discussion.

• • •

Two weeks after the classification unit, Therese went to see Marie Sharp, the third-grade teacher whose classroom was next to Therese's. Marie had been teaching for more than twenty years, and she was a wonderful resource for her new colleague. In the year and two months that she had been teaching, Therese had come to see Marie as her mentor: Marie was able to help when Therese wasn't sure what to do with a problem in her classroom, and Marie's years in the district had "sharpened her eye," so she was also Therese's source of advice about political issues. Since Therese considered her problems with the science curriculum as both academic and political, she was again turning to Marie for counsel.

Marie smiled as Therese walked into her classroom. "Hi, how was your weekend?"

Therese returned the greeting and went on: "Actually, my weekend was lousy, since you asked. I spent hours working on my lesson plans for the next science unit. I thought I'd get some help at the grade-level meeting on Friday, but I seem to be the only first-grade teacher having a problem with the curriculum. You should have heard the other teachers when Carol asked how

LITTLETON SCHOOL DISTRICT
K-2 Science Program

TEACHERS' GUIDE
Lesson Plan Ideas

Level: K-2 Science Curriculum
Topic: Science Skill—Classification
Week: 6

Lesson 1

Objective: To enable students to see that objects can be grouped and regrouped according to certain characteristics.

Method: In this lesson the teacher will model the skill of classification. Using one or more shapes familiar to the students, demonstrate how to sort the shape(s) by different characteristics. These characteristics may be color, size, texture, etc.

   Once the initial classification is understood, demonstrate that the shapes can be reclassified by another characteristic.

Lesson 2

Objective: To provide guided practice in grouping and regrouping objects according to certain characteristics.

Method: Using animal crackers (or something similar), have the students sort the animals by different characteristics, such as the number of legs, the length of tail, the humps on body, etc.

   Once the initial classification is understood, help the students to see that they can reclassify the shapes by a different characteristic.

Lesson 3

Objective: To give students independent practice in grouping and regrouping a variety of objects according to certain characteristics.

Method: Using materials available in the classroom (erasers, pencils, chalk, books, etc.), have the students sort the objects by different characteristics. These characteristics may be shape, size, color, usage, etc.

   Then have the students reclassify by another characteristic. Be sure that the students understand the characteristic that is common to each sorting.

teaching the new curriculum was going. I couldn't believe it. I can't be the only teacher having trouble with the lessons, but no one said anything except how well the classes were going. I was the only one to bring up problems."

   "What did you say?"

   "I explained that I felt some of the lessons were impractical for young students. Remember the lesson on classification I told you about? The manual called for the students to use animal crackers as part of the lesson. The kids ate the cookies as soon as I handed them out. I told that story."

"And what was the response?"

"That's just it. No one agreed with me. I said that I thought some of the units were unrealistic. I also talked about how elaborate some of the lessons were and how much time I'm spending making the 'props' I need for the lessons. First-grade classrooms aren't equipped for science. And not one other teacher said anything. I really felt like a fool."

Marie looked sympathetic, so Therese went on. "What's going on, Marie? Why the silence?"

"Don't forget, Therese, Carol's got a lot invested in the new science curriculum. She's still pretty new as science coordinator, and the science curriculum is her first big project. The teachers are probably changing the lessons. I'd guess that they've figured out how to work around the curriculum, and they're just not talking about it."

Marie's last comment actually gave Therese some relief. "Then I really don't have to use this curriculum," she thought to herself. "I can pretty much do what I want."

Therese hadn't told Marie that she was going to be observed the following week and that the principal had specifically told Therese that she wanted to see a science lesson. But now that she and Marie had talked, she knew what to do for the principal's visit. She was feeling better already.

Joyce Davidson

A high school English teacher is not making much progress with a remedial English class and is particularly concerned about an extremely shy student.

Joyce Davidson gazed unhappily at the folder of papers on the table in front of her and then raised her head to scan the study hall she was monitoring. Students were whispering quietly or working. Joyce knew that she should concentrate on grading the papers she had brought, but the next period was her ninth-period remedial English class, and she often used this study hall just to regroup mentally and try to find the reserves of energy she would need to manage the class. "This just wasn't such a problem last year," Joyce thought ruefully. "Maybe Beth's lack of participation is getting to me."

This was Joyce's second year teaching in the English department at Littleton High School. Joyce enjoyed her job partly because it was demanding, but dealing with this particular English class for ninth- and tenth-graders was a special challenge. The class was loud and boisterous and tough to control, except for one quiet little girl. Beth Martin had been in the same class with Joyce last year, as had six others of her thirteen students, but this year the child seemed increasingly withdrawn and indifferent. Joyce herself was an outgoing, gregarious person, and a withdrawn child caused her concern.

"Well, for one thing," Joyce thought, "last year I had this class first period. Ninth period is the worst time of day for everyone." It wasn't so much that Beth was tired or difficult at the end of the day; it was that the rest of the class was so much louder and intimidating. "At 7:45 in the morning they've hardly woken up," Joyce thought with a smile.

Beth was a short blond girl of 16. She had a slow gait and a timid manner; she entered the classroom every afternoon with her books held tight to her chest as if it were the first day of class. All the students in Joyce's class were reading well below grade level, but Beth seemed to have the most difficulty. Most of the rest of the class exhibited more behavior problems than academic ones. Beth's file reported a slight speech delay, which Joyce thought was a considerable understatement, since Beth almost never spoke in Joyce's class. Beth was not an independent thinker and worked best on worksheets or with rote material. Her

49

Littleton High School

Class: **Tenth-grade English**
Teacher: **Joyce Davidson**
Period: **Ninth**

Name	End of ninth grade MAT scores*	Total reading†	Reading comprehension‡	Vocabulary‡
Antiero, Angela	33	4	6.7	6.9
Ayagari, Mahon-Rao	55	6	7.9	8.1
Booth, David	31	4	6.4	5.5
Bowen, Harold	9	2	5.0	5.1
Diaz, Ernesto	18	3	5.8	5.0
Espitia, Luis	49	5	7.7	7.8
Fernandez, Carlos	8	1	4.9	4.9
Lawson, Jesse	28	3	6.0	6.1
Martin, Elizabeth	5	1	4.4	4.6
Maxwell, Leon	30	2	5.1	5.2
Sanchez, Pedro	10	2	5.4	5.8
Washington, Tyrone	35	4	6.0	6.4
Wilson, Anton	11	2	5.5	5.6

*Metropolitan Achievement Test scores, reported in percentiles.
†Stanine scores: 1 = low, 5 = average, 9 = high
‡Grade-equivalent scores: 6.7 means seventh month of sixth grade

reading grade level was about 4.5, and her written work matched her reading level.

Joyce thought that Beth was immature in her outside activities as well and that this contributed to her isolation. Beth seemed to be overprotected by her parents. Joyce's mental image of Beth being picked up at the bus stop by her mother, going home, having a snack, and watching cartoons crystalized for her the challenge of getting this 16-year-old girl to interact with a class full of loud and rambunctious teenagers in order to learn.

Last year, Joyce had wondered whether assignment to a special education class might serve Beth better than the remedial track she was now in. She had inquired about Beth's placement and learned that Beth had been evaluated in middle school and that the test results indicated that she was not eligible for special services. Joyce agreed in principle with the concept of regular classroom instruction whenever possible, and she had vowed to make Beth's time in her class productive.

There were four levels of classes in most academic subjects at Littleton High, which the administration tried not to refer to as "tracks." Joyce's ninth-period English class was a remedial class. Most of the students in it were in remedial classes all day except for art, music, and gym, which were not grouped by ability. Joyce's class this year was also larger than the one in which Beth had been placed last year: Last year Joyce had had only ten students in the sophomore remedial English class. She knew that had been a real luxury; in fact, she was lucky to have only thirteen students this year. The class was made up of eleven boys and two girls; the other girl was as flamboyant and aggressive as Beth was reserved. Angela was Peruvian and, at 17, was one of the oldest students in the class. She had confided to Joyce that when she first arrived in the United States four years ago, she had been as quiet and shy as Beth, a claim Joyce thought preposterous. Angela was Beth's antithesis.

The boys in the class were an engaging mixture of personalities: enthusiastic, friendly, loud, and occasionally hyperactive. There was one other shy student in the class, but his reserve was very different from Beth's. Rao, who was West Indian, was intellectually alert and conscientious; his assignment to Joyce's class was the result of difficulty with English as a second language. Rao's withdrawal was probably due to fear of being drawn into misbehavior by his peers; Beth's isolation seemed to be the result of indifference.

The boys in Joyce's class were black or Hispanic. All were sophisticated and worldly; their poor reading skills had not prevented them from becoming social creatures who participated actively in life outside the school. This participation was not all positive: Pedro, for example, was fond of flashing wads of bills and occasionally wore a beeper in class.

Joyce worked hard to ensure that her students were comfortable in her class so that they could participate freely. While the price of this atmosphere was an occasional behavior problem, Joyce felt that it was crucial to establish a positive, risk-free climate if her students were to learn.

Joyce actually jumped when the bell rang signaling the end of the eighth period, and she thought once again what an irritating sound it was. She sighed as she stuffed her unopened folders into her book bag and headed toward ninth-period English. "Still all questions and no answers," she thought.

Joyce opened the solid, heavy door to the small classroom and immediately saw Beth sitting at a desk. Beth was always the first to arrive. "Hi, Beth," Joyce said with a smile. "How was your weekend?"

Beth did not answer, at least not audibly, and Joyce quickly began setting out materials for the day's lesson. Not having a room permanently assigned made teaching much more difficult. Joyce could not decorate, post students' work, or otherwise personalize the classroom. The L-shaped room was longer than it was wide, making seating difficult, and it seemed crowded even though furnished with only fifteen desks. By ninth period, the desks were awry, the wastebaskets were full, and the air was thick with the smell of lunch recently served in the cafeteria next door.

For weeks, Joyce's class had been working on nouns and adjectives: What are they? How are they identified? How are they used? Joyce was permitted some latitude in course content, and she tried to choose reading and writing activities over grammar whenever she could. But at least two-thirds of the sophomore curriculum was mandated, and parts of speech were unavoidable. Joyce was having trouble getting her students to focus on these lessons, and she found it difficult to make the material interesting and meaningful.

Today, Joyce planned to review the subject *again* and then group the students for an exercise designed to give them practice in what they had been learning. As usual, she had tried to design a lesson that would hold her students' attention in spite of their distractibility and boisterousness.

"OK, settle down and listen up," Joyce said loudly enough to be heard as soon as the bell rang and the last student let the door slam behind him. "I know everyone had a good weekend, but it's time to get to work!"

"Yo, Miss D, what are those magazines for?" called a tall boy who lounged comfortably at a desk by the window.

"They're for you, Tyrone, and your teammate, after you come up here to the board and help me out," replied Joyce with a big smile. General laughter greeted Joyce's invitation to Tyrone, as he groaned and affected great reluctance. In fact, it was no easy matter for him to pull his long, powerful legs from beneath the desk to come to the board.

When Tyrone was beside her, Joyce handed him the chalk and said, "Write an example of a noun, Tyrone."

Tyrone took the chalk and turned to look at Joyce. "I can't think of no noun."

"Sure you can, nouns are everywhere." Joyce gestured widely with her arm.

Tyrone's eyes followed Joyce's gesture, and then they lit up as an idea occurred to him. Joyce just loved seeing that look on her students' faces. Tyrone turned to the board and wrote the word *air* with a flourish. Looking pleased with himself, he pivoted to return to his seat. "Wait, Tyrone. That's fine," said Joyce, and she put out a hand to keep him with her. He rolled his eyes good-naturedly. Joyce knew he loved the spotlight. She turned her attention to the class. "*Air*—that's a noun, right? Luis, tell Tyrone a sentence to write using this noun."

Luis's desk was at the back of the classroom, and he was leaning back in his chair, pulling at the cord of the telephone on the wall near the door. He pulled it and let it snap back a few times as he thought. "Tyrone is a air head," he finally said solemnly. The class erupted in laughter, and Tyrone threw the chalk in Luis's direction as he, too, laughed.

Joyce was smiling even as she tried not to laugh. She mentally rehearsed the sentence in her head and contemplated a response. She realized that Luis had stumbled upon one of the few possible usages of the word *air* as an adjective, and she could not resist the urge to use his contribution positively. Joyce knew she risked fanning the fire with these students, since insults were the "stuff" of their constant confrontations, but she couldn't let the opportunity pass.

"Write it," she said to Tyrone, gesturing toward the board and handing him a new piece of chalk. Her students loved to write with new, long pieces of chalk.

"No way," Tyrone laughed, and he refused the chalk. Joyce was laughing with her students as she went to the board herself and wrote "Mr. X is an" and "head" around the word *air,* which Tyrone had already supplied. As Joyce turned to the class, the students were still laughing. Joyce held up her hand and waited, indicating to Tyrone with her eyes that he could return to his seat. In a minute the class quieted down enough for her to be heard.

"*Air* in this sentence is not a noun, Luis," Joyce said matter of factly. "What is it?"

Luis looked at Joyce blankly. Joyce persisted. "Luis, how is the word *air* used in your sentence?"

Luis looked around, as if trying to find the answer on the walls or the ceiling, and Joyce waited. Slowing herself down had been one of her biggest challenges in this job, but she had learned. Only when Luis reached for the phone cord again did Joyce help him out. "Luis, look at the board." When he was looking up, she continued. "Everyone look at the board. Is air what the sentence is talking about? Luis, what is the sentence talking about?"

"Mr. X," Luis replied slowly. He and the other students were following Joyce now. Joyce saw that Beth was looking in her direction also, and Joyce thought about calling on her. But it was unlikely that Beth would respond, and these moments came too rarely with this class to break her momentum now.

"Right!" Joyce exclaimed. "*Mr. X* is one noun in the sentence. We know it's a noun because it's the name of someone." Joyce underlined *Mr. X* and continued. "What else is the sentence talking about? What other word is a noun? Angela?"

"Head!" Angela shouted. The class laughed at Angela's style as much as at her answer, and Joyce waited again.

"OK," Joyce said when she could be heard. "You are right. *Head* is a noun because it is the name of something. Now, listen, here it comes. What kind of head? David. What kind of head?"

"Air head!" David answered.

"Right. Luis, what is the word *air* in this sentence? It tells us what kind of head we are talking about. How is the word *air* used in the sentence?"

Luis was really concentrating as he looked at the sentence. "It's an adjective!" he said. The class was looking at the board with him.

"Right!" Joyce smiled. She sat on the corner of the teacher's desk and let her shoulders drop a little. Her relaxation seemed to touch the class. As the students sat back in their chairs, she repeated Luis's words. "*Air* is an adjective in this sentence, not a noun. We are not talking about air in this sentence. *Air* tells us about the word after it. *Air* describes the next word; it modifies the next word. *Air* is an adjective here. Usually, in most sentences, *air* is a noun, but in the sentence Luis made up, *air* is an adjective."

Joyce got up and went to the board. She erased the sentence and wrote "Beth flies through the air." "Beth, where is a noun in this sentence? Beth?"

Beth was looking at Joyce, and Joyce made eye contact, but she was not sure the girl had heard her. Tyrone called out from the rear, "*Beth* is a noun."

"I want to hear from Beth," Joyce said. "Let's give each other time to answer. Beth, Tyrone was right. The word *Beth* in this sentence is a noun—a proper noun because it is a person's name. What is another noun in this sentence?" Joyce leaned a little toward Beth as she held her left hand under the sentence on the board. This time the class waited, although as the seconds passed, the inevitable whispering, shuffling, and laughing began. Finally Beth softly said, "I can't fly."

As her class broke into new peals of laughter, Joyce glanced at the clock. By now she was running short on time. The class's earlier laughter had been for a good cause, but it was time-consuming. Joyce knew that Beth was not trying to be obtuse, but she was slowing the class down.

"Quiet down," Joyce admonished. She took a deep breath. "Beth, pretend you can fly. Think about the sentence here on the board. Your name, the word

Beth [Joyce underlined the word *Beth* as she spoke], is one noun in this sentence. What other word in the sentence is a noun?"

Beth looked a long time at the board. Noises from outside the room filtered in. (The school dismissed some students early to catch buses, and the bus stop was right outside the classroom windows.) Joyce prayed she wouldn't have to wait so long that the rest of the class would start throwing things at the kids outside.

Finally Beth spoke, so softly that Joyce had to read her lips to hear her. "Air?"

"Louder, Beth. Say it so that the class can hear you."

"Air?" Beth repeated, still hesitatingly.

"Right! Air! *Air* is a noun in this sentence. It was an adjective in the sentence before." Joyce scanned the class to look for expressions of comprehension or confusion. "Do you all understand?"

Sure enough, the delay in waiting for Beth to answer had broken the other students' train of thought. Joyce saw a few quizzical looks and a few expressions of understanding, but the rest of her class had forgotten the topic. Joyce felt frustrated: Learning had been happening a moment before, but now she had lost the students. Joyce seldom proceeded without ensuring complete understanding, but she had to move on if she was to get her next activity done.

"Now we are going to pair off. I want each of you to work with one other person. We have a project to do about nouns and adjectives." Joyce began to pair students sitting next to one another. "Angela, you work with Pedro. Beth, you work with Tyrone. Luis . . ."

"I don't wanna work with her," Tyrone interrupted.

Joyce used grouping often in her class, and she usually allowed students to work with whomever they chose, especially when they were working in pairs. Most of the time the students were fairly tolerant of Beth, seeming to recognize her differences, but they did not socialize with her and seldom wanted to work with her. Joyce did not tolerate rudeness, but Beth was often so blank and indifferent that Joyce thought simple remarks like Tyrone's went right over her head. In any event, Joyce elected not to challenge Tyrone. "You may work with whomever you want." Tyrone happily rose and walked over to Luis. Their earlier exchange had apparently made them fast friends.

"Miss Bartino, will you please work with Beth?" Joyce indicated Tyrone's vacant seat for her assistant, who had been watching quietly from the back of the room. Joyce often used Anita Bartino to work individually with Beth, anyway. When they were working in pairs, Joyce needed Anita to round out the number, and Beth certainly needed the extra attention.

Joyce got all the students teamed and explained their assignment. They were to search for examples of nouns or adjectives in the magazines she had brought and were to cut them out and paste them onto construction paper in an appropriate arrangement or design. Joyce gave the students some examples, showing them how they could choose just nouns, just adjectives, or nouns and adjectives all on a certain theme (all about fashion, for instance). She told them that supplies—scissors, glue, markers, crayons—were available at the center of the room on a supply table. Joyce usually orchestrated projects in this way so that the entire class was required to cooperate in order for individual teams to obtain materials.

The students were more or less occupied with their task as Joyce walked from pair to pair. She worked for a time with Tyrone and Luis, and then she turned and saw Beth sitting alone, looking quietly at the magazine on her desk. Anita had partially turned her chair away from Beth and was answering a question for another group.

Joyce approached the girl and spoke softly. "Beth, do you need something?"

Beth looked at Joyce without much expression. "Scissors," she answered softly.

"You know we have to share materials in this class, Beth," Joyce said. Beth did not reply. "How do you get supplies that you need?"

"Ask?" Beth asked quietly.

"That's right, Beth," Joyce replied. "Ask the other kids for what you need. We have to share."

Beth looked doubtfully at Joyce and then spoke in the general direction of the rest of the class. "Can I have the scissors, please?"

"Louder, Beth" persisted Joyce. "You have to speak up to get what you want in this class." Anita turned away from the other group and began to move her chair toward Beth, but Joyce stopped her with a glance. Beth remained mute.

"Beth, this is a loud, noisy class. You have to talk loud enough for the others to hear you and ask them for what you need. Just ask again so that they can hear you."

Finally Beth repeated the phrase. "Can I have the scissors?" Her voice was still soft, but Pedro, her nearest neighbor, heard her. He handed a pair of scissors back to Beth without turning around.

"There! See!" Joyce spoke brightly, verbalizing her pleasure with Beth's accomplishment. "You just have to ask!" Joyce nodded toward Anita, who then moved her chair around to work with Beth.

Joyce walked back to the front of the room to collect the students' work and dismiss the class. She was really worried about Beth. Joyce thought her approach and personal style were beginning to work for the rest of the students, and she did not want to jeopardize their progress. But after a year and a quarter she still had not found the combination that would unlock Beth's mind and bring her into the group.

Alice Peterson

An experienced elementary school teacher is having problems with a prefirst-grade class in which every student brings unique (and difficult) problems into the classroom, leading her to wonder if she is reaching anyone.

Alice Peterson drove to work mentally agonizing over the same dilemma that faced her every school day: how to help her students learn. Alice taught a class of prefirst-grade children at the Mason Elementary School in Eastvale, a small town outside Chicago. This year was proving to be the most challenging and the most frustrating of Alice's twenty-eight-year career.

The Eastvale school district served a heterogeneous school population. More than 40 percent of the students were black or Hispanic, and about a quarter of the school population qualified for the free or reduced-cost lunch program. There were also many students from middle- or upper-middle-class families.

Three years ago the school district introduced a prefirst class in an attempt to serve developmentally latent children. Over the past ten years or so, the kindergarten curriculum had become more academic, with less attention paid to readiness and group social skills. For some children, an academic kindergarten was not the best preparation for formal schooling; they needed more time before they faced the demands of first grade. On the basis of testing and the recommendations of their kindergarten teacher, such children were placed in a prefirst class rather than first grade at the end of their kindergarten year.

Alice held strong opinions about the prefirst concept, both as intended and as actualized. If it was used properly by parents and educators together, she knew that the opportunity to spend another year growing and developing could work magic for some children.

But many parents, particularly well-educated ones, saw assignment to prefirst grade as an indication of failure; they argued adamantly to have their children placed in first grade, despite test scores and teacher recommendations. Parents' attitudes were crucial to the success of this program. If a child detected a negative attitude about prefirst grade from his or her parents, the child would be likely to develop the same attitude and might benefit less from the extra year. Accordingly, the district often accommodated parents' wishes.

Since it was typically the middle-class parents who rejected the prefirst class for their children, the students actually placed in these classes often came from poor, disadvantaged, minority backgrounds. Furthermore, since there was only one prefirst class in any school, all the least mature 6-year-olds were placed in one classroom rather than distributed throughout several first-grade rooms. Despite these two drawbacks, Alice initially had seen the prefirst assignment as a challenge and believed that she could make a difference in these children's lives.

Alice tried to ensure that her students developed a sense of confidence and self-worth, which the experience of "failing kindergarten" had already undermined. She began the school year using kindergarten curriculum and in January began to introduce first-grade materials. In this way, she hoped that her students would have a head start relative to their peers when they entered first grade the following fall. Alice had followed her game plan this year and started using more advanced materials after Christmas, but she knew it wasn't working. This class just didn't seem ready for more advanced academic work.

Minority children were usually overrepresented in prefirst classes, but the presence of a few white students assured Alice that placement was based on age, maturity, or stage of development rather than race. This year, however, Alice thought her class configuration made teaching almost impossible. The two white children in her class were not simply immature; they each had serious deficits, physically, mentally, and emotionally. Therefore, the other children, all of whom were black or Hispanic, saw the "normal" white children being promoted to first grade and saw themselves placed in prefirst with other minorities or with white children who had obvious handicaps. Alice felt sure that these children had internalized a negative self-image as a result. Because they believed that they were dumber, slower, and naughtier than the other children in the school, Alice thought, they performed below their individual potential and ability.

At 6 years of age, these children were still enthusiastic and endearing; they each very much wanted to learn to read, for instance. But their home environments and individual histories had made them emotionally needy, and they often "acted out" to gain attention. Alice knew that children this age all craved a teacher's attention, but most children wanted to be noticed for positive things. It seemed to Alice that her students this year were happy even with negative attention. As a result, her class was often rowdy, rude, and inattentive.

Alice turned into the staff parking lot, which was framed by mounds of dirty snow plowed aside after last week's storm. As usual, she was the first to arrive. The February morning was cold, and Alice walked briskly to escape the chill. She unlocked the school door and headed toward room 105.

As she unlocked the door to her classroom, Alice was already beginning to rehearse the opening minutes of the phonics lesson she was going to conduct with her students this morning. She tried to arrive at least an hour and a half early every morning in order to finalize preparations for the day's instruction. Throughout her career Alice had invested long hours in order to teach effectively, but the fact that the results this year were so disappointing made expending the effort increasingly difficult.

Alice Peterson began her career teaching in the Chicago school system, and after three years she moved to Eastvale. She had taught every elementary grade, although most of her experience was in third and fourth grades and kindergarten. She accepted the position teaching prefirst at Mason last year because she was promised flexibility and control over the choice of curriculum. Increasingly, however, Alice felt that even though she had the flexibility to design unique instruction, she did not have the time.

Alice took off her coat and sat down behind her desk in the back of the room. She scanned the empty classroom, which she could view clearly from this vantage point, and enjoyed the peace and quiet, which would end soon.

Alice had carefully designed the arrangement of furniture and supplies in the room. The twelve desks at which the children sat for instruction all faced the front of the room, where they could see only the chalkboard and an alphabet banner above that. All the toys, art supplies, and decorations, as well as the bulletin board, were in the back of the room near the play rug. Alice had planned the room in this way in order to minimize distractions for the children as they sat at their desks and listened to lessons. For the same reason, she had their desks arranged in four rows of three each, far enough apart to minimize each child's opportunity to irritate others. Alice would have liked to group the children at tables in order to foster better cooperation and communication, but she was sure that this would only lead to arguments or collusive misbehavior.

Alice knew that she should review her objectives for the morning's lesson, but she sat instead just looking at those twelve desks, so neatly aligned and soon to be thoroughly askew. She let her mind wander, thinking of the children as she looked at their desks.

Barry sat at the front of the classroom, at the desk to Alice's right as she faced the students. She had purposely placed Barry at arm's reach so that she could physically assist him if necessary. Barry was one of the two white children in the class, and he had muscular dystrophy. Although he could walk, he was much slower than the other children and fell down five to ten times each day. He had been placed at Mason because it was the only elementary school in the district without stairs.

Alice thought Barry was a spoiled brat. He was self-centered and did not adjust well to the social environment of the classroom. Barry did not display much respect for authority and was very headstrong. He had temper tantrums when challenged, complete with screaming and kicking.

Yet Alice was most concerned for his safety. Barry would topple over with the slightest shove from a classmate, and Alice found herself constantly maneuvering to be near him in order to catch him if he fell. This, of course, was an unacceptable situation, since the frequently rowdy misbehavior of the other students also demanded her physical proximity.

Realizing this, Alice had requested an aide for Barry after the first two days of the school year. Yesterday the aide had arrived, but Anna Brown was only 17 and the mother of an infant. After her first day Alice was concerned that Anna would be more of a distraction than a help. In any event Alice would have to take time to train her explicitly in what she needed her to do. "They'll put me on the committee to hire the principal, but they won't give me a say in hiring my own aide," Alice thought as she gazed at Barry's desk.

Theresa sat at the desk behind Barry; she was a quiet, cooperative girl who generally did as she was asked. Alice's thoughts, though, quickly skipped to the last desk in the row. In a few minutes, she knew, Peter would sit there, constantly disrupting class, calling out, and harassing her.

Peter inspired Alice's sympathy when she thought about him objectively and out of the context of his misdeeds. He was a black 6-year-old whose family situation was truly sad. Peter's mother was handicapped. He was cared for by his aunt, but she could not speak because of a stroke. Peter had two brothers, one of whom was recently jailed; the other one was in the army. Peter was very attached to his 18-year-old sister, but she was living in a halfway house for drug abusers.

Peter was a chronic behavior problem. He was loud and impulsive and had developed few inner controls. He was very jealous of other children and tended to bully them. His sense of humor and his affection for adults were the traits that kept Alice trying with Peter. She had found that he responded to physical affection and to gentle teasing, and she hoped to help him develop the self-discipline he would need to succeed in school and in life.

Shoma sat next to Peter, in the last desk of the next row. Alice nearly grimaced when she thought of this child. Shoma represented an escalating problem for Alice. She was a black Haitian-American who was very tall and looked about 8 years old even though she was only 6. She was jumpy and easily distracted and displayed little interest in schoolwork. Alice thought of Shoma as an angry child. Shoma often reacted defiantly to Alice's instructions, and Alice worried about the constant frown on the child's face. Shoma's mother had so far been unavailable for a conference in spite of Alice's repeated attempts to solicit her help.

Alice's gaze continued along the desks at the rear of each row. Don, the other white child in the class, sat at the desk to Shoma's right. Alice thought Don might have a neurological problem. He was deficient in his small motor skills—he couldn't hold a pencil correctly, for instance—and he just didn't seem to make mental connections. All his work was rote, with no evidence of thinking taking place at all. Even in behavioral issues, Alice could not reach him or break through to reason with him. It was not that he was purposely dense; he seemed unable to understand the relationship between his behavior and consequences. Alice would never forget the time when Don screamed an obscenity at another child, was sent to the office, and still asked for a star at the end of the day. Alice had been unable to communicate to him the relationship between his behavior in the morning and his reward in the afternoon.

Don's parents were trying not to panic over their obviously handicapped oldest child, Alice thought. Don had two sisters, ages 4 and 3, who could do more than he, and this was having an impact on Don's self-confidence. There had been some discussions between Don's parents and school personnel about special testing at a private rehabilitation center in town, but they were all concerned about the messages that this additional testing would send to an already insecure child.

Alice realized that special education placement was a possibility for Don, but she hoped, along with his parents, that this could be prevented. In fact, Alice knew that prefirst was in some instances an attempt to make the regular curriculum and the mainstream system work for children on the edge. She wanted very much to make it work for her students.

Thinking about special education made Alice's mind wander to Luis, who sat in the desk next to Don. Luis was Hispanic, and even though English was spoken in his home, he was practically nonverbal and very shy. Alice had heard rumors that Luis's mother was on crack and that she supported her habit through prostitution.

Whatever his true home situation, Luis did have difficulties in school. His shyness made it difficult for him to relate to the other children, and when he did engage them, it was often in a belligerent or impulsive way. When he expressed himself verbally, it was often by cursing.

Luis sometimes lapsed into silly moods in which he could not control his giggles or his need to rock in rhythmic patterns. At these times, Alice would ask Luis to help clean the room. His interest in picking up toys or sweeping the floor was the antidote for his private pain.

Alice tried to shake her reflective mood and reached into her desk for the phonics worksheets. But as she did so, her mind traveled involuntarily from thoughts of Luis, in the back of row four, to little Darryl Washington, in the front. Darryl's birthday was in August, which made him one of the youngest in his grade; he was born two months prematurely to a mother in her forties and a father in his fifties. Both Mr. and Mrs. Washington were retired employees of the school system.

Alice thought that both of Darryl's parents were overprotective of him, and it seemed that they were in school almost daily checking on him. Darryl was in occupational therapy for fine motor skills and was in private counseling because of his behavior problems.

Actually, Darryl's behavior had improved since the first of the school year, although he still had lapses such as sneaking around behind Alice's back or being physically disruptive by jumping or yelling. Alice thought he perpetrated these antics mostly to attract friends. Like almost all her students, Darryl had a temper tantrum from time to time, and his typical reaction to discipline or even mild correction from Alice was, "I'm gonna' tell my mama on you!"

Alice began to hear the sounds of children in the halls and bus traffic at the front of the building. "Where did the time go?" she wondered as she moved from behind her desk to look at the clock in the back of the room. It was 8:40.

The students in Alice's class were beginning to line up in the hallway outside the door. She opened it to invite the first three inside. "Good morning, Shoma. Hi Don, Darryl," she said pleasantly as they entered.

Alice had found that permitting all the children to enter the room at the same time invited bedlam. The lockers were inside the room, and the process of removing outerwear inevitably led to pushing and shoving if the children were shoulder to shoulder when they took off their coats. Children were placed in this class in part because of language deficiencies, and they tended to express themselves physically rather than verbally. Although the students might jostle and argue in the line outside the room, Alice preferred that to misbehavior in the classroom.

Shoma, Darryl, and Don moved toward their desks. The children knew that after they put their things away, they were to go to their desks, where work was waiting for them. Last night, Alice had set out a copying exercise, designed to practice handwriting.

Alice, who still stood at the classroom doorway with one eye on the hall and the other on the room, gestured to the next students in line. "Barry, Peter, good morning." She then greeted the new aide. "Oh, hello, Anna. I'm glad you're here."

Just then Peter stopped short in front of Barry at the lockers, causing Barry to bump into him and teeter to the left. Anna had been looking at Gumdrop, the class rabbit, and she noticed too late that Barry was about to fall. She reached out to catch him but missed, and Barry hit his hip on a desk as he fell to the floor. The desk, luckily, was fairly insubstantial, and it was pushed noisily to the side by the force of Barry's fall.

Barry looked momentarily as though he might cry, but he visibly held his feelings in check and began to collect his things, which had scattered when he fell. As Barry picked himself up with Anna's help, the children waiting in the hall pushed forward to investigate the commotion. Peter turned and laughed, enjoying the fact that he had captured the attention of the other children.

Alice had not been sure that Peter's abrupt stop was intentional until she saw his expression. She put a hand out to signal that the children in the hall should stay put, and then she went to Barry and Peter.

"Peter, what you just did to Barry was mean and rude," Alice admonished. "Turn around and apologize."

Peter was facing his locker, acting as if he had not heard Alice. A little louder, and with a touch of impatience, Alice repeated herself. "Say you are sorry, Peter!"

Peter turned to Barry, who was now on his feet and trying to escape any further notice. "Sorry," he mumbled. Barry looked up fleetingly at Peter and headed toward his desk. Anna followed him and pulled a small chair beside it for herself.

Alice ushered the rest of the children into the room and glanced at the clock as they made their ways haphazardly to their desks. By the time the last students to enter were seated or standing in the vicinity of their desks, the children who had entered first were now out of their seats and talking. Alice moved to the front of the room to begin her day.

She started each day with a routine the children could depend upon. She noted that Luis was absent, made her introductory comments, and walked back to her desk and located the phonics worksheets. The instant she left the front of the room, the conversation and activity that were a constant in her classroom escalated. Alice walked from desk to desk, handing a worksheet to each child, and began to speak more loudly than usual in an attempt to recapture the group's attention.

"Let's start by looking at the blue side of this paper," Alice said. Most of the children turned to the correct side. "On this worksheet we're looking for the *eh* sound. Look at the first picture. What is that?"

As Alice began talking, the din subsided somewhat, but there was still noise in the room. Peter was humming quietly at his desk; Shoma was alternating between rocking in her chair and jumping up and down in her seat. Other children were just talking—sometimes to themselves, sometimes to each other. Alice was used to the constant hum in her classroom and usually addressed it only when it became overpowering.

"Darryl, what is that in the top picture?" Alice repeated.

Darryl had been sitting sideways at his desk, but now he turned to the front to face Alice. "A elephant," Darryl answered.

"What sound starts that word?" Alice continued, looking at the entire group. "Do you hear the *eh, eh, eh* sound? Circle that elephant. Now what is the next picture?"

About half of the children were involved now with Alice's lesson, either watching and listening to her or focusing on their worksheets. A few of these mumbled an answer to Alice's question. "Bird," she heard faintly.

"It's a special kind of bird," Alice replied. "An ostrich. *Oh, oh,* ostrich. Do you hear the *eh* sound there? *Eh, eh, eh?* No. Get rid of that ostrich. Now what is the next word? Barry?"

Barry had his head on his desk, and Anna sat beside him craning her neck to see over his head in order to follow along. Barry's eyes were on Alice even though he was bent over. "An egg," Barry replied.

Before Alice could respond, she heard Peter speaking from the back of the room. "My teeth are falling out," he said.

Alice walked back toward Peter's desk. "I know they are falling out, Peter. And there is nothing I can do about it, unless I knock them out." She smiled as she reached Peter and playfully touched his chin with her fist. "I could knock them out." The rest of the children laughed loudly. Alice particularly heard Don, laughing more raucously than the joke justified.

"Shh," Alice said gently as she turned to walk back to the front of the class. "I know your teeth hurt, Peter, and I'm sorry they hurt. But there is nothing I can do about it."

When she was back in front, Alice tried to pick up where she had left off, momentarily hunting in her book for the picture she had been asking about. "*Eh, eh,* egg," Alice said. "Right. Circle that egg. Now the next word—what is the next picture?"

As she spoke, Alice realized that the noise level in the classroom was slightly higher. She also saw that Shoma was becoming a real distraction in the back row as she bounced in place or stood up, leaning her elbows on her desk, and wiggled her hips.

"Shoma, what is the next picture?"

Shoma took a minute to find the picture. "A apple." Shoma seemed to spit her reply at Alice.

"*Ah, ah,* apple. Do you hear the *eh* sound?" Alice was again addressing the entire class. "No. Throw out that apple; get rid of that apple. Now what is the next picture? An igloo, right? Do you hear the *eh* sound in the word *igloo?* No, not in igloo. Now the next picture—Peter, what is the next picture?"

Peter looked up at Alice with a vague expression, and Alice walked down the row of desks to his. She gestured toward the picture in question on his worksheet. "What is that, Peter?"

Peter answered promptly, "A elevator."

"*Eh, eh,* elevator. Hear it? Yes! Circle that picture. Now what is the last picture?"

"An arm," Darryl called out exuberantly.

"No, it's a special part of your arm," Alice replied, holding her right elbow with her left hand as she bent her arm. "An elbow," she said. As she spoke, Darryl said "elbow" with her simultaneously.

"*Eh, eh,* elbow. Hear the sound?" Alice was now walking up and down the rows between the desks as she spoke. "Circle that picture."

"You should each have four circles on your papers. Do you have four?" Alice bent over each paper as she moved from desk to desk. "Sit still, Shoma," she said as she came to Shoma's desk.

When Alice had glanced at most of the papers to see that the children were following her, she walked back to the front of the room. "Now I don't know if we should do the green side of the paper. It's awfully hard." Alice looked doubtful. "Let's turn to the green side."

Barry said something unintelligible, which Alice took to be "no." With a smile she said to the class as a whole, "Don't you like trying hard things?" She got no answer from the five or six children listening to her, but she did see Peter's hand waving in the back.

"You didn't check my paper," Peter called. Without commenting, Alice walked back to his desk and drew a star on his worksheet; she then pivoted to look at Shoma's paper and drew a star on it also.

"Do you remember last week when we were doing word families?" Alice asked. She got no response. She moved to the side of the room where a large poster hung on the wall from a previous lesson, in which like-sounding words (*mix, fix, six*) were written in groups. Alice thought briefly of drawing a parallel to an earlier lesson but then thought better of it. She walked back to the board and picked up the chalk. Alice wrote the word *bed* on the board.

"Now are you looking at the green side of the worksheet? Now look up here. See this word? *Bed.* Hear the *eh* sound in the middle of it? Now if I erase the middle letter [Alice did so with the heel of her hand] and change it [Alice wrote an *i* where the *e* had been] the word becomes *bid.* 'I bid my mother hello.'" Alice smiled, acknowledging the stilted sound of the sentence she had used. "The sound we are listening for is in the middle of the word."

Alice wrote a series of other words on the board: *bud, bed, bid, bad.* Don called out from the back of the room, "I know! Bug!"

"We are working with the sound in the middle of the word," Alice said, not really in reply to Don's contribution but to the class as a whole. She drew a line on the board and a circle in the middle of it. "Not the sound at the beginning and not the sound at the end; the sound in the middle.

"Now look at the picture on the top of your worksheet. What is that picture? A bed, right? See the bed?" Alice left the front of the room and walked from desk to desk as she spoke. "*Eh, eh,* bed. Hear the *eh* sound in the middle of the word? Circle the bed."

"Now what is the next picture? Theresa?"

"Sock," said Theresa.

"Sock," repeated Alice. "Sss…oh…ck. Hear an *eh* sound? Who hears it?" Alice gestured a thumbs-up sign with her hand, indicating to the children that they should signal with their hands if they heard the sound. She had found that any physical activity she could weave into a lesson helped them listen and remember. But too few children were with her this morning. "It's always worse on a Monday," Alice thought to herself as she persevered. "Who doesn't hear it?" she asked, gesturing thumbs down. A few children responded. "Who isn't really sure?" Alice got no response. "*Eh, oh.* No. Get rid of that sock."

Alice realized as she paced the rows that nine of the eleven children were lost. Several were engaged in conversation with their neighbors, and the rest were looking out the window or at the wrong picture on the paper. "Let's finish this another time," Alice said as she walked back to the front of the room. "I'm going to collect your papers now. We'll do the green side later." Alice walked to each child's place, collecting worksheets.

As she walked to the back of the room to deposit the worksheets on her desk, Alice said, "Please take your storybooks out now." A few groans greeted this request, which Alice ignored. She exchanged the worksheets for her storybook guide and went back to the front of the room.

The children shuffled possessions inside their desks, looking for the right book, and the general din increased. Suddenly Don spilled a plastic container of arithmetic rods onto the floor, and they bounced on the linoleum, scattering under desks in the back third of the room. Don laughed and began picking them up, crawling around on his hands and knees. Alice had found there were too many of these interruptions for her to wait for their resolution, so she continued in spite of the distraction Don was causing.

"Turn to page 30. Are you all on page 30?" Alice went to a few desks to help each child find the right page. The picture on the page was entitled "Dressing Up" and depicted children in an attic playing with old clothes. Alice saw, out of the corner of her eye, that another boy had joined Don on the floor, but they were almost finished picking up the rods, so she let it go.

Alice began the picture story by asking the children to define an attic. As usual, she got no immediate response from the class, but this time she didn't know if it was due to the children's language deficiencies or the fact that most of them had never heard of an attic. She went to the chalkboard and drew a house, placing a big star under the roof.

"This is an attic, children," Alice said. "It is right under the roof, and sometimes people store old things up there. Do any of you have an attic in your houses? Barry, do you have an attic in your house?"

"I don't know," said Barry.

Alice decided to go on. She looked at her teacher's guide for another item to discuss, but she couldn't immediately locate anything that would be familiar to the children. The picture in the guide was only a black-and-white outline of the picture in the children's books. Alice walked to the back of the classroom, toward Luis's empty desk. "I'll use Luis's book, since he's not here. My book doesn't have the big colored picture that your books have, and I can't see everything we are talking about."

"You can have my book," Don volunteered.

"No, that's all right. I'll use Luis's." Alice sat down at Luis's desk and resumed the lesson from there.

Alice returned to the conversation about attics by asking the children where, in their houses, their parents stored old things. "Where does your mother store your old baby clothes, Theresa?" she asked. The children indicated various storage spots in their homes or said that their parents didn't store things at all. Alice then asked the class to identify various things in the picture: a dresser, a trunk, a rocking chair.

By now, Alice was again on her feet and walking up and down the rows. "What else is in the picture?" She heard no reply. "Name some things you would use to decorate the walls of a house."

The conversation about the picture continued haltingly for a few minutes, until Alice glanced at the clock and saw that it was almost 9:45. She closed her book and walked back to Luis's desk to replace his.

"Tomorrow we will talk about the picture on the next page and do some rhyming," Alice said. "We will have fun with that. For now, you may close your books and put them away. Take out your reading workbooks." The children began closing their books and putting them away in their desks.

Alice walked from desk to desk, getting each child started on a workbook exercise. A few children sat still at their desks and began to work, and Alice went to sit at the round reading table. One child, then two, then several left their desks. Some of the children stood talking in small groups; a few others stood at the reading table, waiting to speak with Alice. Shoma, who was still at her desk, began to call out to no one in particular but generally in Alice's direction.

"I need help!"

"You know how to do that page," Alice called back. She turned to Darryl, who was first in line at the table.

"I need help," Shoma repeated. She looked around the room and saw everyone occupied, either in work or play. She began to walk about aimlessly, carrying her workbook.

Alice helped Darryl with his question and then spoke to Theresa, who had completed her current workbook and so needed a new one. Peter was next in line. "OK, Peter, read to me, sweetheart."

As Peter read haltingly from a paperback storybook, seven other children also stood around the little table, listening to him and waiting their turn for help. Alice began sorting books and other materials into piles on the table as she listened to Peter. Occasionally she heard him stumble and looked over to his book to help him with a word. When he had finished three pages, she stopped him.

"OK, Peter. Do you want to work in your blue phonics book?" Peter's expression was her answer, and Alice relented. She saw that Darryl was in line again at the reading table. "You and Darryl can go read together." Alice looked up to see if Anna was available, but Anna was still sitting next to Barry, working with him and another boy. They were the only children still sitting at their desks. Shoma was standing behind Anna, trying to get her attention. "Ask Anna to get you mats."

Peter bounded over to a tall cabinet and tried to climb onto a chair to reach the carpet samples which served as mats. "No, you're not tall enough," called Alice. Anna looked up, saw the activity, and stood to go help Peter.

Peter and Darryl happily grabbed their mats and ran to the opposite corner of the room. They pulled the chair back from Alice's desk and crawled in under the desk. Peter reached out and pulled the chair back into the opening, enclosing the two boys in the space underneath.

Alice noticed that Shoma was again roaming the room, occasionally asking a child to look in her book and identify a picture. "What is this?" she would ask. Alice waved her back to her seat and then turned to the next child waiting at her elbow. Alice listened as he began to read. "Page 7 is a hard one, isn't it, honey?" she said after a moment. "You keep working on page 7. Go ask Anna to help you read if you get stuck." Alice turned to the next child, and the student she had dismissed carried his book toward his own desk. He saw that Anna was busy and looked momentarily confused. Then he tossed his book onto the top of his desk and went to talk to Tyrone.

Alice quickly spoke to the remaining children at the table, answering their questions and steering them back to work independently. Shoma came up behind her as she finished with the last child in line.

"Can I have a snack now?" asked Shoma.

"No, you may not have a snack," replied Alice sharply. "Get back to your desk and get some work done!"

Alice was ready to work with Barry, but she saw that he was still engaged with Anna, so she sat quietly at the reading table, observing the groups of children talking or playing in various corners of the room. The two boys who had been hiding under her desk now surfaced and began to wander around the room. They headed toward the lockers and opened them. Alice thought about getting them back on task but realized that snack time was imminent and that any new activity would probably be interrupted. Alice generally resisted the urge to rein her children in too tightly, believing that the opportunity to pursue self-directed activity was a gift for children who were unable to control much else in their lives.

In a few minutes Barry brought his book to Alice at the table. As Alice bent over the workbook with Barry, Anna walked to Shoma.

"Have you done any work yet this morning, Shoma?" she asked.

"Yes. Mrs. Peterson checked me out already, just now."

Anna looked at Shoma skeptically and glanced toward Alice, but Alice was busy, so Anna turned away to help another child.

"That's good, Barry," Alice said to Barry as he finished the exercise. "You and John are the hard workers in here today. Bring me your other book now." Barry smiled and walked back to his desk. Alice called loudly to the class as a whole. "All right, children, I am still waiting for some work from Barry, and I think Theresa is doing extra work today. The rest of you can go get your snacks." Alice sat as Barry returned with a second book, and they looked into it together as the children gradually disengaged from their various conversations and activities and went to their lockers.

Some of the children took lunch boxes or bags from their lockers and sat down with their treats. In a few minutes Alice finished with Barry, and she walked back to her desk to retrieve a package of graham crackers. She walked from desk to desk and offered a cracker to those children without a snack. She also took one for herself. The class was fairly quiet as the children ate and spoke softly to each other. Alice began setting out cards that the children would use to indicate what they wanted to do during playtime.

As the children finished eating, they moved toward the toys and began playtime activities. Some of the children first went to the front of the room, where a large poster entitled "Playtime" was hung. Alice had set out cards on which were printed the available playtime activities: "Blocks," "Lego," "Puzzles," etc. Each child chose a card—sometimes with Alice's help, as the children could not yet read—and then went to find the item named on the card chosen.

Alice went from desk to desk, wiping up crumbs and straightening the mess from snack time. Don had spilled raisins all around his desk, and she enlisted his help to pick them up.

Playtime was centered in the back of the classroom, where Alice had placed a large, colorful, inviting rug, patterned with letters and numbers. Most of the children were now busy at some activity. Two boys were playing together with wooden puzzles, and three others were playing with blocks, building airplanes and flying them at each other. Three girls were in the front of the room, using a Bright Lite toy.

Darryl and Don wanted to play with blocks when playtime began, but since all the cards for that activity were gone, Alice told them to find something else to do. Instead, the boys wandered back to the rug and slowly injected themselves into the activity. Gradually the noise from that corner became more and more irritating. Darryl and Don's conversation was escalating.

"Darryl, Don, I want you to stop shouting!" called Alice. She was sitting at her desk trying to grade papers, but she knew she wasn't going to get much done.

Just then, Luis walked into the room. Alice stood up and helped him off with his coat, noting the time as she did so: 10:20. Luis stood in the center of the room and seemed to need a minute to get oriented.

"Did you miss the bus?" Alice asked sympathetically. Luis nodded. "Did you have breakfast?"

Again, Luis nodded affirmatively, but Alice was doubtful. She went to the snack supplies and brought back a graham cracker.

Alice offered the cracker to Luis, who took it and began to eat. "What do you want to do for playtime, Luis?" she asked. Luis looked thoughtful and then walked over to the big box of waffle blocks next to Alice's desk.

"Do you want to do waffle blocks?" Alice asked. "Could you say that for me?"

Just then Alice heard shouting from Darryl and Don, who were arguing over a tower one of them had built. Alice walked quickly to the scene of the altercation. "Darryl, I want you to put that down and go sit at your desk. I told you before to stop shouting!" Darryl suddenly looked cowed, and he complied, walking quietly to his desk.

Alice turned back to Luis and saw that he had built a large maze from the giant waffle blocks. She walked over to him. "Do you want me to get Gumdrop?" she asked quietly. Luis nodded, so Alice gently lifted the rabbit's cage from a table by her desk to the floor next to Luis's structure. Ensuring that the rabbit could not escape at the point where the cage met the blocks, Alice opened the door.

"She got really scared this morning, Luis," Alice cautioned. "We have to be especially gentle with her now." Luis watched as Gumdrop sniffed at the open door of her cage and then tentatively hopped to the rug inside the maze he had constructed. Alice smiled at Luis as they watched together.

Alice used animals extensively, not only by selecting stories about them but also by providing real experiences whenever she could. She had found that sometimes the children could relate better to animals than to people. Inner-city children, in particular, often had no other opportunity to learn about nature or to know what "cuddling" a bunny felt like.

Sometimes Alice wished Gumdrop could know how important she was to the children in the class and how instrumental she had been in helping Alice make connections with some of them. Luis, for instance, really seemed to love the animal. He helped Alice take care of the rabbit, and he often built a pen for it out of the plastic waffle blocks, as he had this morning. On those mornings when the other children joined him in this activity, Alice felt that she was really making progress.

The classroom had gotten very noisy, and several of the boys were chasing each other. Alice felt ambivalent about restraining their play, for she knew that they had nowhere else to run or to pretend. Often Alice let the play escalate as long as she could, drawing the line only when safety became a concern.

Alice witnessed a near collision between one of the boys and a desk and reacted. "Don, Darryl, stop that running around! If you're going to play with blocks, you get back on the rug!" The boys returned to the rug.

Alice saw that it was 10:55 and almost time for the children to leave for gym. The school was on a six-day cycle, and the children alternated between music, art, and gym at this time each day. Each of these special sessions was conducted elsewhere in the school.

"It's time to clean up, children," she called. Some of the children began to pick up their toys, but others continued to play. Still others stopped their games but sat without helping to straighten the room. Alice put a carrot in Gumdrop's cage to lure her back in; after the rabbit was inside, she closed the door and picked up the cage. As she tried to step over the waffle blocks to put the large cage back on its table, she banged the cage against the side of her desk.

"Oh, I'm sorry, Gumdrop," said Alice sadly. She opened the cage and petted the rabbit. "Now you're scared again. It was my fault, Gumdrop," she crooned.

Anna was helping the girls put away the Bright Lite toy, which had at some point spilled, showering tiny pegs over the floor in the front half of the room. Alice helped Luis pick up the rest of the waffle blocks and then walked to the classroom door.

"May I have Shoma and Barry at the front of the room, please?" she called. The two children quickly complied, gladly interrupting their contribution to cleanup. "Now the rest of you line up behind them," called Alice.

By eleven o'clock most of the toys had been put away, and the children were in two lines behind Shoma and Barry. "Now I want a good report from gym, do you hear me? I want no problems with gym," Alice admonished. Several of the children nodded and grinned. "Now everyone follow me."

After escorting the children to the gym, Alice returned to room 105 grateful for the opportunity to collect her thoughts and take a mental break. Teaching always required constant vigilance in the classroom, but Alice found managing these children even more mentally exhausting than usual. As she opened her grade book to annotate comments on the morning's activity, she wondered if she could approach the problem differently.

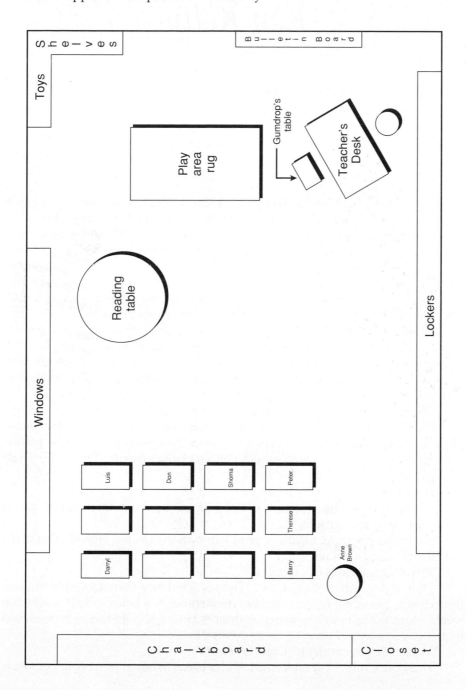

Ken Kelly

A first-year social studies teacher having trouble encouraging discussion in his high school classes visits a fourth-grade philosophy class taught entirely through discussion.

Ken Kelly looked out across the four neat rows at his twenty-four ninth-grade students. Each seemed to have one eye on the clock and the other on the door.

After spending a week lecturing about simple economic principles, Ken was trying to engage the group in a discussion of the differences between free and planned economic systems.

Communism had been unraveling in eastern Europe for many months, and Ken had asked his students to watch the news each night for current information. The students were showing by their written assignments that they understood the issues, but still they were slow to open up in class and discuss them. Ken's questions elicited only simple, two- or three-word answers.

He looked out at the sea of empty faces and pushed on. "Christie, who owns the factories in communist countries, private businesspeople, or the government?"

"The government?" Christie answered, hesitatingly.

"Exactly. Very good. Any why's that? Because, as we studied last week, the governments of communist countries own the means of . . . " Ken waited for a second, hoping someone would volunteer the answer. "Of . . . of what? Carlos?"

"Production."

"Exactly. Production. Good, Carlos." Ken got up from his desk and paced across the front of the room.

"And who owns the means of production in the United States? Who owns the factories here? Tell us, Craig."

"Private people do. Lee Iacocca."

"Half right, half wrong, Craig. The stockholders own Chrysler Motors. Iacocca was president of the company. Remember, we talked about stocks last week? Now, tell us which system you think is better. Should factories be owned by the government or by . . . "

"Yeah. The government," Craig said.

"Hold on, Craig. Don't interrupt. We've already heard from you. Let's hear from someone else. Besides, you should wait until I finish my question. You can't answer a question until I tell you what it is. So, should factories be owned by the government or only by the people who can afford to buy them? Should we be able to have private property as we have here in the United States, or should the property belong to the government so that it can be shared equally by the people? Jessie, how about you? You've been quiet all day. What's your answer?"

Silence.

"Jessie?"

"I like it like we have here."

"OK. Why?"

"You should have to earn what you own."

"Excellent. Good answer. Does anybody disagree?"

Silence.

"Anybody?"

More silence. Several students shifted uneasily in their seats or found ways to occupy themselves. Keith, a typically inattentive student who also was captain of the Littleton High School junior varsity track team, stared at the clock with a hand on his wrist, apparently taking his pulse. In front of him, Maria worked attentively on a braid in her hair.

"Keith! Tell us. What are the advantages of a planned economy? The government can control prices, right? Give me another one. Come on. You should have read this in your text last night."

"Taxes are lower? Ah, no. I mean . . . "

"Oh, really? You want to show me where you read that in the text? Tara, Keith said taxes are lower in a controlled economy. Is that right?"

"I'm sorry," Tara responded. "I couldn't hear the question. May I go to the girls' room?"

Ken walked across the classroom and stood behind the lectern by his desk. "This isn't working," he thought. "These kids know this material, but they won't talk about it meaningfully. They're just not interested."

His anger growing, Ken decided to change his tactics. "Maybe if they saw that the alternative to a discussion is a test, it would motivate them to open up," he thought.

"All right. Everyone take out a pen and a piece of paper," Ken said. "Write your name at the top of the paper, and answer the question I just asked. Should property be owned privately or by the government? You've got until the end of the period."

• • •

Ken collected the papers and walked from the classroom when the bell rang, annoyed that he had to resort to the test and bewildered about why his students were pulling back from him. He remembered that discussions in the first few weeks of class were more lively, but participation gradually declined until only one or two regulars spoke up anymore. "These are all bright kids, all in the upper tracks of their class," he thought. "Many of them are friends, which should make them feel at ease in the classroom and facilitate discussion."

Ken was free for the next two periods. He headed for a nearby elementary school, where he usually ate lunch with a friend who taught there. Walking down the hallway on his way to the cafeteria, Ken saw Sybil Avilla, a teacher in the gifted program who had been teaching philosophy to her gifted students in the elementary school and was now using the same method in regular elementary classes.

Ken had been skeptical when he heard that philosophy would be taught to third- and fourth-graders. Now, still festering at the way his last class had gone, he wondered how students that young could be engaged in philosophical discussions if he couldn't get his ninth-graders to discuss simple economic systems. But Avilla's class had been gaining a reputation among teachers. Ken decided to skip lunch and drop in.

He looked into the classroom and waved at Sybil. "Good afternoon, Mrs. Avilla. I'm Ken Kelly. I teach social studies at the high school. I've heard about your class, and I'm free now. Mind if I sit in a corner and watch? I've been meaning to stop by to see how you do this."

"Sit in a corner, or sit in our circle. We're happy to have you, Mr. Kelly," Avilla responded. "I've had several teachers from the middle school in here already. You're my first high school teacher. Take a seat anywhere."

The period was just beginning, and the seventeen fourth-grade students were settling into chairs that had been arranged in a circle. Sybil, sitting with the children in the circle, turned her attention back to the class.

"Last week, I asked you to think about this question: Would you be different if your name were different?"

Several students began speaking at once. "Just one, please," Sybil said, nodding toward a girl with her hand in the air. "Maria?"

"I was thinking about it the other day," Maria said. "Actually, it depends. Because if you have a name and somebody starts to tease you about it, well that might change your attitude. And you might be a different person. Or you might do different things."

From her seat in the circle, Sybil held up a book. "Well, this is a book about a name. And while I read it to you, I'd like you to think about that question—would you be you if you had a different name? The book is called *The Bear Who Wanted to Be a Bear.*"

Sybil began reading. "Leaves were falling from the trees. Flocks of wild geese high above were flying south. The brown bear felt a cool wind on his fur. He was feeling very sleepy. . . . "

Sybil read for ten minutes from the book, which described a bear who wakes after a hibernation to find that a factory has been built in the forest over his den. He tries to convince the factory officials that he's a bear, but they say he's only "a lazy, unshaven worker in a fur coat" and order him to work on an assembly line. The bear works through the spring and summer at the factory, coming to believe he may not be a bear. The following fall, as a new hibernation season begins, the bear begins falling asleep on the job. He's fired and eventually finds his way back to a den in the woods to sleep through the winter.

Sybil closed the book and looked up.

"I wouldn't forget I'm a bear," Rita said, leaning forward into the circle.

Sybil asked, "Why?"

"Because even after an amount of years, I wouldn't forget. I'm a bear. I would look like a bear, even if I shaved."

Kathy raised her hand and began talking. "But if you were in a totally different environment, would you still act the same? Would you think you still looked the same? I mean, maybe there weren't any mirrors. Maybe there was just one, to shave or something. So how would you know you were still a bear and not a person working in a factory like everyone else?"

Craig, who had raised his hand when Kathy did and responded to Sybil's nod, spoke next. "If I were surrounded by machines, and all I did was press a button all day long, I really wouldn't think about my normal activities because I'd be concentrating on pushing the buttons. So I'd think I looked the same and acted the same as everyone in the factory."

Rita shook her head. "Well, I'd remember that I was a bear at least."

"But you'd be surrounded by humans," Kathy said.

A chorus of voices filled the room. Sybil raised her voice above the din, nodding toward one of the children. "Go ahead, Camille."

"I know how it feels. I'm surrounded at home by grown-ups and sometimes I feel like I'm a grown-up, and so I do grown-up sorts of things because everybody around my house is grown-up."

"So that brings us to the question we asked last year," Sybil said, turning again toward Camille. "Would you be you if you had white skin?"

Camille thought for a moment. "Well . . . "

Several students began talking at once.

Sybil held up her hand. "Wait. Wait. Just let her think for a second."

Camille went on, "Yes. You'd have the same personality. It's like on Halloween. When you dress up as somebody else. But you're not that person."

"But that's temporary. It's not for a long time. If it was permanent, would you be you?" Mickey's voice rose as he finished.

Terrell responded, "Yes and no. You wouldn't be yourself because you'd have white skin. But you would be yourself because you'd do what you normally do."

Maya, who had been listening quietly, leaned forward and spoke to Terrell. "What if you were in a completely different environment? Say you moved to California and became a kid star. And every morning you'd go to work. And you didn't go to school. You got a tutor every afternoon, at lunch break. Would you still be you? Would you still run around and play and everything? Or would you be practicing your lines all the time and everything? You'd probably have a different personality if you were always around a different environment."

Terrell started to respond, "Well, yeah, but. . . ." and was interrupted as several students began speaking and several hands went into the air. Sybil interjected again. "Let him finish. Then we'll get to you. Put your hands down for a second."

Terrell continued with the series of questions he had been formulating. "You'd forget that you used to live in this town? You would forget that you were white? You'd forget that you have to go to school every day? You would forget all that stuff?"

Paula spoke next, "You wouldn't forget it. But it wouldn't be a part of you anymore, so you'd change from how you are now. If you lived in a different environment, then your personality or whatever you thought or think would be different."

"When I lived in Florida, everybody was kind of shy and didn't speak up," Allison began. "So I was shy and I didn't speak up. But then I moved to the north, and all the kids say what they think and what they want to do. So that's what happened to me. It just changed my life totally. Because now I can speak out and say what I want to. Before, I was holding everything in. So you change with your environment."

Sybil addressed the whole group, "If that's true, then we shouldn't be surprised that the bear didn't know he was a bear. Can you make that connection with me now? Do you follow me?"

Several students nodded, and Sybil continued, "If what Allison just said is true, if you accept her statement, then we could understand why the bear didn't know he was a bear. Even though we know he was a bear. So is your bearness or your humanness an outside thing or an inside thing? Who determines what you are? Sonya, good to see your hand up."

Sonya smiled at Sybil as she began to speak. "Well, if you have friends that are rich and other friends that are not too rich, you hang around with the rich people. You'll become like them. You'll act like you're rich."

"So is your personality defined by other people?" Sybil asked.

Sally, whose hand had been up for several minutes, said, "No, it's not. Because if you hang around with rich people, it's not like you're rich. You can act like them, but you're only pretending."

Again, Sybil responded with a question. "So then what is it that makes you who you are?"

Sally continued, "Only you should. Yourself. Suppose some kids are from rich families, and you go and hang around with them. Say they're really 'Jappy,' and they talk like 'Like, totally, and for sure.' And say you start to talk like that. That won't be good. If you hang around people that aren't like you and you become like them, then don't try to go back to your old friends. Because they'll see you've changed a lot, and they won't like you."

As Sally paused, Sybil said, "I'm sorry. We have to stop right now. The period is about to end."

Several students spoke up in protest.

Sybil stood and waved her hand to quiet the chatter. "Wait a moment," she said. "Just because we're done with this in class doesn't mean you should stop talking about it later. I would like you to talk about this with whomever you have dinner with tonight. Try to remember the story of *The Bear Who Wanted to Be a Bear*. And I want you to talk about what it is that makes us human. Is it other people who define us, like they defined the bear? Or do we define ourselves? And if we define ourselves, then how come we change when we're with different kinds of people, as we've been talking about? Or maybe who you are can change."

The chatter among the students continued as they reorganized their desks back into rows. A few approached Sybil and began explaining their ideas about the discussion. After a minute, Sybil waved the remaining students toward their seats and gathered her materials as the regular fourth-grade teacher returned to the classroom. Motioning Ken to follow her, she said, "We can meet in my office across the hall."

As they walked from the room, Sybil turned to Ken and asked, "So, Ken is it? How did you enjoy the class? Different, don't you think?"

"There's no doubt you had them going. I haven't heard that much from any of my students, particularly in my ninth-grade global studies class, since the semester began. But . . . " Ken stopped himself short.

Sybil seemed to sense his hesitation. "But what, Ken?"

"Well, where's the teaching? You didn't do anything. You said only a few words, and the kids just . . . talked."

"If you assume that teaching is telling, you're right," Sybil responded. "I tell them very little in this class. But if what you want to do is create a community of inquiry, you have to assume that a teacher's opinion stands as only one. My job is to get students actively talking together and doing their own thinking, not to get my agenda across."

"Agenda? We've got to be realistic, Sybil. The school district and the state have given us an agenda—the curriculum. At the end of next year, my global studies students will have to take the state curriculum exam. I need to cover the world with them in just two years, and I don't think I could do it using freewheeling, open-ended discussions very often."

"Certainly you've got to help your students prepare for the exam," Sybil said, "but you also can use the Socratic technique you just saw. A good teacher needs many techniques. A teacher delivers a lecture when it's important to get a lot of information across in a hurry, but there are times when the teacher has to be more of a coach, a facilitator of information. There are times when it's appropriate for students to listen and take notes, and times when they should participate more actively: talk, respond, react, analyze, personalize, think. That's what these dialogues are for. Every teacher could use them, in any subject."

"Every teacher?" Ken asked. "Maybe there's a place for these dialogues in some of the social sciences I teach, but how could they be used in the hard sciences, or math? Kids won't learn long division by sitting in circles chatting with each other about it. C'mon, Sybil. Aren't you stretching the point?"

Sybil started to respond but then paused. She shrugged and said, "Maybe so, Ken. I probably do stretch the point." Ken wasn't sure if she was angry or not, and he didn't know what to say next. He watched Sybil organize materials for her next class.

"It's a valid technique, Sybil. I enjoyed watching you work at it. And thanks for talking to me. I don't know if I could ever give up so much control. I don't know if it would work for me."

"Maybe that's true," Sybil responded. "It's interesting, isn't it? The children adore this method, and the teachers are scared to death of it. To make it work, teachers have got to change their point of view, to look at their place in education. They've got to be genuinely interested in asking questions for which they're not looking for the almighty right answer all the time. It's tough to do."

Ken nodded good-bye and headed for the teacher's lounge, hoping to find the friend with whom he usually ate lunch. He needed another reaction to what he'd just observed, but the room was nearly empty. Ken bought a sandwich and a soda from the vending machine and took a seat at an empty table. He opened the newspaper he carried with him but found his thoughts continually returning to Sybil Avilla's classroom.

"I'm a teacher, not a talk-show host," he said half out loud. "I've got to get through a mountain of curriculum—the history of the eastern and western worlds—and she wants me to suspend the lessons every fourth or fifth day so that I can let my kids just chat about it.

"There may be no right answers in Sybil's classes, but when my tenth graders sit down to take the state curriculum exam next June, they'll need to know a lot of right answers. And they're not going to find those answers sitting in circles and talking some bear through an identity crisis."

Ken picked up the newspaper again and thumbed to the sports pages, but his thinking returned to Sybil's class. "Certainly, there are arguments for what Sybil does," he thought. "Clearly, the class was more lively than any of mine have been in a while. But so much of what she does, or doesn't do, contradicts some of the basic strategies I studied in education classes; her lesson had no real advance organizer. It needed more closure. She never praised a right answer. She never corrected an incorrect one. The obvious point of the lesson was that only you can define the kind of person you are. But when a few of the kids said exactly that, she didn't even acknowledge them. Kids need that feedback.

"And the class lasted forty minutes, but only half the kids said anything at all. I'm not sure the other half were even listening. I don't think they got anything out of it. She never called on kids, even those that were obviously daydreaming. And when the discussion wandered, she never stepped in to bring it back. I wonder, really, what Sybil's kids learned today."

Ken looked down at his unread newspaper and then at his watch. He picked up the paper and his trash from lunch, tossed them into the garbage, and headed back toward the high school for his afternoon classes. "She's just too radical," he thought as he swung open the door from the elementary school and let it close gently behind him.

Molly Clark

A first-year teacher in a private all-girls high school teaching eleventh-grade English plans and executes a unit on Macbeth. *This case reveals in detail her unit and lesson planning, several teaching sessions, and her thoughts about her instructional decisions.*

My feet tread softly on the sacred dust of my ancestors
I feel the hot sun beat down on my back
I am held captive in a land and time that wants no part of me
Walking on a lonesome trail of tears. . . .

Molly Clark smiled openly as she listened to the last student read her Native American-style poem. This was a sad poem, but some had been wonderfully funny. Both styles were exemplary of the kind of poetry they'd studied. As the eleventh-grade students read their work, Molly realized she was proud of their efforts and pleased with their final products. On the other hand, she was not looking forward to January when her class would tackle *Macbeth.* In September, Molly had left a seven-year career in commercial art to take an English position at Holcroft, a small, private, religious girls' school. Miriam Franklin, the principal, had told her that she had been hired because of her creativity, which she showcased in an interdisciplinary model lesson she taught as part of the interview process. Though Molly was an artist, both her bachelor's and master's degrees were in literature, and she was just finishing a master's in teaching. Despite all her education she had not studied much Shakespeare in any of her programs, and she secretly worried about how she could teach such complex literature without having any background in it—especially to *this* class.

Holcroft placed its students in one of two tracks, labeled H and E. Students called the tracks "Hard" and "Easy," but the school considered them to be high and low ability respectively. Students in the E class were thought to be weaker students because their performance was inconsistent across their classes. If they shined in foreign language, they often failed in math or science. If a student did particularly well or poorly in a subject, she had the option to switch tracks just for that subject; however, most of the girls chose to stay with their group despite the fact that another track might better meet their needs for that subject. Consequently, it was possible to have a student in a low-track class who exhibited a real aptitude for a subject. However, the principal and other teachers usually discussed classes as if they were homogenous. This class was an eleventh-grade

E class, and two of the fifteen students, Sarah and Rachel, had been bluntly described to Molly as "illiterate" and "learning disabled," respectively, though they had never been formally tested. Molly had discovered that Sarah did quite well in her math class, while Rachel was a budding artist. Another student, Ellen, clearly had a writing gift, but had been described by the principal as "a very poor student." Though Molly recognized that the class was not as academically homogenous as its label implied, she noted that it appeared homogenous in other ways. The girls were all white, from the same religious background, and from middle- or upper-class families. Despite the supposed homogeneity, however, the girls viewed themselves as radically different. There was a clear split in the class between those who labeled themselves as smart, well-mannered, and conservative and those who saw themselves as low achievers, appropriately talkative, and worldly-wise.

Molly glanced around the circle of tablet-arm desks, which had been arranged as comfortably as possible for the day's poetry reading, in the oppressively small room. The chalkboards sagged on either side of the front windows and the teacher's desk sat at the front, like an obstinate dinosaur encroaching on the classroom's precious little space. "Maybe *Macbeth* will be too big for these students, too big for this room, too big for me to teach," Molly worried. "After all, Janet Lerner had these kids last year, and she told me they were 'dull, dull, dull' and that I should stick to the 'easier literature.'"

"On the other hand," Molly thought, "the principal is always on my back to 'keep the class moving' and 'teach to the top.'" Molly could not figure out exactly what Miriam meant by the "top." It seemed she wanted Molly to teach the class as if these were advanced students, yet she had warned Molly that most of the class would probably fail the state proficiency exam. Several times, she had stopped Molly in the hallway to find out which books and plays Molly was teaching and how many she had done to date, even though Molly had a reading list and was supposedly free to design the curriculum. "Are you going to do Shakespeare?" she had asked. "The kids always do Shakespeare."

A little confused, Molly wondered why she was being pressured. At any rate, she felt obligated to do what Miriam was hinting at, so she shelved her plans to do American short stories after this Early American literature unit and scheduled a *Macbeth* unit instead. It seemed that the play would fit best at this juncture anyway, since Molly had done a class that touched on the fact that the colonists left England while Shakespeare was alive and still writing plays.

Now that the unit was scheduled, however, Molly felt uneasy. She wondered, "Is *Macbeth* doomed to travel over their heads?" Nevertheless, the sound of the students' poetry still filled her ears. If they could write such delightful verse, why couldn't they understand Shakespeare? "There must be some way to make it work for them," she thought. "Besides, maybe students like Ellen, Beth, and Rena could help some of the 'slower' students out."

At home, with her cup of tea, Molly began preparing for the *Macbeth* unit. The first order of business was to reread *Macbeth*. She tried to read it for pleasure a few years before and found it difficult going. However, this reading seemed to be proceeding much better. At one point, she thought, "I feel like I actually understand this. I never felt this way before reading Shakespeare. I wonder what's changed?" She decided it must have been her accumulation of life experiences and her advanced reading level. But these were things she couldn't really give to her students as they tackled *Macbeth*. She could, though, try to connect the themes to students' lives, and she could definitely find a way to make reading a support activity rather than the central approach. Maybe she could use videotapes? Or, she could have students act out some of the major scenes. She jotted down some ideas and kept reading—continuing to make notes on her perceptions of the play and to record questions she felt would be important to include in class discussions.

When Molly finished reading, she arranged her observations and questions into categories: half-truths, temptation, ambition, sin, guilt, death, childlessness, and manhood. The categories clearly suggested possible interpretations, such as the Fall of Humankind or The Development of Manhood. A few hours with some critical sources, particularly the work of literary critic Harold Bloom, confirmed her ideas. *Macbeth* could be framed as Adam, Eve, and God in the Genesis account or Son, Mother, and Father in the Oedipal cycle.

With her ideas in place, Molly felt ready to start formally planning the unit. The first step would be to write her objectives. Though she felt she didn't write particularly good objectives, she believed in the value of the activity. The process seemed to clarify her thinking and provide a unit road map. In a sense, she always had the same objectives for literature reading: students will have fun, understand what they read, find personal relevance in the story, and remember the central ideas. These objectives were particularly important if students were going to be able to recall and comfortably use the literature when taking the proficiency exam in June. From these broad objectives, she wrote related ones that were more specific. For *Macbeth,* some of these included: (1) Students will identify the essential qualities of Macbeth and Lady Macbeth; (2) Students will remember the relationships between Macbeth and Lady Macbeth, Macbeth and the witches, Macbeth and Banquo, Macbeth and Duncan, and Macbeth and Macduff; (3) Students will understand how Macbeth's and Lady Macbeth's actions affected themselves and others; (4) Students will discover that complex literature can have multiple interpretations; (5) Students will find personal relevance in Macbeth; and (6) Students will explore the key characters' motivations. Difficult as the objective-writing stage could be, the next stage was even more challenging: choosing activities that would achieve the objectives and arranging them in a coherent sequence. Molly examined her entire set of objectives. How would she accomplish them? She decided to design a project that would unify the set. By assigning a project, she could make each unit lesson seem relevant to students, since each would provide an important "piece" they would need to complete the "puzzle."

She thought back on her initial ideas. An acting project might just be the thing. After all, she had recently read that students remember 90 percent of what they say as they do something versus only 10 percent of what they read. Also, she knew that an active approach could boost student motivation. Of course, each student would not get a chance to act each character, and each student would only be part of one or two scenes. But the project would give students a purpose for studying the play. If class discussions, reading assignments, and student journal writing could "make up the difference," students would get a comprehensive picture of *Macbeth*. Besides, she could mix members of her class in small groups and facilitate the razing of some walls students had built over the years. Excited by the possibilities, Molly went to the library and looked up Shakespeare in the *Education Guide to Periodicals.* She discovered that *English Journal* had recently run a series of articles on acting out Shakespeare in the classroom. One article featured a project that required students to interpret, direct, and act out a scene. Students were also responsible for keeping a prompt-book, which was a record of their decisions. Molly decided that this was the project she was looking for. She added another piece: playbills. The playbills would feature play reviews, actor biographies, a biopoem on a major character, and copies of Shakespearean art that she would provide for students to use for the covers and throughout the body of the playbill. For Molly, this aspect of the project would help take students beyond the boundaries of the one or two scenes they would be acting out. It would also give students like Rachel a chance to contribute their artistic skills, thus making them a valued part of their group.

Molly toyed with how to open the unit and had settled on an activity called KWL. It was a multi-purpose activity, assessing students' prior knowledge, allowing them to set some of their own objectives for the upcoming unit, and encouraging them to monitor their new learning.

Molly opened class by introducing the activity and its purpose. "As we begin *Macbeth,* I want to see what you already know about Shakespeare and the play. I also want to hear about what you'd like to learn. This information will help me plan lessons to meet your needs and aims. It will also generate material for you to address in your weekly journals. We're going to use an activity called KWL to find out what you know and want to learn." Molly wrote the first category on the board. "The *K* stands for *What I Know.*" Then she wrote the second category on the board. "The *W* stands for *What I Want to Know.*" She turned and finished, "The *L* stands for *What I Learned or Still Need to Learn.* I have handouts that describe how you can use your journals to do the *L* step on your own. I'll give them out at the end of class."

"We don't know anything," said Rachel.

"Yeah, and how can we say what we want to learn when we don't know anything about the book?" added Stephanie.

Molly smiled. "Well, why don't we try? I'll bet you know **something** about Shakespeare or *Macbeth.* We'll save the category *What I Want to Know* for after we finish our *What We Know* category. How about it? Somebody tell me something about Shakespeare or *Macbeth.*" Molly waited and eventually the first student spoke.

"There's always death in Shakespeare," Rena offered.

"OK," said Molly. "What kind of Shakespeare plays contain death?"

"Tragedies," said Jennifer.

"Yes, tragedies," said Molly. "So I'll write 'tragedy' and 'death' together. Is that OK, Rena?"

"Yeah, that's fine."

"Is that it? Are all Shakespeare's plays tragic?" questioned Molly.

"No, there are funny ones too," replied Stephanie. A general chatter arose and students quickly decided that the funny plays were better.

"What do we call those funny plays?"

"Comedies," said Sarah.

"Yes, comedies," said Molly. "So I'll write 'comedy' and 'funny' next to each other. What else?"

"They're hard to read," said Rachel. A general murmur of agreement went throughout the room.

"Yes, they are," said Molly. "I have trouble understanding Shakespeare, too. Why is he hard to read?"

"It's old," said Nina.

"That's true. Our language has changed a lot in three hundred some years. Shakespeare's audiences understood his plays, but we'll have to work a little harder to accomplish that. Let me put 'middle English' on our list to show the type of language the plays are in."

"There's a Lady Macbeth!" exclaimed Melissa. "And she kills a baby! I know because I was in a play when I was little, and I was Lady Macbeth, and I carried around a baby doll. We even put ketchup on the doll!"

"You know, I don't remember that part. I'm going to put Lady Macbeth on our list, but I'm going to put the rest of what you said under the category *What I Want to Know*." Molly wrote "Lady Macbeth" under the *Know* title and "did Lady Macbeth kill a baby?" under the *Want to Know* title. "Anything else?"

"There's always a deeper meaning," said Beth.

"Very true," said Molly and recorded Beth's response on the board.

The activity continued and students offered a few more ideas about Shakespeare and the play. When they seemed to be out of ideas, Molly directed their attention to the second category. "Now, tell me what you want to learn," she said.

Answers came flying. "What's the deeper meaning in *Macbeth?*" "Who are the characters?" "What's the conflict in the play?" "What's the relationship between Macbeth and Lady Macbeth?" "Did they use masks?" "How come there weren't any women actors?" "What kind of costumes did they wear?" "What kind of theaters did they perform in?" Molly recorded each question as it came until the students couldn't think of any more.

Then she went to the desk and retrieved the handouts on the *L* step and spoke as she handed them out. "We've asked some questions today that may or may not be answered in our readings. Remember, you can use your journals as a place to record any answers you discover, as well as new questions that arise. The handout will show you how to do this in case you forget what you're supposed to do. Tomorrow, I'll hand out the play." As Molly distributed the final copies, the bell rang, signaling the end of class.

Later, Molly reflected on the first *Macbeth* lesson. Students knew some things about the play, but not much. They had asked several questions that fit in with her objectives, like, "What's the relationship between Macbeth and Lady Macbeth?" and "What's the conflict in the play?" They also showed an obvious interest in acting information, and this made Molly glad she'd chosen an acting project. It was clear, though, that she would need to create lessons that relied on other prior knowledge students had because they didn't know much about Shakespeare or *Macbeth*. Since the students also seemed interested in the play's "deeper meaning," Molly thought she should present at least two interpretations. The interpretations could be linked to the project by serving as perspectives from which the groups could act out their scenes. However, Molly didn't want the groups to feel that these were the sole ways to see the play, so she decided to require them to provide at least two perspectives of their own. From the total of four, groups could then settle on a perspective they would use when making decisions about their scenes.

The next day, Molly opened class by introducing the project. "OK," she said. "I want to talk about a project that you'll be doing for this unit."

Rachel, who sat in the front row, looked down at her feet.

Nina exclaimed, "I hope it's not going to be too hard!"

Jennifer smiled and waited expectantly. "Sshh," she said.

"Yeah, let her finish," chimed in Rena, as she shot an annoyed glance at Nina.

"It's not going to be hard. It's going to be fun," said Molly.

"That's what you always say!" Stephanie exclaimed.

"Well, that's because it's true. It **is** going to be fun," returned Molly.

Molly began to distribute handouts as she spoke. "This handout has all the information you'll need to complete the project successfully. It also has your group assignments. The group names are names of real acting groups that existed during Shakespeare's time. There are three main parts to the project, which I'll go over separately, but I'd like you to read the sheet silently first."

Molly noticed that Ellen was already frowning and showing her sheet to Rena, when suddenly Melissa called out, "What if we don't like our group?"

"The groups have been assigned very carefully, so it doesn't matter if you don't like your group—the groups will stay as they are," said Molly.

"But why should we have to be with people we don't like?" asked Nina.

"Yeah," said Melissa.

"Yeah," said Mary.

Rena turned around and glared at the protestors, and Jennifer rolled her eyes.

Molly cringed inside as she heard and watched this display of disaffection, but she felt even better about having grouped the students as she had. They obviously needed to learn how to value each other and work together. Prior to this project, Molly only grouped the students for short in-class activities. Because she knew that she was the first teacher who had ever grouped them, she had initially stuck with "safe" groups—mixing and matching students who were friends or who seemed neutral about each other. But these groups would be constant throughout the unit, and Molly had assigned them based on differing abilities and talents, as well as on her observations of students who fell on either side of the "split." The most critical group would be Melissa, Ellen, and Heather, because it brought together respected members of the opposing groups and the neutral group. Molly felt these three students had the potential to work well together, and she was counting on the success of this group to spark the healing of the divisions between the girls.

Molly calmly answered Nina's question, "Because this classroom is not about always doing what's most comfortable. Sure it's more fun to work with our friends, but you're here to learn how to work with everybody. The makeup of the groups is not negotiable. Now, let's make sure everyone understands the project. Please continue reading, and then we'll go over it together."

The students read, after which Molly answered their questions. Then they moved on to a brainstorming session on the meaning of one of the first lines in the opening scene: "Fair is foul and foul is fair."

Molly wrote the line on the board. "I want to consider the meaning of this line, which is from the opening of the play, because it's an important idea that underlies what goes on in the play. Let's start by defining the important terms. Then we can decide what the line might mean."

Molly wrote the headings *Fair* and *Foul* on the board. "Give me some meanings for fair," said Molly.

"Beautiful," said Beth.

"True," said Brenda.

"Right?" Sarah hesitantly continued.

Molly wrote each response under the appropriate heading. "Anything else?"

"Justice," said Jennifer.

"Correct," said Nina.

There was a long pause. "Is that it?" asked Molly. When no one could think of anything else, she moved to the next heading. "Could we define this word by stating the opposites of what's under our other heading?"

She heard students saying "Yeah" and "Sure."

"OK, then, give me the opposites."

Students decided on "ugliness," "false," "injustice," "incorrect," and "evil." Molly then led a discussion on how it would be possible for something fair to be foul or vice versa.

Ellen offered the first insight. "Well, somebody could be beautiful on the outside but ugly on the inside."

Molly turned the observation into a graphic by drawing a circle and writing "ugly" inside, then drawing a bigger circle completely around it and writing "beauty" in it. Then, she asked, "What will the outsider see if he looks at the person, based on this graphic?"

"Just the beauty," said Ellen, "because it surrounds the ugliness and hides it."

"Is that deception?" asked Molly.

"Yes," said Stephanie.

"No," said Jennifer. "It's only deception if you do it on purpose."

Stephanie began to protest, but Molly held up her hand in a 'quiet' signal and kept eye contact with Jennifer. "OK," said Molly, "but isn't it true that the outsider will be deceived?"

"Well, I guess so," said Jennifer, "but I still think it's different if you do it on purpose."

"Maybe we need another word to help us out. What is deception that's on purpose?"

"It's evil," said Jennifer.

Molly wrote "deception/evil" under the graphic, then addressed the class, "Do you see how Stephanie and Jennifer are both right? Ellen noted that what's on the outside hides what's on the inside. So, the outsider can be deceived, which is what Stephanie agreed to. But, Jennifer added that there is a purposeful deception we call 'evil.'"

Valerie shyly raised her hand, so Molly stopped talking and motioned her to speak. "I think that an outsider probably makes assumptions," said Valerie.

Molly wasn't sure what Valerie meant, and, since this was the first time Valerie had ever spoken in class, Molly hesitated to push her. But she wanted Valerie's comment to add to the discussion, so she asked, "What kind of assumptions do you mean?"

"You know, he'd maybe be deceived because if he saw one thing on the outside, he'd assume that the same thing was on the inside too."

Molly was pleased when Mary excitedly added, "So the only way you can get past the assumptions is to get to know a person! I mean, if they look beautiful on the outside you can't know if they're also beautiful on the inside unless you talk to the person and stuff."

Molly summarized, "So, in order to avoid making assumptions and end up being deceived, the outsider needs to get more information." Then she pointed to the paired ideas under the headings and asked, "What could happen in any of these cases if the outsider doesn't get more information—whether that's through getting to know someone or digging for facts?"

"You could get hurt," offered Rena, "or you could hurt somebody else, because you might do things based on your assumptions."

"Good!" Molly said with emphasis. "Now, I want everyone to read the opening of *Macbeth* together. See if you can pick out some things that appear to be either fair or foul but might turn out to really be the opposite."

Molly broke the class into groups. Each group read a character's lines chorally and Molly narrated several transition sections. Then the class briefly discussed their ideas about possible fair/foul elements, and Molly noted that this week she'd be introducing an interpretation of the play that was based on the concept of "Fair is foul and foul is fair": the fall of humankind. She had decided to start with this interpretation for two reasons. First, it could easily be woven in with their early readings, and, second, it was a framework they were very familiar with through the religion curriculum required by the school. If the students could see *Macbeth* as Adam, Eve, and God, this would probably help them in their readings.

The next day, Molly opened class with a question designed to get the class thinking about the "fall of humankind" interpretation she'd be starting the following day. She also wanted to provide a foundation for their reading homework. The question, "Someone is contemplating performing an action that is clearly wrong. How could we convince the person to 'Go ahead and do it!'?" urged students to explore the effect of temptation on a person. Students generated a list of things they could tell the person, including: "It won't hurt you"; "It's not really wrong"; "It'll be a secret"; "It won't hurt your reputation"; "You **need** to do it"; "You don't want to stay in suspense"; and "I dare you." At the end of class, Molly told students that Macbeth was a character who was contemplating performing a wrong action. Students were to read the "temptation" scenes for the next day and answer two questions:

1. What tactics do the people around Macbeth use to tempt him? Give examples.
2. Do you think Macbeth would have **done it** anyway even if no one else had discussed the matter with him? Support your answer.

The following day, Molly started with a mini-lecture on why *Macbeth* might have been understood by Shakespeare's audiences as an Adam/Eve/God motif. She reminded them of King James's divine-right-of-kings theory that posited the king as a "little God" and discussed the popular conception of women as either an Eve or a Mary—providing the students with a photocopy of a painting that illustrated the Eve-Mary dichotomy. She then wrote two headings on the board, *The Temptations* and *The Fall*.

"Yesterday, I asked you to read for homework and note the kinds of tactics people around Macbeth used to get him to **do it.** Today, I'm going to call these tactics 'temptations,' since these are the things that urged him towards the deed. Somebody tell me what they noted as tactics and who used them."

Tracy called out, "Lady Macbeth puts him down!"

"Yes, she does, doesn't she? Can somebody find an example of when she does this from the text?" Molly replied.

Beth began rapidly to turn pages. "On page 56, starting with line 35, she basically calls him a coward."

Nina found the reference in her book and said, "I don't get it. And, what does she mean about the cat?"

Molly looked at the lines. "Well, obviously there must have been some kind of saying that Shakespeare's audiences were familiar with. Let's look at the footnote. Yes, here it is. It had something to do with a cat that wanted fish but was afraid to get its paws wet. So Lady Macbeth is saying he's like that cat. He wants to be king, but he's not willing to do what it takes to be king—kill Duncan."

"Oh," said Nina.

"She plays on his manly pride," said Stephanie.

"Mmmm. Yes, she sure does. How does she do this?" asked Molly.

Beth raised her hand. "She tells him that if he were really a man he would do it, and then she says that she's a **woman** and even she would do it."

"That's sort of like what we talked about yesterday. It's the 'I dare you . . . Prove yourself to me!' tactic," Molly commented.

Students continued to share what they had noted as tactics, and then Molly moved the discussion to "The Fall," asking them to recount the biblical results of the fall of humankind. Together, they generated a list: Adam and Eve are thrown out of the garden (separation from God), their relationship deteriorated, life became more difficult, nature degenerated, guilt plagued the couple, and sin led to more sin and death. Molly ended class by giving a homework handout that specified the required reading and posed two questions:

1. What are the results of Macbeth's fall?
2. Do you see any parallels between this fall and the fall of humankind?

Over the next week, Molly finished the first interpretation and started the second one on the Oedipal cycle, using the same method of helping students construct knowledge prior to readings, assigning readings with accompanying questions, and weaving the students' answers into the next day's discussion.

When she had finished with the interpretations and the reading of the play was completed, she planned to start the group work. Students were to finalize their scene choices so they could plan for their scenes during the upcoming week's mid-semester break. Molly also planned an assignment that required students to watch the movie and compare it to their reading. For any student who had difficulties with the reading, Molly hoped this would fill in some gaps. But, she was awakened the next morning by a call. "No school today," said the secretary. "Have a great vacation!"

Molly looked outside at the heavy snow and sighed. "Some great vacation," she thought. "Now they won't have that 'extra' time to help them out." Little did she know that school would be canceled for three days at the end of vacation too, starting a string of snow days and vacation that would interrupt school for a total of twelve days.

• • •

The first day class reconvened after the extra-long break, Molly had groups pick three scenes they'd be willing to do and rank them in order of preference. That night, she assigned scenes based on their requests, making sure to include all the "major" scenes so their performances would piece together like a mini-play. The next day students worked on their biopoems, and the day after they began work on their promptbooks.

Molly explained the first step groups should take before working on their scene interpretations. "Remember, I gave you two interpretations of *Macbeth*, but I also told you that you'd have to come up with two perspectives of your own from which to see the play. I want you to record your perspectives in your promptbooks. Then, later, you'll choose one of yours or mine to use for conceptualizing your scenes."

"Can't we just use yours?" Jennifer asked hopefully.

"No, I'd like you to do some thinking of your own," answered Molly.

"But it's too hard!" called out Stephanie. "You're the teacher, so you can come up with this stuff. We can't."

"I have great faith in you," said Molly. "Besides, I'm going to walk around and work with each group, so don't worry."

Several students glanced at each other doubtfully.

"If you're still working on your biopoems, you should finish them before you start discussing your perspectives. Also, if you finish developing your perspectives today, you can move to the next step, which is choosing one and using it to help you conceptualize your scenes," said Molly. "All right, please get into your groups and start working."

Students began to shuffle chairs, and Stephanie came up to the front of the room. Whispering, she spoke rapidly, "Ms. Clark, we can't do our work. We didn't finish our biopoem yet, and Beth is sick and she has our work with her! We can't do anything until she comes back, and you know she always gets sick for a long time. Can we do something else? Can I read instead?"

"No," said Molly. "You can still do work without her . . ."

"But we can't!" Stephanie interrupted emphatically.

"Yes, you can. You don't have to finish the biopoem right now. You can move on to the next step, which is developing your perspectives," said Molly.

"But you don't understand," said Stephanie. "Rachel doesn't say anything. Beth and I did all the work on the poem and when we ask Rachel what she thinks, she says, 'I don't care. It sounds good to me.' She doesn't do anything! How can I work on this with her? I don't want to get a bad grade or anything. Can't we wait until Beth gets back?"

Molly quietly answered Stephanie, "Look, I want you and Rachel to work on this together today. I'll be circulating, so I can help you if you need help."

"But Ms. Clark . . . ," Stephanie pleaded.

"Stephanie, I want you to go start working with Rachel. I'll come by in a minute and help you get going."

Stephanie frowned and relented. Still looking upset, she retreated to where Rachel was sitting.

In the meantime, several hands had raised in different groups around the room. Molly walked to the group furthest from her, telling other groups "I'll be right with you" as she walked by. She pulled up an empty chair and faced Brenda, Mary, and Nina. "How can I help you?" she asked.

"We're not sure what to do," said Mary. "We were thinking that Lady Macbeth reminds us of Jezebel, and Macbeth is like the king of Israel. Is that right?"

"That's fine," said Molly. "I just want you to find other ways to see the play. Then, when you do your scene interpretation, you'll have some choices about how to develop it. Now, how is Lady Macbeth like Jezebel? And, how is Macbeth like the king? You should let me know by writing your ideas in your promptbook."

"OK," said Mary.

"Let me go help some of the other groups now and you keep working on your ideas," said Molly.

Valerie, Jennifer, and Rena were sitting silently when Molly approached them. Jennifer was writing in her weekly journal, and the other two were staring at their promptbooks. "Jennifer, please put that away," said Molly. "You need to be working on today's task. Now, how's it going? You guys look stuck."

"We can't think of anything," said Rena.

"Do we *have* to do this?" Jennifer asked. "Why can't we just use your viewpoints? Aren't two enough?"

Molly looked sympathetically at the girls. "I know this is hard. It might be one of the hardest things you've done yet this year. But I think it's important for you to do your own thinking."

"But it's so hard," said Jennifer.

"Well, let me give you an example of what some other groups are doing. Brenda, Mary, and Nina compared the play to Jezebel and King Ahab . . . "

"That's wrong," said Rena testily. "It's not the same at all."

"Well, that's what they came up with. I'm just giving you an example," Molly responded.

"But Jezebel is nothing like Lady Macbeth," Rena asserted, and her face began to redden.

"That's true," said Molly, "but the point is not in the literal comparison. You need to look at the spirit of the story. The spirit of the story is that a woman urged her husband to do unforgivable things and the result was destruction. This is the same thing that happened in *Macbeth*."

"It's not the same!" Rena said, raising her voice slightly.

"I don't want to argue about this with you, Rena," said Molly. "The important thing is that the group found another way to see the play, and I wanted you to hear about it. You don't have to make comparisons to Bible characters. You can compare the main ideas in the play to natural phenomena, or historical events, or current events, or other literature, or movies. I compared the play to the fall of humankind and the Oedipal cycle. Now, as a group, you need to find two more things to compare it to." Molly stood up as she finished speaking and moved toward Stephanie and Rachel.

"How are you two doing?" asked Molly.

"We've just got dumb stuff," Stephanie answered.

"Like what?" asked Molly.

"We thought maybe Lady Macbeth was like a cat playing with a mouse," said Stephanie.

"That's a good start! I don't think that's dumb at all," said Molly. Then she shared the Jezebel/Ahab example and gave them ideas on the other types of things the play might be compared to, after which she moved on to the next group.

Jill, Sarah, and Tracy were quibbling when Molly joined them. "That's stupid!" said Tracy to Sarah.

"What's stupid?" asked Molly.

"Sarah thinks the play is like the story *Little Red Riding Hood*," Tracy said. "That's stupid."

"What made you think of that comparison, Sarah?" Molly asked quietly.

Sarah answered haltingly. "The wolf pretends to . . . he tries to . . . he's going to eat her . . . she doesn't know it's him . . ."

"So, he's trying to fool her?" Molly asked.

"Yeah," said Sarah.

Tracy jumped in, "But how is that like the play?"

"Maybe it's not," said Molly, "but you can't give up on an idea before you consider how it might be. Was that the only idea you've had so far?"

Jill looked up and caught Molly's eye. "Did you have something?" Molly asked.

Tracy jumped in again. "She thought Macbeth is like a flower. How can a person be like a flower? It doesn't make any sense."

"Oh, I think it could make sense," Molly said to Tracy. Then she turned to Jill and asked, "What made you think that Macbeth is like a flower?"

Jill answered, "In the beginning he's beautiful, but as the play goes on he loses his petals—his beauty—until he's nothing but an ugly dried-up bare stalk."

"OK," said Molly. "Now, what if you choose that perspective to interpret your scene? What could you do to communicate that Macbeth is like a dying flower?"

"We could change his clothes as the scenes go on," said Tracy.

"You mean like go from a bright color to a dark color?" said Jill.

"Yeah, or even go from nice clothes to old, ripped-up clothes," returned Tracy.

"That's the idea," said Molly. "You might also want to do something with physical position."

"What do you mean?" asked Tracy.

"Well, like at first Macbeth could stand tall and stately and as the scenes go on he could start to hunch over and crumple up like a dying flower," Molly offered. "Does that make sense?"

The girls began to come up with more ideas about physical position, then Molly directed them to finish developing their perspectives. She excused herself and moved on to the group in the corner. Melissa, Heather, and Ellen were whispering intensely, but when she approached they stopped abruptly. "You don't have to stop on my account," she said. "I'm just here to listen in and see if you're on the right track."

No one spoke. Ellen looked down at her desk, while Melissa and Heather looked at her expectantly. Molly realized that Ellen, who seemed to have recently taken a negative attitude toward her, was not about to speak while she stood there. "If you need any help, just let me know," Molly offered and moved away. Ellen immediately continued speaking when she left the group, and Molly felt a twinge of disappointment about the girl's increasing coldness towards her. She was glad to see, however, that Ellen appeared to be bonding with her group.

For the rest of the period, Molly continued to move from group to group, monitoring the students' progress and assisting them as needed. She left the corner group to themselves, but made a mental note that she'd need to find a way to make sure they were on track. At home that evening, she decided to have each group share its perspectives with the whole class so that she could help them consider how the perspectives could affect scene interpretation and direction.

Molly opened class the following day by asking each group to report its perspectives. Mary, Brenda, and Nina shared first. "We thought the play is like the movie *Beauty and the Beast*," Mary said.

"How so?" asked Molly.

The three girls looked at each other, then Mary attempted to explain. Within a few sentences, she gave up. "Maybe it's not like that," she said.

Molly had not seen the connection and was confused by the faltering explanation, so she let Mary stop. To her surprise, the "secretive" group offered one of their perspectives. Melissa spoke, "We thought the play was like *Snow White*. You know, the witch deceived Snow White by being nice and giving her a shiny apple, but the apple poisoned her."

Mary questioned, "So how is that like *Macbeth?*"

"Macbeth was deceived by Lady Macbeth and the witches and his mind became poisoned, so he killed the king!" Melissa returned.

"I don't get it," said Tracy.

Molly turned the conversation and asked, "If this group decides to use this perspective, how might it affect the way they play their characters?"

"It wouldn't," said Rena matter of factly.

"Yes, it would," said Melissa. "The deceiver would have to act nice and tempting."

"I agree!" announced Tracy. "You can't convince somebody to do something if you're scaring them or being mean."

Molly added, "I think that's interesting. Remember when we saw the play as Adam, Eve, and God? Just like the witch in *Snow White*, Eve and the snake were very sweet and convincing."

Rena spoke up, "But that's not the only way to get somebody to do something!"

"That's true," said Molly. "We're talking about how these specific perspectives might influence the way we play the characters. Another perspective might influence the scene differently. That's why it's important for you to choose a perspective and go with it."

"Ms. Clark, I have another idea!" Nina blurted out.

"Yes?" Molly asked.

"Macbeth is like Jafar in *Aladdin*. And Lady Macbeth is like the parrot Iago who was always whispering in his ear, telling him what to do!" she declared triumphantly.

"I think we're on a Disney theme!" Molly said playfully, and the class started laughing. "Now how would this perspective affect a scene with Lady Macbeth in it?"

"You'd have to play Lady Macbeth kind of quietly," said Brenda.

"No you wouldn't!" returned Melissa. "A parrot is persistent, so Lady Macbeth would have to be played stronger."

"Actually," said Molly, "the character could be played with quiet persistence, couldn't it?" The class agreed that this was possible, though they might choose to go with one extreme or the other.

Valerie, Jennifer, and Rena still hadn't come up with a perspective to share, so they didn't offer one during the class discussion. However, by the end of the period, after more individual group work, they shared with Molly, "Lady Macbeth is like a spark and Macbeth is like wood. She starts a fire she can't control in the end."

As the unit continued, Molly scheduled time for groups to conceptualize and practice their scenes, and she showed them how to write personal biographies and reviews. Random snow days interrupted the groups' progress, but eventually everything fell into place. The week of the performances, Molly's principal stopped her in the hall. "What are you doing with the 11E kids?" she asked.

"I'm just finishing *Macbeth*," Molly responded.

"Just cut your losses and finish it today," Miriam said. "Several kids came to me and said you've been doing the unit for two months."

Molly felt her annoyance rising. "That class has been cancelled twelve times. It's an afternoon class, so we lost more days than morning classes."

"I don't want you to defend yourself. Just finish the unit today," Miriam answered.

"I'm sorry," Molly said, "but I can't finish it today. The kids have to do some performances as part of the evaluation. But, I promise we'll finish it this week."

"Fine," Miriam replied. "Just remember, it's OK to be creative, but you've got to keep the class moving. If you don't do more books, then the parents will blame you when their kids fail the proficiency exam. What are you doing next?"

"I thought we could do *Frankenstein*."

"Good, good," Miriam said in her clipped manner. "You're such a good teacher. Keep the class moving!" she said as she walked away.

Molly thought about how to finish the unit in the time frame she'd specified to her principal. Originally, she'd planned to stagger performances with postperformance discussion, which would require two days. By dropping the discussion, she could fit all the performances into one day. "This is what she wants," she thought and scheduled in one performance day.

When the day of performances came, Molly's spirits were raised. Excitement filled the room as playbills were distributed and groups gathered props and costumes.

During the 43-minute period, tin foil swords flashed, sending a great paper head rolling. A Macbeth with a twentieth-century vocabulary told the witches, "And, by the way, whatever you're cooking smells absolutely horrible." An entranced Lady Macbeth talked to walls and windows. Playbills were splashed with famous Macbeth and Shakespeare art and student-penned calligraphy. Molly observed that the groups had worked well together despite their initial doubts.

Now that *Macbeth* was over, Molly had so many questions. Would the class continue to become more cohesive? Would students remember the play in four months and feel comfortable enough about it to use it for an essay question on the proficiency exam? Had the students learned anything? What would she do differently next year? Only time would tell.

Frank Oakley:

The Classroom

A teacher plans a unit in metric measurement for his students, reflecting on what he has tried in previous years and why those plans didn't work. He tries to develop a teaching strategy given the needs of the students and the inadequate materials.

Frank Oakley unwound the plastic wrap from his sandwich and turned to the stack of student papers sitting on his rubber-topped desk. The thin, blue-lined papers were rumpled, smudged, and ripped. "No matter," Frank thought, biting into peanut butter on whole wheat. "Bring 'em on."

It was lunch period at Littleton High School, but Frank was surrendering his free time to grade a graphing exercise his ninth-grade physical science class had completed the period before. This was the third week of the year, and Frank was so eager to size up his new crop of students that he had not left their now-empty classroom. "All right," he said out loud, as if the papers were the kids themselves. "Let's see how well you can graph."

Wolfing down the rest of his meal, Frank uncapped his red pen. His enthusiasm soon dissipated, though; about half the students in the class had turned in unacceptably sloppy work. Many had mislabeled the axes or had drawn graphs on an illegibly small scale. Some had misplotted points. A few had not even bothered to draw straight lines.

"Aw, this is terrible," Frank thought, as he slashed another red X across a graph. From the students' work on homework assignments, Frank knew they understood the concept of plotting coordinates. But some of them obviously had not cared to follow through in class. And Frank thought he knew why: he had let the students work in pairs.

Allowing students to work in groups was a technique Frank remembered from graduate courses in education. It was supposed to be a fun way to teach teamwork, a method for inspiring less motivated students. What it had become with this class, Frank realized, was an invitation to goof off. Ruefully, he conjured images from the period: two boys pushing their chairs to the back of the room out of his line of sight; two motor-mouth girls giggling straight through the class.

"The trouble with students picking partners is they usually end up with someone as lazy as themselves," Frank thought. "Jerks pair up with jerks."

Frank pulled another paper from the stack. It was a perfect paper, so far the only one he had read. Frank remembered that Michael, the freckle-faced red-head who had drawn it, had worked alone. "That's it," he thought to himself. "Pairing doesn't work."

Pairing doesn't work. Here was a new addition to Frank's small but growing collection of truths about teaching high school students. By training and incli-nation, Frank was a deducer of truths. For most of his professional life, he had taught at a local medical school. With a Ph.D. in microbiology and an assistant professorship at a medical school in his resumé, Frank was a published re-searcher and a specialist in lung disease. But four years before, Frank had faced a difficult decision. To climb higher on the academic ladder, he would have had to find a job at a university that would offer him a tenure-track position. And that would mean moving his wife and four children from the Littleton area, where they had sunk roots.

Instead, at the age of 35, Frank decided to return to high school, this time as a teacher. He enrolled in a science-teacher certification program at a local uni-versity. Because of a shortage of science teachers, Frank had no problem secur-ing a job. Littleton hired him the day his notice of certification arrived in the mail.

Now he was beginning his third year at the school. This semester, his course load included four classes geared mostly for first-year students: three physical science classes and a biology class. None presented a bigger instruc-tional challenge than the average-level physical science course he taught third period.

Every fall, the science department dispersed incoming ninth-graders to five different classes: honors biology, above-average-level biology, above-average-level physical science, average-level physical science, and remedial-level phys-ical science. Considered poor bets to pursue higher education in the sciences, physical science students at all three levels usually wound up taking watered-down versions of the biology and chemistry courses offered to the college-bound, although good above-average-level students in physical science often made it to the harder upper-class courses.

The average-level track was a particular challenge in that it typically en-rolled students with a greater range of ability and motivation than the others. Frank's third-period class illustrated an extreme of this rule. The students were both intellectually and demographically diverse. The class had twenty stu-dents, eleven of whom were black, six Hispanic, and three white. There were ten boys and ten girls.

The male-female ratio and the relative crowding contributed to making third period very noisy. Every day before the late bell, Frank could count at least four flirtations in progress, and they usually continued at a stage whisper through class. "Ninth-graders are ruled by the pituitary gland," Frank had de-cided. Another problem in third period was that several of the students liked to "disrespect" or insult each other. Frank had assigned seats the first day of class, but after a week of noise he reorganized the seating, banishing the loudest mouths to opposite sides of the room. He called this trick his "four-corners de-fense."

There was nothing Frank could do about the students' range of abilities, however. He had never seen such extremes. Most of the kids were considered slightly below average. Yet some seemed so bright Frank thought they could have handled the work in his biology class. At the other extreme were three tenth-grade students repeating the course after flunking it the year before. "Half of this class could have an A average, and the others don't know what an average is," Frank told his wife after work one day. "I have no middle this year."

Picking at the whole-wheat crumbs on his desk, Frank finished recording marks in his grade book and looked up at the classroom clock. He had two minutes to make it to biology. The biology classroom was just around the corner, but compared to the atmosphere of the physical science classroom, it could have been a world away.

The physical science room had one sink, no plants, and a row of old posters celebrating "Famous Black Scientists"—so faded the scientists looked white. Four rows of tables, each with two chairs, filled the room. The two-seaters had been coated with stain-resistant black rubber; since the room had no lab counters, students had to perform labs at their tables.

The biology room, on the other hand, looked like a real laboratory. It had anatomical and chemical models, a virtual greenhouse of terrariums and ferns, and a row of experiment counters, each with its own gas spigot and sink.

When Frank thought about the contrast, he realized that the makeshift conditions in the physical science room were indicative of physical science's low status in Littleton's science department. For a long time, average-level physical science had been a dead end, a holding pen for students who needed science credits to graduate. Two years before, however, a new principal had begun a crusade to improve the school's average and remedial classes. Frank shared his enthusiasm. He knew the first year in high school was virtually a kid's last chance to escape the stigma of low tracking. He wanted his physical science classes to be a platform for his students to leap to more rewarding science courses. And he was proud that every year 30 to 40 percent of his students qualified to move on to above-average biology.

Frank gathered up the crinkly graph papers and restacked them in a rumpled pile. As he did, he wondered who in this year's pile would make it around the bend to biology.

Michael, the boy who had worked alone, would do it with ease, Frank thought. Owner of the highest average in class, Michael was a quiet, ghostly pale boy who every day took his seat silently and flipped open his notebook. Though Michael preferred to work alone, he never complained when paired with a partner, and his work never faltered. In fact, Frank had no idea why Michael wasn't in biology already.

Another likely survivor was Hank, a black student with a taste for designer clothes, who wore a "buzz" haircut with floral patterns shaved into his hair. Like Michael, whom he sat behind, Hank displayed real originality on homework. But he was careful not to appear too smart in class. He was always pestering his deskmate, Ali, to the point that Frank had to repeat questions to both. Hank often drifted into the class late, usually with a loud, disruptive "Yo!" to Yusif, his friend across the room.

Darryl was *not* prime honors biology material. Chubby and heavy-lidded, he sometimes appeared to be hibernating inside his oversized bomber jacket. His grasp of basic concepts was shaky. Once, when he was called on to define volume, Frank had to repeat the question four times before Darryl supplied the answer.

Darryl could usually be found pitched halfway into the aisle that separated him from a Hispanic girl named Maria. Maria invariably tilted back toward him; sometimes the couple's heads would touch in a midair V. Maria was repeating physical science, and if her flirting kept up, Frank suspected she'd end up there for a third time.

Jane and Yvonne, on the other hand, would do fine, especially if they could be kept on task. Yvonne was a mature black girl whose sharp tongue and quick wit made her a class leader. Jane, a junior-varsity cheerleader, was white and equally popular. Frank had assigned the two students to the same desk, and they had proceeded, when focused, to set a positive tone for the entire class. Frank remembered one time when a dizzy student had flounced in late, announcing that she had lost her homework. "Good for you, retard," Yvonne had snapped with a cold stare that frightened the girl into doing her homework for a week. Lately, however, Yvonne and Jane had done as much disrupting as policing, chatting their grades to below the C range.

"Pairing *doesn't* work," Frank muttered, as the bell burst his reverie about his physical science class. Picking up his satchel of papers, he bustled into the biology room.

"Mr. Oakley! Mr. Oakley! I think you made a mistake on my test." A blond girl wearing an expensive sweater accosted him before he could make his way to his desk.

"Hold your horses, Daphne, I promise you I'll answer your questions soon," Frank responded.

He looked at the girl and past her to the rest of the class. Once again, all twenty-two students had beaten him to class and were gossiping in their seats. The kids in biology were typical products of above-average tracking, Frank thought: the majority white, all accepting of daily routines and all reasonably motivated, if not by love of science then by grades and college plans.

What they needed, Frank thought, was to have their routines shaken up every once in a while. That was why he occasionally used cooperative learning activities with this group.

"All right! Listen up," Frank said. "A couple of you had some questions about last week's cell exam. But instead of me talking during the whole class, maybe you can answer the questions yourselves. What I want you to do is break up into your four-person lab groups. I'll be around to each group in a few minutes to help out. But first, see if you can help solve your group's mistakes yourselves."

Cooperative learning was another one of the theories he had learned in graduate school that both intrigued Frank and gave him migraines. There was, for example, the dilemma of integrating diverse students into lab work. Inevitably, Frank had found, the one or two best students in a group conducted the experiment while the rest copied results. Enforcing autonomous work was virtually impossible since, in effect, it entailed policing six or seven groups simultaneously. There was simply no way to keep an eye on the kids who needed the most watching. "Rule 3," Frank thought. "In groups of three or more, someone always gets lost in the shuffle."

As the kids piloted their chairs into their groups and began to work, Frank found his thoughts returning to his third-period physical science class. In two days it would be time for their first lab, and Frank had not yet decided how to organize it.

Required by the course curriculum, the first physical science lab was an experiment in graphing and using the metric system. Students had to calculate and plot the volume of a series of wooden blocks using both linear measurement and fluid displacement. They also had to calculate and plot weight and density. In his first year, Frank organized the activity into stations: weighing, block measuring, beaker filling, and so on. Students worked with lab partners and were instructed to start at any free station and move on when finished. The result, Frank remembered with gruesome clarity, had been chaos. Many kids, unsure of where to go and when, had frozen in confusion amid the hurly-burly of activity.

Last year, Frank had imposed more order by assigning one process per period. Now, however, he worried that a rigidly structured approach would not work with the rambunctious and disparate students of third period. He could already envision the student who would be working with Michael pushing the balance scale in Michael's direction and letting him do the work. Hank would also scuttle away from his partner, no doubt theatrically and loudly complaining about messing up his clothes in the experiment. And Darryl would play while his lab partner worked. Frank winced as he mentally pictured Darryl idly fooling with a glass beaker until it shattered on the ground.

"That won't do," he thought. Frank mentally checked off his available materials. The physical science classroom had eighteen graduated cylinders, nineteen beakers, eighteen rulers, twenty-three sets of measurable blocks, sixteen sets of colored pencils for bar graphs, and ten scales. He could ill afford to lose any lab equipment. As it was, the shortage of scales and colored pencils already posed a serious problem. Mastering measurement and graphing were the most important skills the students would learn this year, prerequisites not just for college science courses but for survival in the job market. No matter how poorly stocked the supply cabinet, it was essential that every student get hands-on experience with the instruments.

"How am I going to engineer this lab so they all learn it?" Frank wondered. "Let's see, what if I had every student . . ."

"Mr. Oakley!" Daphne's shrill voice brought his musings to a halt. "You said you would help."

"I'll be right there."

Time had run out for this pass at the problem. But in the back of his mind, Frank kept the wheels turning, aware that if he could manage to work out a plan for lab day, he might fit at least one piece into his larger puzzle of how to meet the vastly diverse needs of his third-period students all year long.

PART THREE

Diversity

Carol Brown

A first-grade teacher, after socially integrating an extremely heterogeneous class, sees her efforts threatened when a child's pencil case disappears and is thought to have been stolen.

Carol Brown locked her car and turned her collar up against the cold January wind as she rushed toward the school. At the outer doors of the building, Carol reached down and picked up a red mitten that must have been dropped as students raced to their buses the night before. She tucked it into her pocket, making a mental note that later she would take it to the lost and found.

Her mind was already on a situation that began yesterday in her first-grade classroom. As the class settled in, John Casey realized that his pencil case was missing from his desk. Some of the children suggested that it had been stolen, but Carol assured them that it was probably misplaced and would turn up soon. However, by the end of the day the pencil case had not been found, and Carol remembered how upset John was when school was dismissed.

Hanging up her coat in her classroom, Carol heard an argument just outside her door. She stepped into the corridor and found two of her students shouting at each other. Managing to separate them, Carol asked the boys what the problem was.

"Robert stole my mitten," yelled Brian.

Robert interrupted, "I didn't steal nothin'."

Brian explained to Carol that he had both his mittens in his pocket the day before. He sat with Robert on the bus going home, and when he got off the bus one of his mittens was gone.

"He's lying. I never took his dumb mitten." Robert seemed very upset at the accusation.

"Brian, what does your mitten look like?" Carol asked as she walked the two boys into the classroom and showed them the mitten she had retrieved from the sidewalk earlier.

Brian grabbed the mitten and said, "That's mine. That's my mitten. Where was it?"

Carol knelt down and pulled both Brian and Robert to her. She looked at Brian and said, "I found it right outside the building when I came in this morning. Don't you think you owe Robert an apology?"

Brian looked down at his feet and then at Robert. "I'm sorry," he said. Brian spoke quietly, but it seemed clear that he really was sorry.

"It's good that you could apologize, Brian. See how bad you made Robert feel by accusing him of stealing? You guys are such good friends, it would really be a shame to lose a friend because you accused someone unfairly. You won't do that again, will you?"

Brian shook his head to indicate that he would not. Carol turned to Robert. "Do you accept Brian's apology?"

Robert shrugged and said, "Yeah, OK."

Carol hugged the children and said, "Let's seal it with a high five."

Both boys giggled, slapped upraised palms, and left the classroom to wait in the gym for the morning bell.

Carol watched them leave and thought to herself, "Why would Brian automatically suspect that his mitten had been stolen? What a strange reaction from him." But, as she remembered the missing pencil case, she suspected that it was more than coincidence that stealing was on Brian's mind. Carol knew that the children had been consumed the day before with talk about the "stolen" pencil case, and she feared it would not be quickly forgotten.

John had brought the pencil case to school just after Christmas, and the whole class had demonstrated an appreciation for what a treasure it was. John did not hesitate to share the case with other students. It was not unusual to see the other children carrying it around, using the ruler or protractor or stapler that were part of the case. Yesterday morning John came back to school after being absent the day before and found that the pencil case was not in his desk where he had left it.

At first, Carol suggested that perhaps someone had borrowed the case and forgotten to return it. To Carol's dismay, none of the students resolved the problem by bringing forth the missing item. When Carol suggested that maybe it had simply been misplaced, John became frustrated and angry. The child was upset about his loss and in his anger did not hesitate to announce openly to the rest of the first-grade class that someone had stolen his property.

The other children seemed affected by the situation because the missing item was something that they all enjoyed using. The class was quick to rally around the idea that this was a theft, and some children began to name possible "suspects." In only one day, Carol Brown's happy, close-knit class of twenty-four children became accusatory and mean.

In the beginning of the year, this class had presented a real challenge for Carol, because the children came from such diverse backgrounds. Of the fifteen girls and nine boys in the class, eight came from economically disadvantaged homes. The Littleton school system had implemented its racial balance program in such a way that this school drew its students from the richest section of the city, where the school was located, and from the poorest areas, from which a sizable number of students were bused. There was only a small representation of middle-class children to buffer these disparate groups. Students in Carol's class who were driven to school in Mercedes sat next to others whose parents could not afford to provide warm winter coats.

At first, as would be natural, the children from the affluent neighborhoods tended to associate with one another, and the children from the poorer areas felt more comfortable with friends from their own neighborhoods. This natural tendency, coupled with the fact that the children shared very few common experiences, made it difficult at first to break down the barriers and create a unified class.

In the first few months of school, Carol implemented as many strategies as she could to help the students interact and to provide shared experiences in the classroom. Early in September, she established cooperative learning groups. She made certain that the groups were balanced socioeconomically and that each group contained no more than three or four students so that small cliques within the groups could not form. The types of activities she created required that the children work together in order to get the most from the tasks. She changed the group composition every two weeks.

Carol also established centers that only a few children at a time could work in. There were centers for playing dress-up games, for building with blocks, for listening to talking books, for working at the computer, for doing art projects, and so on. Children drew lots for which center they could go to, guaranteeing that there would always be a diverse population at each one. Since the children typically had "center time" twice a day, there were many opportunities for the children to interact and to get to know and trust one another.

The classroom also featured what Carol called "the author's seat," which allowed all the children to share stories they had written. This helped the students get to know one another and begin to understand each other's backgrounds. Carol's early efforts paid off, and by Thanksgiving the children were mingling easily and interacting across socioeconomic groups on their own.

This was an accomplishment Carol felt very proud of because her approach to teaching had always stressed respect. In her class, Carol often discussed the importance of individuality and the ways in which all students shared equal rights within the classroom community. But the current incident certainly put her philosophy to the test. In just one day the missing pencil case created an air of suspicion among the students that Carol feared would undermine the integration she had achieved.

Carol began to wonder what had really happened to the pencil case. It was clear that John's friends thought that one of the poor children had stolen it, and Carol nurtured the same suspicion. While all the children coveted the special pencil case, Carol understood that the affluent children had many treasures and the poor children had few.

Carol had been teaching for many years in elementary classes. Early in her career, she spent three years teaching in an economically deprived urban area and encountered many situations involving classroom theft. She understood the pressure and sorrow of poverty and knew that the egocentrism of children could translate envy into action. This very heterogeneous class, however, added a new dimension to this classic problem. Before, she had been able to handle a theft situation without worrying about whether it would undo the foundation of a successfully integrated group.

Carol looked at the clock and saw that class was about to begin. She knew that she had to handle the pencil-case situation today and that she had to do it very carefully. More important to Carol than the $10 pencil case was the preservation of trust among the students. How could she carry on her investigation discreetly in order to solve the problem of John's missing property and perhaps further her agenda of mutual trust and respect?

As the children spilled into the room and began to sit in a circle on the area rug where the class always started its day, Carol resolved to use the pencil-case incident as a means of strengthening the class's unity rather than permit the situation, through inaction, to cause divisiveness. She also knew this was an ideal opportunity to use a real-life situation to help the children grow. "A good offense . . ." Carol thought as she took her place in the circle.

"Good morning, boys and girls. Are you all warm now that we're inside and together?"

"Yeah." "Sure." "It's so cold!" A chorus of replies rang around Carol.

"What day is today, Fernando?"

"Um . . ." Fernando, a dark-skinned Puerto Rican child dressed in an oversize sweatshirt looked toward the posterboard calendar that hung on the wall above the play area shelves. "Um . . . Wednesday."

"And what number day is it?" Carol continued addressing Fernando.

"Numero 15. Of January."

"Good! Would you go put the number 15 in the Wednesday slot so that we can all remember the date?" As Fernando uncurled himself to update the calendar, Carol turned her attention to the rest of the children.

"Today we are going to finish the story we began yesterday about Eskimos, and we are going to make pictures of igloos and snowmen at art time using cotton and glitter. Then after recess we're going to bring some snow inside for science time and look at it and feel it and talk about what happens when we heat it up. But, first, I want to talk to all of you about something I think is on our minds—John's pencil case, which we lost yesterday."

"Somebody took it," a girl with blond pigtails called out indignantly.

"Did you find it?" John Casey asked excitedly.

"No, it was stolen. It's gone," Fernando said to John with a "forget it" gesture.

"Well, children, I don't know where it is, and we may not find it. But let's talk about your feeling that the pencil case might have been stolen. Karen, you said you think someone took it. Why do you think that?"

"Because it was so nice and somebody that wanted it an' couldn't buy it would just take it."

"Would you take something that you didn't have the money to buy?" Carol asked.

"Well, maybe, if I really wanted it." Karen seemed to sense she was on thin ice with this admission but obviously answered honestly.

"Then you'd get caught an' go to jail!" cried Brian. "You can't steal, or you go to jail!"

"Why do we send people to jail for stealing, Brian?" pursued Carol.

"Because it's wrong!"

"Yes, it is wrong to steal. But why is it wrong? Yusef?"

"Cause you might go to jail. My brother is in jail 'cause he tooked some stuff ain't his. He ain't never comin' home!" Yusef's eyes were huge and hurt, and a few of the children looked frightened and subdued as they digested this information.

"That's dumb. Kids don' go to jail," ventured Robert confidently.

"An' if nobody was looking an' you knowed you wouldn't go to jail you might take it," Janey spoke quietly.

"Sure, you only go to jail if the teacher sees," volunteered Arlene.

"Well, we already said that children don't go to jail, Arlene, and certainly teachers are here to help children learn what is right, not to catch children or punish them. But I want you to think about whether or not there are other reasons not to take something that is not yours." Carol's manner was warm and encouraging as she smiled at her class.

There was silence in the circle as the children thought. "Well, just if you get in trouble," Robert finally concluded.

"And if John is sad his case is gone," Brian mused.

"Yeah, if your mother finds it or you get caught!" Another student's elaboration on Robert's point drowned out Brian's contribution.

"What if we all took each other's things whenever we wanted?" prompted Carol. "What would happen then?" Again the students concentrated on their teacher's question. The seconds ticked by, and Carol fleetingly thought about getting through story time and art before recess.

"Well, we'd all get in trouble, I guess," speculated Yusef.

"Yes, that's right," agreed Carol. "Classrooms need rules just like grownups do so that students can all work together happily and not worry about their things being taken. We need to trust each other and care about each other." Carol studied the open faces turned toward her in an attempt to read the children's reactions. She saw acceptance in their eyes because she was the teacher, but she felt a nagging doubt that they really understood or believed her.

"So who took my case?" John suddenly called, addressing his classmates accusingly. They looked at him miserably, and Carol saw that the discussion hadn't served its intended purpose.

"What," she wondered, "do I do now?"

Mary Ewing

An experienced high school math teacher moves to the middle school and has problems with grouping in a remedial math class where each of the eleven students is working at a different level.

"Forget it! I have to do my own work!" Joe Johnson's anger at his classmate's interruption was way out of proportion to the concentration he had been investing on his worksheet.

"Well, *excuse me!*" Anna Jones affected great indignation to hide her embarrassment at having her request for help rejected.

Mary Ewing was bending over a worksheet of word problems with one of her students, and she looked up in irritation when she heard this outburst from the other end of the room.

"Miss Margolis, would you please help Anna when you have a moment?" Mary addressed her teacher's aide, who was across the room helping Hank with a division problem. Miss Margolis looked up and nodded, although she was clearly frustrated by the number of students clamoring for help. Mary knew that Betty Margolis was no wizard in mathematics and that it took all her concentration to make mental leaps from addition to division to fractions in order to accommodate the four groups into which Mary had divided her class.

"Miss Margolis promised to help me next!" shouted George, who had been waiting more or less patiently with his head on his folded arms. "This stuff don't make no sense no how!"

Mary sighed and marshaled her characteristic patience and understanding. It was six weeks into the school year, and she was enjoying the year in most ways, but she dreaded the constant disruption and noise that seemed endemic to this seventh- and eighth-grade remedial math class. "George, you have been very patient. I will help you when I finish with group B. And Joe, next time someone in your group asks for help, you give it!" Mary realized that this outburst had distracted all the children, and she had exacerbated the disruption by addressing the principals from her seat beside Jesse. But Jesse was so close to grasping the arithmetic operation that had been eluding him since September that she did not want to leave his side until they had finished. Too often with this class Mary wrestled with just such a choice: disrupt her group instruction to control the class or risk overall bedlam.

This was Mary's tenth year teaching math, but all her previous experience was on the high school level. Mary had been excited last spring when she was offered the chance to teach at Littleton Middle School. She saw the change as a chance to meet new challenges and to stay "fresh" in her field. She was assigned four regular math classes, which ranged from general math to honors geometry, and one remedial math class during the second period. The latter was a group of eleven children, ages 12 to 15. The class was nearly balanced racially: six black and five white students, but that was where the symmetry ended. The skill levels and math backgrounds of the children were widely diverse. In this class Mary had some students who were working on two-digit addition and others who were ready for fractions. Individualization of instruction was required in all classrooms, Mary knew, but she had never found it so difficult to accomplish until now.

Mary had known that this would be the case when she first began planning during the summer. She familiarized herself with each child's needs through his or her test scores and other records and devised a plan for math that had worked well in her high school classes. She divided the eleven students into four groups according to their readiness and skill levels. On the first day of class she assigned groups as follows:

Group A: **Division and fractions**
- Hank Donovan
- Sheila Arjoon
- Sara Black

Group B: **Times tables and multiplication problems**
- Jesse Smith
- Jimmy Lyons

Group C: **Four-digit addition and subtraction with regrouping**
- George Sanders
- Adam Garth
- Jack Myers

Group D: **Simple addition and subtraction**
- Anna Jones
- Joe Johnson
- Peter Marks

By the second week, Mary modified her plan, as her personal experience with the children led to a refinement of group assignments. She moved Sheila to group B and Peter to group C. While this rearrangement resulted in groups of different sizes, Mary thought she had like-skilled students grouped fairly closely.

Mary spent the first week of the school year teaching cooperation and group learning skills almost as much as she taught math. Mary had attended a seminar on cooperative learning at her district's Teacher Center a few years ago when the technique was first introduced, and she implemented aspects of the approach with her high school classes, modifying it as she felt necessary to fit the characteristics of her students. Mary duplicated her group formula in most of her classes this year. She arranged the desks in a horseshoe so that she could sit at the open end when working with one group. The children in other groups sat next to their group-mates around the horseshoe, working independently but sitting close enough to each other for help to be exchanged as necessary. Mary also introduced a token system modeled after one that served her well in her high school remedial classes. Each child earned tokens, redeemable for free time, bathroom privileges, computer time, or library time. Tokens were earned by completing one's own assignments successfully and on time, and they were also awarded on the basis of the success of one's group-mates.

By the second week in October, however, Mary was concerned. Total individualization was required, even within groups. Some students responded more easily to word problems; others to arithmetic operations. Some could use the school-supplied curriculum, but others needed customized worksheets and instruction. Within each group, some of the children had yet to grasp the concept of the arithmetic operation under study, while other students were ready for practice and application of the skill involved. Mary often found herself preparing eleven different math lessons each day, drawing upon four different math textbooks, the curriculum used by the regular math classes, worksheets, workbooks, and her own intuition about what would click with each student.

Besides the time required to prepare so many lessons, a big disadvantage of such extreme individualization was its negative impact on group cooperation. When Mary was working with one group and Miss Margolis with another, the remaining two groups were to work individually at their desks, helping each other with questions and explanations as needed. But because the children were working on different operations even within their groups, they were distracted by one another's requests for help.

Furthermore, Mary was not used to the immaturity of children of this age. In spite of her instruction on group behavior, she soon discovered that the children could not work effectively together without an adult present. They would tease each other when they discovered mistakes, and the more advanced students occasionally made fun of those working on more basic skills. Joe Johnson, in particular, was the butt of many jokes, for at 15 he was the oldest student but was working on the most elementary material. Those students who did try to help their classmates often just confused matters with explanations that were unclear or incorrect.

In spite of the fact that general murmurs of conversation were audible around the room, Mary returned her focus to the students in Jesse's group. She forced herself to recall their conversation even as she listened to—and ignored—the escalating din.

"I'm sorry, Jesse. Sheila, put that down and listen too." Mary glanced sharply at Jimmy Lyons to be sure he, too, was paying attention. "Now tell me, Jesse, again. How many popsicles did the Good Humor man sell on Tuesday?"

"Mrs. Ewing, we done this problem yesterday!"

"Sheila, we are going over this again to be sure your whole group understands it, and then we will move on. You know, using multiplication in everyday life takes lots of practice. Listening to this review won't hurt you."

Sheila grumbled something inaudible under her breath and rolled her eyes. Jimmy and Jesse looked at each other with expressions of disdain, but Mary knew they were trying to mask their embarrassment over the fact that they had not completed this assignment. Mary decided to let the boys off the hook.

"All right, Sheila, since you know the answer to this problem, why don't you show the rest of us how you got it."

Sheila looked down at her worksheet and tried to gather her thoughts. "Well, the ice cream truck sold 439 popsicles on Tuesday; 63 of them were ice bars, 244 were frozen eclairs, and the rest were ice cream sandwiches."

"Sheila, what are we trying to figure out in this problem? What is the overall thing we want to know?" Mary wanted to be sure these children really understood the concepts of problem solving behind this example, and so she started again at the top.

"Well, what do you mean?"

"Pretend you are the Good Humor man. I mean woman." Mary smiled. "What do you want to know at the end of the day?"

"How much money I made!" Jimmy was paying attention and even enjoying himself.

"Right, Jim. OK, Sheila, if you want to know how much money you made and you sold different kinds of ice cream bars that sold for different amounts of money, what do you have to do?"

Sheila was on track again. "You have to multiply how many you sold of each kind by how much each kind costs."

"Good! Jesse, do you see what Sheila did? Did she just make sense?" Mary reached for Sheila's paper as she spoke and slid it to the right so that Jesse could see it.

"Uh, yeah, so he sold, um, 63 that cost a quarter and the eclairs cost a dollar. . . . " Suddenly they all heard laughter coming from across the room. Jesse looked up from Sheila's paper and turned toward the sound. Mary turned with exasperation and saw Anna and Peter laughing.

"Hank, look at this!" Peter grabbed a paper from the desk in front of Joe Johnson and sailed it across the horseshoe. As it fell to the floor in front of his desk, Hank noisily leaped forward in a futile attempt to catch it.

"Slow Joe just added 13 and 38 and got 41!" laughed Peter. "Can you believe it?"

"Group D for *dumb*—I'll never get any chips with Joe on my team," moaned Anna.

"Well, you aren't the smartest girl in school either!" shouted Joe. As he spoke, he sent Anna's open book, paper, and pencils flying to the floor with a sweep of his arm.

The noise of the book striking the floor stunned the class into silence, and Mary reacted swiftly and decisively. "All right—*no more!* I am appalled at you! Peter, Anna, I expect you here after school. I will not tolerate this sort of criticism of each other." Mary turned and spoke just as sharply to the rest of the class. "We will all work alone for the rest of the class period. It is obvious you cannot work together today. Miss Margolis and I will do our best to help those who need it, but I do not want to hear one more word from anyone except to a teacher. Is that understood?"

• • •

Mary opened her second-period class the next morning with mixed emotions. She had decided overnight to make some changes in the class in order to structure it more realistically in light of the children's attitudes and abilities. She believed that she was bowing to the inevitable, but she also felt a sense of defeat. Mary had always enjoyed teaching classes that could work well together, and she felt that important skills were learned when children cooperated. But this class was simply not responding to that formula, and math was not being learned. Since she had to individualize so much anyway, Mary decided to capitulate.

"Good morning. I have some changes to explain to you this morning." Mary spoke as the bell rang. The children were arranging their notebooks and taking out pencils, but the tone of her voice captured their attention.

"Each of you is working on different concepts in this class, and I have decided that working in groups is not helping you as much as it is distracting you. From now on, we will have a system for individual work. No more groups."

This sank in for a moment, and then Sara Black waved her hand in the back of the room. "Yes, Sara?"

"Does that mean no more chips? How do we earn free time?"

"You will each earn chips on the basis of your own work. Just as before, you get one chip for turning in work on time, one if you get only one problem wrong, and two if your work is perfect. But you get no chips for anyone else's work. Just your own."

"All right!" Jimmy's comment underscored the general nods of approval visible around the room. The students' reactions made Mary sad, but again she was convinced of the necessity of this action. These kids just didn't like working together.

"You will each have your own work folders, which I will prepare with your assignments." Mary walked around the horseshoe placing closed manila folders on each student's desk. "No one else even needs to know what you are working on." When she got back to her desk, she held up a chart with two columns entitled "Need Help" and "Work Complete." "This chart will always be kept on my desk. If you need my help as you are working on your assignment, get up and write your name in the 'Need Help' column; then sit quietly while you wait for me or Miss Margolis to get to you. We will cross off names as we go, so you will know when your turn is coming up."

"What do we do while we wait?"

"You may do other work."

"Even other class work?"

"Yes, as long as you are quiet. When you finish your work, write your name in the 'Work Complete' column; I will check your papers when I am free."

"This might be a little boring," ventured Joe. "Can't we . . . "

Mary interrupted abruptly. "Joe, this is our new procedure. Do you have any questions on how we will work?" Joe remained silent, and Mary gazed around the room at the rest of the class. "OK, then, let's do some math!"

Mark Siegel

A fourth-grade teacher is irritated by a parent who visits him regularly, demanding better teaching for her son. The teacher believes that he has tried everything and that the problem rests with the child and the demanding mother.

Mark Siegel shifted uncomfortably in his chair. This latest conference with Kyesha Peterson was going no better than the earlier ones. Realizing he had stopped listening to her, he tuned back in and heard her say, "Karim isn't learning enough in your class. It's November, and he still isn't catching up. What are you going to do for him?"

"Mrs. Peterson, we've had this conversation before. I'm continually trying to help Karim."

"We certainly have had this conversation before. And I don't see any evidence that you've made things better for Karim in your class."

"You're right. Karim has not made any great breakthroughs since our last meeting. He isn't responding to any of the strategies I use in my classroom. He simply shows no interest in participating in class activities."

Mrs. Peterson continued to look out the window. "Well, it seems to me that it's your job to make school interesting for the students."

Mark gritted his teeth. He tried to recall if he had ever met a parent who treated him so rudely. He thought, "This woman has a lot of nerve coming in here and telling me what my job is." And since Kyesha Peterson had been coming to see him at least once every two weeks since school started, Mark was feeling both hounded by her and stung by her criticism.

By four o'clock, Mrs. Peterson had said her piece and allowed Mark to escort her to the front of the school. The conference ended with Mark assuring her that he would give Karim more attention and make further efforts to make school more compelling for the boy.

Walking back to his classroom, Mark thought about Karim Peterson. A part of Mark felt sorry for Karim because, in addition to the child's academic problems, he seemed like such a social outcast in the class. When the difficulties with Mrs. Peterson began, Mark went to Paula Fowler, Karim's third-grade teacher the year before. She told Mark a little bit about Karim's background.

Karim was a 9-year-old who came from a stable black family in which he was the youngest of three children. African culture and heritage were strongly emphasized in their home. The mother seemed to be the dominant figure in the family and, according to Paula, her beliefs and values were firmly impressed upon the children. The Petersons celebrated African holidays; American holidays were ignored. The year before, Karim had been kept home the day of the class Christmas party. His mother had explained to Paula that if academics were not going to be taught, Karim didn't need to waste his time at a party for a holiday the family did not recognize.

Paula told Mark that the family seemed to be very conscious of racial issues and that Karim and his siblings tended to have negative ideas about white culture. On one occasion Karim had challenged Paula by rudely asking why there were no black children in the highest reading group.

Karim's father was a bus driver for the city transportation system, and his mother worked in the Littleton public library. Paula believed that education and career opportunities were extremely important to the family.

Karim had difficulty socializing with the other children in Mark's class. He could be verbally abusive to the other children, and he seemed to be a loner. The children teased him for talking "like a baby." When he was nervous, he had a habit of sniffing his fingers, and the children made fun of him whenever he did.

During the two months that Karim had been in Mark's class, it became obvious that the other children did not like to be grouped with him. When Mark asked the children to choose and work with partners, Karim had to be assigned a partner. Most of the time he was reluctant to participate in activities that involved peer interaction. When the class had free time, Karim usually sat by himself. His classmates did not include him in their activities, and he did not express any interest in joining them in play.

Despite his seemingly antisocial behavior, Karim was a reasonably verbal, bright child. His standardized test scores suggested that he should easily be doing grade-level work. Mark understood why Mrs. Peterson expected better school performance from Karim, given his verbal skills and his test scores. While the boy was working only about half a year behind grade level, his oral reading was slow and labored enough to concern his mother. Mark thought that Karim's limited reading skills contributed to his poor school performance, and he felt that Karim's inability to focus on his work and maintain his attention contributed to his problems. Karim's short attention span and slow reading meant that he worked very slowly, and he often was unable to finish in-class assignments.

Since Karim's mother began demanding that her son receive special attention, Mark had used all the tricks he'd learned in his nine years of teaching fourth and fifth grades at Roosevelt Elementary School. His goal had been to improve Karim's reading skills and bring them up to at least grade level. At first, he thought that if he could spark more interest, Karim would respond with increased attention. Mark tried some high-interest reading materials, using topics like sports, music, and extraterrestrials—guaranteed winners with other fourth-grade students. None captured Karim's attention; he did not seem to share many of the interests of his peers. Mark also tried a reward system, offering Karim free time for completing work within an assigned time. Karim didn't respond. Mark then sat down with him and tried to find out what would act as a reinforcer, but he found Karim uncooperative. The boy seemed unwilling to discuss his interests with Mark or to tell Mark what rewards he would be willing to work for. Mark learned nothing he could use from their meeting.

While Mark was frustrated by Karim, his frustration was exacerbated by Karim's mother, whose demands for after-school conferences were increasing. Since Mark was unable to report any successes with Karim to Mrs. Peterson, these meetings were now making Mark feel particularly anxious. He had had no luck reaching Karim, improving his reading, or getting him to respond to either teacher or classmates. Mark felt he could honestly say that he had tried his best with Karim, but he also felt that there were some kids who could not be reached. It seemed to him that Karim might be one of them.

Mark slumped down at his desk and thought to himself, "I've only got to make it until the end of the year; then Karim will move on to fifth grade and take his crazy mother with him." That thought was not much help, however, since it was now November 4, and Mrs. Peterson was sure to return in two weeks.

Maxine Korns

A teacher is having problems coping with her students, many of whom come to school with emotional problems. The number of difficult students has increased recently, and the school district has instituted rules and procedures for dealing with behavior problems.

"It's all right, Malcolm. Shh . . . it's all right." Maxine Korns leaned down and picked up the jumpy, angular 5-year-old, shifting slightly in her child-sized chair to keep her balance as she settled him in her lap. She began to rock gently, turning so that one arm entirely encircled the wiggling child and the other held the book open toward the twenty-seven children sitting in a circle on the floor. Maxine wondered how such a small child—he seemed to weigh less than her cat—could maintain such perpetual motion. "Another one who suffers from the sins of the mothers," she thought briefly, even as she returned to her lesson.

"You know that people who write books are called authors, boys and girls. The author of this book is Eric Carle, and he called his book *The Very Hungry Caterpillar*." Maxine opened the book to the title page as she spoke. "What do you think *The Very Hungry Caterpillar* is going to be about?" Maxine smiled and nodded toward the students at her feet while simultaneously holding her chin clear of Malcolm's bouncing head. She kept up the rocking motion and nodded toward a little girl who was anxiously waving her hand. "Angelina?"

"I think it's about a bug."

"That's an interesting idea. What makes you think that?" queried Maxine.

"The picture on the front," replied the child brightly. As she spoke she swished her head from side to side, apparently feeling her long dark hair brush against her face in a motion seemingly unrelated to her response.

"Authors can use more than words to tell their stories when they write books, can't they?" asked Maxine. "Mr. Carle used a picture on the front to start us thinking, too. Let's see what happens." As she spoke Maxine tried to turn the page of the book one-handed, but she could not separate the worn pages with her fingers and simultaneously hold the book. "Dead time"—even a few seconds—was treacherous in this class, and she quickly tried to stretch her other arm around Malcolm to turn the page. The child's unpredictable movements were hard to judge, though; just as she reached for the book he lurched forward, and in order not to drop the child she had to drop the book.

Three children nearest Maxine's feet reached for it; two of them knocked heads and began to cry. Several children at the outside edge of the circle began to rock and laugh. Maxine knew the class was on the verge of pandemonium.

"Oh, clumsy Miss Korns!" Maxine admonished herself with a smile and made sure that Malcolm, who had tensed at his near fall, was steady. His frail little body never felt relaxed, but he didn't seem on the verge of panic. "Hand me my book, please, Les." Maxine ignored the escalating movement and noise in the room until she had the book in her hand and opened to the first page. "Shh . . . shh. I'm ready." She sat quietly and locked eyes with every child whose gaze she could capture. "I am waiting . . . shh . . . Richard, watch Miss Korns. Bobby, stop leaning on Jake. Shh . . . " Maxine rocked and tried to remain patient as she waited for order.

Such gentle tactics used to work right away. But in recent years the children seemed to have become rowdier and naughtier and more frustrating. Now, instead of responding to her quiet call for attention, the children's misbehavior began to escalate.

"Bobby!" Now Maxine raised her voice. "I said to stop bothering Jake. You come sit here by me." When Bobby did not quickly stand, she spoke even more vehemently, "Now!" The child—one of only four white children in the class—sheepishly left his friend and crawled toward Maxine. His route took him past Jercisse, a large, frequently disruptive boy, who laughed loudly. "Jercisse, please be quiet and listen to this story. Children, hush!" Since she was anchored by Malcolm, Maxine had no choice but to use her voice to command attention; often she left her chair to separate partners in crime or to command attention by grabbing a child's upper arm. She had become much more physical, she realized, in her past few years of teaching.

Finally, the children settled down enough for Maxine to resume. "Let's read Eric Carle's story, now: *The Very Hungry Caterpillar*. 'In the light of the moon a little egg lay on a leaf.'" This time Maxine managed to turn the page and balance Malcolm at the same time."'One Sunday morning the warm sun'—Ouch!" Maxine could not help her startled cry as Malcolm's bobbing head forcefully connected with her jaw, forcing her teeth together and causing her to bite her tongue. She had no idea how such a small child could be so strong. Reflexively, she pushed him off her lap and put her hand to her mouth. Now her rocking was for herself. "Oh, Malcolm, you hurt Miss Korns." She put her hand to her face and tried to smile at him and the class over her pain. She could taste blood.

Malcolm, suddenly adrift amidst twenty-seven rapt witnesses, looked terrified, and Maxine quickly tried to recover. "It's all right, honey . . . I'm all right." She reached for him and pulled him back onto her lap, returning to her reading before the disruption's surprise gave way to silliness again. "'One Sunday morning the warm sun came up and . . . '"

"' . . . He was a beautiful butterfly!'" As she closed the book, Maxine gently sat Malcolm on the floor; his wriggling had not really subsided but she was simply too tired to hold him any more, and she needed to talk to the class. He leaned against her leg and at least stayed put. "Was Angelina right? Was this about a bug?" A few children raised their hands and a few others nodded; several paid no more notice to this question than they had the book, but their inattention was not disruptive so Maxine ignored it. The discussion of the book continued haltingly for the few remaining minutes until art.

In her twenty-seven years of teaching, Maxine Korns had never felt as physically exhausted and mentally drained after each day in the classroom as she did this year. Only a few credits shy of earning her doctorate in education, Maxine considered herself a professional in the business of child development and education and had really dedicated her life to her work. She had been teaching at Lincoln Elementary School in Alton for twenty-two years and willed herself not to regret the changes that had enveloped the school during the recent past.

Maxine had tried her best to adapt to the different teaching environment caused by the court-ordered busing which was intended to integrate schools in this northeastern city-suburb. Lincoln was located on the city's affluent west side and had served the children of Alton's white middle class successfully for years. Even as poverty, crime, and homelessness crept into Alton's east side from its adjacent big-city neighbor, Lincoln had enjoyed high test scores, loyal taxpayers, and involved parents. But five years ago, with court-mandated busing, the school and Maxine's life had changed forever.

Now, fewer than 30 percent of the students at Lincoln were residents of the neighborhood; most parents had opted for parochial schools as the barely affordable alternative to integration. The school's staff was largely unchanged—the principal and seventeen of eighteen teachers remained. But the character and spirit of the school had shifted dramatically now that the students came from such different backgrounds, and the parents were either completely absent or long bus rides away.

As the children returned in a scraggly line from art, Maxine greeted them with smiles and affectionate pats and herded them gently toward the science corner in the large and airy room. In early March the children had begun what Maxine called the "incubator vigil," and right on schedule, four baby chicks had hatched twenty-one days later. Today, Maxine intended to discuss their growth after four days out of the shell and to let the children feed them. Then she would talk about how all animals must eat to grow before the class left for lunch.

"I am proud of your quiet walk back here from art," Maxine crooned as she shepherded the children to the back of the room. "Let's all find a place to stand or sit around the chicks. How do you think Tweety looks today, Jason?" Maxine directed her question at a gentle child who had adopted and christened the most pitiful of the hatch. "Is he stronger, do you think?"

Jason knelt and leaned his head far into the box, which was elevated a foot above the floor by a small stepstool. "He's still pretty quiet. Look, he just let Sylvester walk right over his head." Maxine had not been surprised by the cartoon theme of the names the children gave the brood.

Suddenly, Jercisse barged past two other children to reach the edge of the box, and he roughly grabbed its sides. Shaking it violently, he gazed in upon the jostled chicks and cried, "Chicky, chicky, chicky . . . cluck, chicky." He began crowing like a rooster in the few seconds it took Maxine to reach his arms.

"Stop that! Stop that now! You will hurt them! Stop it!" Maxine's reaction was swift and instinctive—keeping these animals alive in the unforgiving environment of a kindergarten classroom was a constant battle. "You know not to touch the box or the chicks. You know that! I have told you that before!" She turned to the class, most of whom looked quite worried. "I have told you all that before." Maxine turned back to Jercisse and pulled him by the upper arm away from the huddled class. "You know better, Jercisse. You cannot be with us for science today. You sit here until lunch." Maxine sat Jercisse on a stool in the supply closet and closed the door two-thirds of the way. "I can see you in there, and I don't want to hear a sound." Quickly realizing that the rest of the class was unsupervised and the chicks were vulnerable, Maxine returned to the fold and managed, for the hundredth time that morning, to pull her mind back onto the lesson and her emotions back into her heart.

Later, as she walked toward the teacher's lounge for lunch, Maxine eagerly anticipated a brief respite from the constant vigilance required of her in the classroom, but she could not shake thoughts of Jercisse and the chicks. She knew she should not have acted so viscerally, and she regretted her outburst. On the other hand, she had patiently and painstakingly reviewed with the children the proper way to behave with the chicks and had tried to use the project to instill in them a respect for living things.

Maxine was troubled by a nagging thought, which she purposefully kept from fully articulating to herself, that she would never have put a student in the closet five years ago. Parents wouldn't have tolerated it. Even though Maxine was pretty sure Jercisse's mother didn't even know where the school was, she was troubled by the knowledge that her teaching was becoming more reactive in spite of her increasing experience and ongoing education.

"At least I'm not alone in this," Maxine thought as she pulled open the door to the lounge. Indeed, the entire district had struggled with its changing student population and with codifying the proper responses to the students' behavior. One result of that ongoing evaluation was the "Zero Tolerance" policy, which held that school was for learning and that disciplinary problems would not be tolerated. Maxine knew that this policy had begun in the middle schools, targeted for the serious disruption and even crime found there. But it had found its way to the elementary schools, and beginning in kindergarten, students and their parents were asked to review the code of conduct and sign it, indicating by their signatures that they would abide by its rules and live with its sanctions. Maxine supported the code and wished that Anne Ackerby, her principal, would enforce it more consistently. She, like most of the teachers at Lincoln, thought Anne was "too soft."

• • •

Three weeks later, Maxine found herself confronting this concern head on. "I can't believe I have to argue with my principal to enforce her own rules," Maxine thought bitterly. Aloud, she repeated the point she had already made three times: "Anne, they were stealing, pure and simple. Either we mean what we say in the guidelines, or we don't!"

Earlier that day, Maxine had caught Jercisse, Richard, and Juan in the hallway just before snack time, red-handed. She had given them permission to go across the hall to use the restroom and had risked leaving the classroom to find them when they did not return promptly. They had taken some popcorn from Angelina's lunch bag and were guiltily eating it as they perched on the open cubbies in the hall.

Maxine scolded the boys harshly and reminded them of the penalty for stealing: suspension. She was now arguing with Anne about that sanction.

"I just think suspending kindergartners is too harsh, Maxine. Let's impose lunch detention, or snack time detention, for a week," suggested Anne.

"The guidelines clearly list suspension as a punishment for stealing. Why do we publish them if we don't intend to follow them?"

"Those penalties are meant for 15-year-olds, or maybe even 10-year-olds, Maxine, not for babies. I worry about those kids' self-image and about what their parents will do to them over this."

"I worry about *finding* their parents to tell them to keep them home," Maxine countered. "And two of those boys have older brothers in this school. The message we send here isn't just heard by these 5-year-olds. It's heard by everyone." Maxine paused, trying to rein in her mounting frustration. "Anne, I am in the classroom with these children all day long. You just don't know!"

Anne sighed. "Maxine, you know I will support you, and I will leave the final decision up to you. But I want you to give this a little more thought. See me at three o'clock and let me know your position then."

Lincoln Elementary School
Anne Ackerby, Principal

Dear Parents,

The staff and parents of Lincoln Elementary believe that all children should have a safe, harmonious, and productive school environment, where they can realize their full potential. Therefore, it is necessary to have appropriate behavioral guidelines which are clearly defined, understood, and adhered to by all concerned.

Attached is a copy of the Discipline Code designed by our staff of teachers, parents, aides, and administrators. Please read it with your child and then sign the form below, tear it off, and return it to your child's teacher.

Keep the code and review it with your child from time to time.

Sincerely,

Anne Ackerby

GENERAL GUIDELINES FOR PUBLIC AREAS

Hallways

1. Walk quietly at all times.
2. Stay to the right.
3. Maintain orderly lines, respecting personal space.
4. Students must carry appropriate passes at all times.
5. Show respect to classes in session by walking quietly.

Cafeteria

1. Walk in and sit down quietly.
2. No talking for the first five minutes.
3. Talk in conversational tones.
4. Remain seated except when getting lunch and dessert.
5. Use appropriate table manners.
6. Only assigned garbage monitors may take the barrels around.
7. Tables and floors are to be cleaned and chairs pushed in before students leave the cafeteria.
8. Food must not leave the cafeteria.

Playground

1. Exit to the yard through the Main Street door, and enter the building through the Maxwell Avenue door.
2. Stay in the assigned yard when playing.
3. No play-fighting.
4. Play fairly.
5. No snacks are allowed on the playground.
6. No student may throw sand, stones, sticks, or snow on the playground.
7. Line up immediately when called.

We encourage the prescribed behaviors through a system of positive reinforcement, such as award assemblies, gold lottos, and other incentives.

For behavior that falls below guideline expectations, the following Discipline Code has been developed. This code covers both *detention* and *suspensions*.

REASONS FOR DETENTION

1. Profanity in classroom
2. No pass in hall
3. Screaming or running in hall
4. Being in wrong bathroom
5. Harassment *anywhere* in building
6. Refusal to identify self to school employee
7. Congregating in bathroom
8. Gum chewing
9. Spitting or littering
10. Taking food out of the cafeteria without permission
11. Disruptive behavior that interferes with instructional process
12. Infraction of Hallway, Cafeteria, or Playground guidelines

Detention will be held three days per week (suggested days: Monday, Tuesday, Friday). Conducted by administrator and aide in room.

GUIDELINES FOR DETENTION

1. Formal detention—in triplicate—copy sent home in mail.
2. Predetermined assignment is used for detention purposes.

Following three detentions, child will be reprimanded to Principal's After-School Detention. (Parent advised.)

GUIDELINES FOR IMMEDIATE SUSPENSION

1. Anyone—K–6—involved in a fight
2. Verbal abuse of an adult
3. Vandalism or destruction of property
4. Stealing
5. Leaving classroom without permission
6. Habitual disruptive behavior which interferes with the instructional process

Jim Colbert

A third-grade teacher in an inner-city school is trying his best to teach language arts using basal readers and a district-required curriculum. He is especially concerned about one Spanish-speaking child who appears to want to learn but who speaks English only at school.

Jim Colbert walked up Seventh Avenue towards Converse Street, appreciating the relative calm of the early October morning. In less than an hour children would be walking this same street on their way to school, passing the dreary, run down, and often abandoned buildings that were now occupied by drug dealers, addicts, and the homeless. "Amazing," Jim said to himself. "Some of the kids in my class call these buildings 'home.'" Jim had been teaching at P.S. 111 in Metropolitan, a large city in the Northeast, for four years, but the conditions in the neighborhood still appalled him.

As Jim turned onto Converse Street, he saw a police car slowly cruising the block. Jim continued down the street, glanced at the garbage-strewn fronts of the row houses on each side, and then climbed the steps to P.S. 111. Watching the rats scurry across, he looked into the school yard next to the building, at the dilapidated apartment building next door, and then to the ever-present drug dealers already hawking their wares. The police patrol had done little to discourage their activity at the end of the block where Converse met Edgar Boulevard. Once school began, the police would become more visible, providing the image of a barrier between the school and the inner-city life around it.

Jim entered the building, the clean and colorful interior offering a welcome contrast to the bleak atmosphere of the street. On the way to his classroom Jim walked at a leisurely pace, enjoying the student work that covered the walls. He passed the other two third-grade classrooms, the 3-C class for 'below average' students and the 3-B class for 'average' students. Jim had been assigned the 3-A class for 'bright' students.

He entered room 308 and quickly set out the materials the students would need for the morning's work. While school policy required at least three learning centers in each room, Jim was currently using five: writing, library, math, listening, and art. Each was equipped with task cards based on the weekly lesson, the materials required to do the assignment, and a time schedule for each group.

The school district required the elementary school teachers to use homogeneous grouping for reading instruction, using the same basal reading program. Jim had divided the class into two reading groups, a 2-2 basal group with thirteen students, and a 3-1 basal group with ten students based on testing done at the beginning of the year. The desks were clustered in groups of three, four, or five and students sat with children who were in their reading group. Each student had been provided with a basal reader and a workbook. Because the district needed to reuse them, the students were not allowed to write in their workbooks.

Jim crossed the room to his desk, sat down, and opened his plan book to review the schedule for the day. The beginning was always the same. Everyone would complete a spelling lesson, and after that lesson one group would go to their assignments at the centers and the other would meet with Jim. When Jim finished with the first group, the students would go to their center assignments, and he would meet with the other group. Because this was Monday they would be starting a new lesson from the spelling book. The class would get ten "words for the week" and would be tested on these words on Friday. The writing-center activities were designed to use these words.

After taking attendance and getting a lunch count, Jim began the spelling lesson. "This week we're going to be working with words that identify the **cause** of an event. These are words that help us figure out **why** something has happened. Here's an example: 'It was raining out, so Carlos played *Nintendo*.'" This was greeted by giggles as the children looked toward Carlos, who was clearly enjoying the attention. "What did Carlos do?" Jim asked.

"He played *Nintendo*," a student answered.

"Right. Now tell me **why** he played *Nintendo*." Several hands went up. "Maria, tell us why."

"He played *Nintendo* because it was raining."

"Good, Maria. What word in the sentence told you that?"

"What was the sentence again?"

"It was raining out, so Carlos played *Nintendo*."

"So."

"Great! Here's another: 'Carlos ate dinner quickly because he was hungry.' What did Carlos do?" Jim paused, then motioned to Tony.

"He ate dinner."

"OK, can you tell us **how** he ate dinner?" Jim probed.

"Yeah, he ate dinner real fast."

"Good, he ate dinner real fast, or quickly. Now Carlos, **why** did you eat dinner quickly?"

"'Cause I was hungry."

"Good. What word in the sentence told us **why** Carlos ate his dinner quickly?" Several hands waved, and Jim turned to Anton.

"Because."

"Good. Now, let's try to say the same thing in a different way. Let's start with 'Carlos was hungry . . .'"

"Oh, I know!" called out Maria.

"OK, Maria, let's hear it."

"OK, 'Carlos was hungry so he ate dinner quickly.'"

"Terrific! We used the words 'so' and 'because' to help us identify **why** something happened." Jim continued with several more sentences using his students' names. He followed this introduction with a page from the workbook where students matched the beginnings and endings of sentences. Their homework was to complete five sentences using "so" and "because" and to draw a picture of the event illustrating what they had written.

The following day Jim went over the homework with the 2-2 group. Each student read his or her answers and showed off his or her drawings. Jim checked each notebook, and when he got to Carlos's work he noticed Carlos had spelled "because" as "becuz." Spelling and phonics had been a problem for Carlos since the beginning of the year. Jim had worked with Carlos on these skills, but he was worried that Carlos wasn't making any progress. He reviewed the correct spelling with the group and asked them to complete one more sentence. This time Carlos spelled the word correctly.

For the remainder of Tuesday's reading lesson with the 2-2 group, Jim introduced and reviewed the vocabulary words from the story *That's What Friends Are For.* Jim introduced each word using a personal context sentence, then went over syllables, decoded each word, and read them in context. The students then did a workbook exercise in which they were asked to write the correct meaning of the underlined word. Homework was to categorize the words by the number of syllables and to put each word into a sentence.

Checking the homework on Wednesday confirmed Jim's concerns about Carlos. His oral reading showed understanding about syllables, and Carlos had written acceptable sentences for each word. However, when Jim checked his workbook he saw that Carlos was spelling words the way they sounded. One sentence read, "I rote that cilly storey about rekreashun club."

At lunch that day Jim spoke with Paul Touron, another third-grade teacher, about Carlos. "I'm worried about him, Paul. His comprehension is good, but his phonics and spelling are so far behind."

"Too bad," Paul said. "Last year you could have sent him to a remedial class, but with the budget cuts they've all been canceled."

As they left the faculty room Jim made a mental note to talk with Carlos when he got back to class. As the children burst into the room, energy renewed from recess, Jim called Carlos over to his desk. "Carlos, I'm really pleased with how well you are coming along with the work we've been doing in class. You also did a great job with the sentences you had for homework last night. I'm worried about your spelling, though. Do you think you could get some help at home?"

"I don't think so. My parents, they speak Spanish."

"Does anyone in your family speak English?"

"Sometimes my sister, she visits and she speaks English to me. That's all."

"What about your friends?"

"Everyone, they speak Spanish. I only use English in school."

"Do you have books in English?"

"No, just what I need for school."

"Well, I'm going to give you this dictionary to take home. Use it to check your spelling when you are doing your homework, OK?"

"Yeah, sure, Mr. Colbert. Thanks." Carlos grinned as he rushed to put the book in his desk.

Carlos's homework was better the next day. The assignment was to answer a series of five reading comprehension questions. Carlos's sentences were basic, but sound. As Jim went over his notebook he thought, "Carlos must be using the dictionary; the spelling is much better." Once the homework review was completed, the students took turns reading aloud while Jim asked comprehension questions and assessed oral reading skills. When it was Carlos's turn to read, he stammered and mispronounced many words. Jim noted he could barely get through a five-sentence passage. However, when Jim asked him about the reading, Carlos's answers indicated that he understood the passage despite his pronunciation problems.

That day at lunch Paul asked about Carlos. Jim told him about the oral reading. "How can he have such a hard time reading but understand what's happening? I remember when I tested him at the beginning of the year his reading was filled with stammering. He couldn't read a 3-1 basal and the 2-2 was still pretty choppy. My first thought was that he was nervous. I talked with him about relaxing and joked with him a little. He seemed to loosen up, but when he attacked the 2-2 passage again the stammering was back. I tried a 2-1 basal and he could read it with ease. So I had to decide if I would send him out of the class to a 2-1 reading group or challenge him in my class with the 2-2 group. I really felt good about him, he had such a willingness to try, and his comprehension was so good I decided to keep him in the 2-2 group. I gave him extra phonics worksheets to do at home, but they usually came back with mistakes. Now, I'm not so sure I did the right thing. Perhaps he should be in a lower group."

"What's your plan now?" Paul asked.

"I've got to immerse him in print. He must take home a library book each night and provide me with a mini-book report. I also want him to create his own stories. He can read or write about anything he wants, comic books, super heroes, anything! I just want that kid reading and writing!"

"Sounds good, Jim. By the way, do you know June Rush? She's a retired school teacher who works as a floating aide. She's here mostly to help out the first-year teachers, but maybe she can give Carlos some time."

"Good idea. I recommended him for the after-school reading program back in September, but he hardly ever shows up. He won't be able to escape Mrs. Rush so easily."

Two weeks later Jim and Paul were on recess duty together. As they headed toward the courtyard behind the school Jim thought back to one of his early conversations with Paul. When Jim first came to P.S. 111 Paul had explained to him why the school never used the large yard next door. "We stopped using it about three years ago. It was just too dangerous for the students to be in such close proximity to the drug dealers at the end of the block. Instead, the kids have to play in the small courtyard behind the school. All in all, it's probably for the best considering there've been about ten shootings in that side yard, and that doesn't include summer when school's not in session." Jim had come to appreciate how true this was in June of that year. He was monitoring recess in the back courtyard when there was the sudden blast of firecrackers from the front of the school. Every student in the courtyard had fallen to the ground, hands over their heads, thinking it was gunfire. Jim had stared in amazement at the yard of students lying on the ground, instinctively trying to protect themselves.

Now, as the students rushed out to the courtyard, Jim saw Carlos head for the basketball court.

Paul interrupted his thoughts. "Isn't that Carlos? I heard he was working with Mrs. Rush. How's it going?"

"You mean, 'How **was** it going?' More budget cuts, Mrs. Rush is gone, and Carlos is back in the cycle of good work at school, terrible work at home," Jim answered, the frustration apparent in his voice. "But I learned a few things about him in the last few weeks."

"What did you learn?"

"Well, I knew Carlos had repeated second grade, so I went and looked at his file to see if I could get some more information. He was in the average second-grade class the first time. Unfortunately his teacher from that year isn't here anymore so all I know is what's in the file. His second year he was still in the average class. I spoke with the teacher, Mrs. Ortiz. She said he was a good kid, he did his work and then some. His math was above average—the first year he scored at the 79th percentile on the math test, and the second year his score was at the 75th.

"Reading was another matter. The first year in second grade he took a phonics based test, prefixes, suffixes and tenses. His score was at the 5th percentile, and since passing is 10th he was held back. The next year the test was changed to a cloze format, and he scored at the 26th percentile and was promoted."

"Why was he put in a 3-A class?"

"I wondered about that. The principal said that because of his math skills plus his potential, they thought he'd be better off in the higher achieving group. In some ways, he really fits there. Just not in reading, unless it's reading comprehension. I've been watching him in the classroom. When he does the SRA cards in the writing center I can see that he really likes that stuff. They're mostly fill-in-the-blank or true/false exercises, and they don't require him to elaborate on his ideas. Since his comprehension is good and the words are all there, these are easy for him."

"Anything else in the file?" Paul asked.

"Well, his family may be part of the problem. His parents are in their fifties; Carlos was a 'change-of-life' baby. They don't speak English and don't intend to learn. Their thirty-year-old daughter interprets whenever I need to speak to them. She also helps Carlos with homework when she has a chance. It's like his parents feel they already did their job raising Carlos's three older sisters, and it's the school's responsibility to take care of Carlos.

"Just living in this part of Metropolitan is another problem. Carlos's family has to worry about their next meal, hot water, clothes, and shelter. Reading and writing aren't very important, I guess. The poor kid's lucky if he can sleep through the gunfire in his neighborhood, then he comes to school, and we expect him to read and talk about places and things he's never seen or thought about."

Paul was listening closely to Jim as he spoke. After a long pause Jim said, "I guess what I'm trying to say is that I don't know how we can expect Carlos's reading and writing skills to improve, given the reality of his life and the limited resources here. I just don't know what to do to help him."

Janice Heron

A teacher does some sizing-up assessments early in the school year and concludes that four of her students will probably be eligible for special education services, although she is reluctant to refer them.

"It's 'pan.'"

Janice Heron beamed at Nancy. "Nancy, that's right! That word *is* 'pan'! I can't trick you today. What did you do?"

Nancy's grin spread across her face, clearly showing the gap where her two front teeth had been. "Turned the key." She giggled and sat up straighter in her chair.

"You certainly did turn that key in your brain. And look at what that brain power did for you!" Janice turned toward the class. "If you think you had the same answer as Nancy, please raise your hand." Janice was pleased to see that almost everyone's hand shot up, although that certainly didn't guarantee that everyone really understood what she was asking.

As Janice scanned the twenty-two earnest faces in front of her, she thought again how different this group of first-graders was from the other first-grade classes she had taught at Roosevelt Elementary School in recent years. For the previous five years or so, the students in Janice's class had come almost exclusively from the lower socioeconomic sections of town, with only a few middle-class students in the group. These poor, often minority, children had accounted for more than 80 percent of her classes. However, recent changes in the Littleton school district's policies, particularly those creating new magnet schools, had resulted in demographic changes in each of the six elementary schools. For the first time in a long while there were equal numbers of white, Hispanic, and black children in Janice's class.

This class had something else, too, that Janice found very desirable. In addition to several very bright students and several with learning difficulties, there were many students in the middle. Janice called this group the "golden mean."

But Janice was growing increasingly concerned about several children who seemed to be at-risk educationally. All had in common marked deficits in reading and language development, and some also struggled with math concepts. Many of these children came from educationally disadvantaged homes, and some of their parents did not speak English as their primary language.

125

Janice had already considered referring four children for special education evaluation. She had a master's degree in teaching; eighteen years of teaching experience, eleven of them in first grade; and three children of her own. Janice could tell almost immediately which children might need special help. However, she had tremendous reluctance to impose a label on children so early in the school year. She had decided to proceed slowly rather than rush into an "at-risk" referral, with the hope that the children might simply need additional time to mature.

While her worries were increasing over the slower children, Janice was also concerned about some of the children at the other end of the spectrum. Several were quite bright, and she was concerned that they were bored when she did large-group instruction.

Over the past several years Janice had come to rely upon whole-class teaching extensively to provide the oral language exposure that many of her students missed at home. This year she believed this approach to be even more appropriate, thinking that her more able children provided role models for the language-impoverished ones. If she grouped by ability for all of her language arts activities—listening, oral language development, phonics, developmental reading, and writing—her slower children would miss the richness of the more language-facile ones. So she ability-grouped only for developmental reading. But she was concerned that the brightest class members were not challenged enough through this formula.

Janice's skepticism that raised hands meant comprehension was not betrayed in her smile. "Look at all of those hands up! Now, what do you think this word says?" Janice pointed to the last of three words with the short *a* sound that she had written on the board. As she scanned the room for responses she noticed Mark and Henry, two of her more able students, leaning toward each other across the space between their desks, laughing and passing papers. "I am awfully proud of the students I see sitting up straight and paying attention." Janice paused a moment to let her remark register; sure enough, all of the children adjusted themselves and faced forward, including Mark and Henry. Then, even though a few children were exuberantly waving their hands in the air, Janice repeated her question in order to give the rest of the group a chance to refocus. "Who can read this word for me?"

Janice was surprised to see a response from an unusual source as Juan's hand climbed tentatively into the air. A chubby, neatly dressed boy, Juan almost never volunteered. When he did, Janice had to walk down the four rows of desks and stand next to him in order to decipher his response.

Juan had great difficulty with school. He was in the lowest reading group, and according to the ESL teacher, even in Spanish his counting was poor. He was not making much progress at letter recognition, and to get him involved during reading Janice had to sit him down and present him with a book. He was also slow to follow directions. Last week he and the others had practiced being bears, crawling around on all fours and then "hibernating." Long after the others were upright again and well into a discussion of hibernation, Janice had to remind Juan to get up from the floor and take his seat.

Juan was particularly handicapped by his speech. It had been virtually impossible for him to say two complete sentences during the class discussion about bears. Janice wasn't sure what to blame for his speech problems—the fact that English was not spoken in his home, his seemingly low ability, a physical problem, or some combination of all these. Although he sometimes pushed other children, Janice felt that this was Juan's way of communicating instead of talking. He was rather a loner, except for a tentative friendship with José.

Juan always came to school with clean clothes and a lunch, and his father picked him up at school each day. His father never spoke to Janice and would not even make eye contact with her. He responded to her comments about Juan with a sort of grunt and a shy smile, yet she had a feeling that he and his wife appreciated the school's efforts.

Janice acknowledged Juan's raised hand with obvious pleasure, but he paused and looked suddenly confused. Outwardly, Janice's expression reflected encouragement and confidence, but inwardly she tried to control the impatience she felt rising within her. "Oh, Juan," she thought. "You're going to slow up the whole class again!" As Juan hesitated, hands all around her shot into the air. Still keeping eye contact with Juan, Janice held out a hand in a restraining gesture and reminded the rest of the class, "Give Juan a chance." She then addressed Juan. "Think about it," she said softly. "Take your time."

Juan still looked bewildered. After waiting for what felt like an eternity, Janice decided to help him so that he could have the satisfaction of answering correctly. She reminded him of the sound of the short *a* in the word *pan*, which Nancy had just identified, and after he had repeated that sound aloud she cued him by focusing on the beginning letter sound in the new word. After several false starts, Juan correctly sounded out the beginning letter, *b*. With Janice's help, he linked it with the short *a*. "Good, Juan. Now put it all together with the last letter: B . . . *ahh* . . . " Janice let Juan think and saw that his concentration was intense; his lips moved as he silently practiced the first two sounds and studied the board. Finally, he announced that the word was *bag*.

Although the word was incorrect, he had properly used the vowel sound that was the point of the lesson, and she praised him profusely. She would have stayed with Juan to correct his misidentification of the final sound, but she felt the rest of the class getting fidgety around her and so expanded the discussion to include others. "Juan has read the first part of this word correctly, but the last letter is not *g* as in *bag*." Janice wrote the word *bag* on the board. "Can anyone else think of another word that sounds like *bag* but ends with *d*?" Janice asked.

By now, in late October, Janice could almost always predict who the likely respondents would be. This morning, however, one of her prime candidates, Bernard, looked inattentive and sulky. Bernard was one of the brightest children in the class. He could read and write well beyond grade level. His father, an engineer, and his mother, a nurse at a nearby hospital, worked different shifts so that one of them could always be home with Bernard and his older brother. The parents had introduced themselves to Janice at the beginning of the year, and she saw that they were determined that Bernard should have every possible opportunity for a good education.

Janice took particular pleasure when minority children like Bernard did well in class, and Bernard was fast becoming one of her favorite students. She had been delighted when he found the word *write* on the board and used it in his journal. He showed initiative and a real capacity for independent thinking, and although he never complained openly he seemed increasingly restless when the slower students kept the class from moving faster. After Mark correctly answered her final question, Janice decided to address Bernard's behavior directly.

"Bernard, you look upset. Did these words make you think of something that made you mad?" The child still looked down at his desk, so Janice approached his side and crouched down to be at his eye level. "You seem unhappy. Is this a bad day?"

Bernard muttered that he was mad because his mother wouldn't buy him a toy. Janice sympathized and then decided to use Bernard's experience as the basis for a brief class discussion.

"Does anyone else ever feel like Bernard is feeling?"

"Yes!" came a chorus of voices. Melanie volunteered that she felt mad when she wasn't allowed to have a puppy, and Janice suggested that Melanie might also have felt disappointed, using the opportunity to discuss and label emotions and to increase the children's vocabulary. Bernard turned toward Melanie with a smile, and his thin body relaxed.

Into the momentary silence came David's voice. "Mrs. Heron, wanna hear what I said to my mother, I was so mad at her?"

"Uh-oh," thought Janice, "no telling *what* we'll hear, knowing the language used at his house." Janice knew that David's parents were in the midst of a bitter divorce. David and his mother had moved on the first day of school from a large house in a wealthy suburb several miles away to a modest apartment in Littleton. David had made some friends on his new block, largely by ringing doorbells and announcing that he had just moved in, and the children at school seemed to like him. But with Janice he could be rebellious and rude.

Janice could tell David was a bright child, and she tried to excuse his behavior because she knew of his private difficulties. But she often felt like putting a bag over his head when he called out in class or publicly criticized her. "You've said that twice now. You repeat yourself a lot, you know?" he had said to her during the second week of school. Janice found that consistent, quiet firmness worked with David. She also praised him for remembering to raise his hand before he spoke out and was beginning to see some success for her efforts. In addition, he frequently helped his seat partner.

David's verbal skills were admirable. It was he who contributed *buttinsky*, *blimp*, and *brunch* and defined each word during a drill on *b* sounds. Although his motor skills were not yet up to his verbal skills and his work was often sloppily done, he was clearly enjoying the challenges of schoolwork, seeking out information in the encyclopedia and other books in the room and always asking questions. David was also complaining more often of being bored during whole-class activities.

Now, David volunteered that he was angry because his mother had refused to allow him to go to a horror movie with some older boys. Janice stopped him before he could get into a discussion that she was sure would involve some choice vocabulary. "Thank goodness your mother is finally beginning to set some limits," she thought. Aloud, she empathized with him over his disappointment.

Janice glanced at the wall clock and said a few closing words about feelings and disappointment to bring group time to an end. She then asked for volunteers for Nature Center, an activity to which she could send six children for the next forty minutes. This was a favorite event. Not only did the children enjoy the lessons provided by the Nature Center teacher; they relished the chance to prove that they were responsible enough to go and return from the Nature Center without an adult accompanying them. She quickly chose six and saw them out the door.

"How many of you are disappointed that you couldn't go today?" Janice asked. All of the remaining children raised their hands, and she reassured them that they would go the following week. José, who had nearly fallen out of his seat with his efforts to be selected, was especially frustrated. He gave Ríos a shove, and Janice quickly intervened.

José and Ríos were of tremendous concern to Janice, and her uneasiness grew as the weeks passed. Both had very poor verbal skills, and José was always ready to use his body to express himself. José often came to school in clothing that was worn or even torn. He had trouble concentrating and tended to drift off by himself during group activities. He had great difficulty with letter recognition, although his math skills were on grade level. Janice felt that he was a spunky youngster whose potential was hard to judge.

This was confirmed when she asked him what he wanted to draw for his bear picture. He was unable to identify a bear, calling it a cat. She placed a teddy bear on his desk and asked his seatmate to remind José of what animal he should be drawing. He then proceeded to draw what he called a "scary bear."

Ríos was the third Hispanic boy in Janice's lowest reading group, and she sometimes attributed his, Juan's, and José's difficulty with letter recognition to their struggle with the language. Janice considered Ríos a very high-risk student. He had virtually no letter association, seemed unable to make connections between letters and their sounds, and had not yet absorbed the "plus 1" concept in math.

Janice encouraged Ríos whenever possible. When he had responded appropriately during the lesson on the short *a* sound, Janice had announced to the class, "Ríos has a hard time remembering. Look how proud we all are of you!" The boy had beamed. His mother was aware of his high-risk status and could not have been more cooperative. He was always beautifully dressed, and his workbooks from home were always complete.

Nancy was the only girl and the only black child in the slowest reading group. She seemed to make absolutely no connection between letters, sounds, and words, and her math skills were equally poor. Nancy came from a single-parent home and had several brothers and sisters. A teenage cousin with her own baby also lived with Nancy's mother and siblings. Nancy's oral language was very immature. She had recently said of her older brother, "Him reads to me at night."

However, Janice had been amazed earlier in the week when she asked Nancy whether she liked a music selection that Janice had just played for the class, and Nancy replied that Monet would have liked to paint to the music. Whenever possible, Janice tried to enrich the curriculum with art and music, tying it in with the language arts lesson the children were working on at the time. Two weeks before, she had told them about Monet, showing them prints of several of his works and a shopping bag that was decorated with a Monet print. They had written a story together about the artist and his work. Janice was delighted that Nancy remembered the lesson about Monet and used it so appropriately.

Now, before starting with the day's first reading group, Janice gave directions to the rest of the class for an activity that involved cutting out words, pasting them in sequence, and writing an accompanying story. She hoped that the variety of activities would keep everyone stimulated, busy, and quiet because she found it difficult to concentrate on a reading group when there was talking in the rest of the room.

The class settled down to work, and she shifted her attention to the average readers sitting in a semicircle around her. As the children read silently in preparation for reading aloud, Janice looked out at the class and noted to her surprise that Juan was offering to help Anton, who was having trouble with the words. She reminded the children that this was an activity that they were supposed to be doing individually, but she was pleased to see this contact between the two boys and remembered that yesterday, Anton had helped Juan color in Juan's alphabet workbook.

Seeing her respond to someone outside of the reading group, David felt free to come over to her with a request for a book about lighthouses. When she suggested he finish his work first, he stated that he had already finished and that the work had been easy. She suggested a book, and he went off to find it. Janice then conducted the reading group with a minimum of interruptions.

At the end of the day, Janice returned to her thoughts about grouping with this class. "Since I have an assistant teacher for an hour each morning, should I be using her more with the bright kids?" she asked herself. "They would really fly with the enrichment from working one-to-one with her." Even silently, she struggled with the companion thought to that one: "The slower ones are probably going to end up in special education anyway." True, she admitted, there were a few signs of progress with the very slow learners. However, as she anticipated their reading group tomorrow, she thought, "What am I going to do with them? I can't just keep doing letters for the rest of the year."

She packed her Monet bag for home, full of work that suggested no answers.

PART FOUR

Classroom Assessment and Evaluation

Sarah Hanover

A first-year high school math teacher is confronted by angry parents when she gives their son, an outstanding math student, a lower grade than expected because he never turned in his homework.

The secretary's voice on the faculty lounge intercom was difficult to hear because of the static. "Mrs. Hanover, there's a call for you on line seven," Sarah heard dimly.

She called toward the speaker, "I'm on my way," and headed down the hall to the math office, wondering who was trying to reach her at 7:40 on a Monday morning.

The caller identified himself as James Kilson's father.

"Good morning, Mr. Kilson. Is James OK?" Sarah asked.

"Well, he's OK except for his math grade," Mr. Kilson responded. "I'm unclear as to why James got a B in your class."

"Did you ask James? I'm pretty sure he knows why he got a B." Sarah softened her voice so that her comment would not seem hostile.

Mr. Kilson responded. "He told us that he got a B because he didn't do the homework."

Sarah said, "That's exactly right. Homework is one of the class requirements."

Mr. Kilson's voice sounded angry. "But he gets perfect scores on the tests without doing homework. Why would you have such a requirement?"

"Not all the students understand new concepts in math as quickly as James. In fact, most students need all the practice they can get. If I didn't require homework and base part of the grade on its being completed, most students wouldn't do it and they'd learn less."

Mr. Kilson sounded puzzled. "I understand that. But why should James have to do the homework when he doesn't need it?"

"All students need to do homework. It's part of learning some discipline."

"Forget that. James is not a discipline problem." His tone moderated as he went on: "You must know how important grades are to high school students, particularly students like James, who plan to apply to highly competitive colleges. This is not a contest between your will and James's. He *needs* high grades for college. All his test scores show that he's doing A work. His math grade should reflect what he knows."

Sarah forced herself not to sound angry or defensive as she responded to Mr. Kilson. "I think you're missing the point here. Homework was one of the course requirements. James got a B because he chose not to do the homework."

"I'm assuming from this conversation that you're not going to change James's grade." Sarah thought that Mr. Kilson sounded frustrated.

"I don't think that he earned a higher grade. When he meets all the class requirements, he'll get an A."

"My wife and I would like to talk to you in person about this. I would ask you to think about what I said so that there might be room for some more discussion between us. When would be a convenient time?" Mr. Kilson did not sound like the type of person who would take no for an answer.

Sarah quickly brought her schedule to mind. "I have a preparation period from 11:06 to 11:48, or we could meet after school. The students leave at 2:50 and I'd be willing to meet you at 3:00, if that would be more convenient."

Mr. Kilson responded, "We'll see you at 3:00 this afternoon, if today is convenient. Where shall we meet?"

Sarah replied, "This afternoon is fine. I'm in room 336 at that time; that's on the third floor of the math wing. When you come in the front door, walk past the office and take the first stairs to your left."

"We'll find it. Thank you for making yourself available."

Sarah said, "You're welcome, Mr. Kilson. Have a nice day." Once the words were out of her mouth, she could have kicked herself. She hated that expression, but in her nervousness she had used it to end her conversation with James Kilson's father.

Sarah replaced the receiver and left the math department office, her heart pounding. She was a new teacher, and Mr. Kilson was the first parent to call her with a complaint. In the two months since school started, her only parent contacts were ones she initiated, and they were made to ask for the parents' help with a problem student.

As she walked to her classroom, she thought about James Kilson. It occurred to her that this call should *not* have come as a surprise. After all, James was the best math student in her third-period honors precalculus class.

James was a pleasant boy, easy to have in the class (although he informed her on the first day of class that he did not like to be called Jim, or Jimmy, or Jimbo, and offered about half a dozen nicknames or variations on his name that he would not answer to). He had a 98 average on the tests and quizzes Sarah had given during the marking period. He was also her best peer tutor and a willing participant in class discussions. James was obviously an A student, except for one flaw: He never turned in homework. And that was why Sarah gave him a B for the grading period.

In September, Sarah was overly prepared to begin the school year—intense preparation was her typical response to anxiety. Although becoming a math teacher was something she had been working toward for the past two years, actually being offered a job had caused her as much anxiety as pleasure.

Sarah described herself as a "traditional rebel"—an oxymoron she took delight in. When she graduated from college in the early 1980s, she was one of only a few women in her class with a degree in business. She married immediately after college graduation (her traditional side) and went to work for a *Fortune* 500 company as a management trainee. Within a few years she was earning as much as her husband, a computer engineer. After ten years with the company, she took a leave of absence to have a child. She returned to work when her son was 6 months old. A year later she was pregnant with a second child, and she and her husband agreed that raising young children was going to be very difficult with both parents pursuing corporate careers; so after her daughter was born, she resigned from the company. As her children grew, Sarah started to think about another career.

Teaching seemed a natural choice. Sarah had done some training on her job and had enjoyed helping others gain new skills. She investigated options and discovered that she could be certified in math with two years of part-time study. By the time her daughter was ready for kindergarten, Sarah was a certified math teacher. She was offered a full-time position at Littleton High School early in June, giving her nearly three months to prepare for her new position.

Her preparation included establishing overt grading standards, which she shared with her students on the first day of class. She even put her requirements on the topic schedule she handed out to each class, believing that she should identify class requirements explicitly so that the students would know exactly what she expected. She didn't want them to be surprised by their grades, as she often had been as a student, and as were so many students she had observed as a student teacher.

One of her requirements was homework, and she made it clear that she took homework seriously. As she explained to her students: "I'm assigning you homework every night but Friday because you will need to practice what we are learning in class, and there won't be enough time in class for you to get that practice. By doing homework every night, you'll get a better handle on the material, and I'll have a better idea of what you know."

In each of her classes, several students asked if she would grade the homework. The first time she was asked the question, Sarah paused before answering. "Let me put it like this. I will go over all your homework as a way of finding out how you are doing with the material. Your homework will let me know who needs extra practice and what I'll need to reteach if lots of you didn't understand something. It will also tell me that we can move ahead faster than I had planned if I see that everyone in the class is doing very well. But I won't put a grade on each homework assignment. You need to have the freedom to use the homework as a means of indicating that you don't understand something. So the only grade will be a check or minus. If you try to do the homework each night, even if you get stuff wrong, you'll get a check. If you don't turn it in, or if you turn in only part of it, you'll get a minus. With a few minuses, your grade will be affected. I expect all of you to do each of the homework assignments."

Sarah thought about that conversation and realized that she was on firm ground with the grade she had given to James. She tried to put her upcoming encounter with the Kilsons out of her mind as she went through her day. Nevertheless, her thoughts kept returning to the afternoon's meeting, particularly during third period. Sarah did not say anything to James about his parents' upcoming visit, and he did not mention the early morning call to her. She wondered if he knew about it.

By the end of the day, the meeting with the Kilsons was all Sarah could think about. When the door of room 336 swung closed behind the last student at 2:50, Sarah stood to erase the board as she nervously awaited Mr. and Mrs. Kilson's arrival. As she mentally went over their position and tried to imagine the additional arguments they might make, she began to wonder, for the first time since she had established her grading requirements, if they were correct. A nagging doubt began to grow that her focus on the explicitness of the grading system had obscured her attention to its content. Were the requirements themselves wrong? Since the conversation with Mr. Kilson hadn't been a lengthy one, she hadn't really had the opportunity to expand on her position or to hear his in detail. Was she really clear about the arguments on both sides of this issue?

Sarah heard a sound at the classroom door and quickly set down the eraser and dusted off her hands. She took a deep breath as she walked toward the opening door.

Diane News

In a school district beginning a gifted and talented program, a first-year elementary school teacher must choose four students to recommend for the program, but she has five potential candidates.

Diane News sat at her desk watching the first gold and orange leaves falling onto the Talner Elementary School playground. "It's time to take down the 'Welcome Back to School' display," she thought. As she pulled a pad of paper toward her to begin sketching ideas for a new social studies bulletin board, she glanced around her room with pride. Diane had been teaching part-time for two years; this fifth-grade class in Littleton was her first full-time position. Her room reflected her love of the arts and her understanding of enrichment materials. A science table invited exploration. Books and magazines in a well-stocked library in the back could be checked out by her students. A bulletin board labeled "Where in the World?" contained a map and photographs. Originally, Diane brought in the photos for the display, but now her students were bringing in pictures, putting them up, and connecting them with yarn to places on the map. The room was bright and colorful. It looked like the kind of place where students could be active and involved learners.

Diane, 27 years old, was married and had recently completed a master's program in arts and education. Prior to her current position, she taught at an alternative school in the district, where she helped to develop afterschool enrichment programs for gifted and talented students. She had become interested in gifted education when she took a course on creativity, and she had taken several more courses in the area as part of her master's program.

As Diane sketched ideas, she began to think about a more immediate problem. She was faced with an issue that she did not know how to resolve. On the surface, the situation appeared straightforward: She had to recommend no more than four students from her classroom for a new gifted and talented program (called "G&T" by everyone) for students in the second through sixth grades. Students were being chosen from each grade level since the program was in a start-up year. The students would be taken from classes to another school twice a week for half a day. Each grade-level teacher was asked to recommend no more than four students because class size would be limited. The G&T coordinator was urging each teacher to pick the maximum number of students, but no one was allowed to exceed four. Of her twenty-seven students, three were obvious choices, but her selection of the fourth was complicated by other factors. However, this decision was only part of Diane's dilemma.

Diane had to choose the four students using criteria that she considered unacceptable. The district required a score at the 90th percentile or above on the Iowa Test of Basic Skills (ITBS) as the primary consideration for admission to the program. Class grades and group-administered IQ scores also had to be high. There was room for a brief personal evaluation of each student recommended by the teacher, but the form stated that this opinion was of less consequence than IQ and achievement-test scores and class grades.

Diane's standards for choosing students had little in common with those of the district. She felt that individual creativity in a variety of areas had to be evaluated when assessing children for placement in a gifted and talented program. For example, creativity in problem solving, choices of imagery in writing, and analytic thinking skills in a variety of subjects all needed to be considered. Diane also thought that some students who did not fit a standard profile and who met only some of the criteria often flourished in the challenge of such a program. She was troubled that she had to ignore these factors as she made decisions about her students.

In addition to having doubts about whether she would be able to make her recommendations according to the district's standards, Diane had other concerns about her decision. While in graduate school, she had taken a number of courses in women's studies. She had read enough in the field to know that girls scored lower than boys on standardized tests and that they were underrepresented in programs for the gifted and in other advanced courses, especially in math and science. Diane was aware that young girls were not sufficiently encouraged to participate in these programs. Yet she was considering recommending four boys.

The dissonance that this created in her was not helped by another recent event. The father of one of the students in her class had called to pressure Diane into including his daughter in the gifted program. Even now, Diane was furious as she recalled the conversation.

George James, a high school teacher and football coach in the district, had called the previous evening. James, who was black, had a reputation for being critical of other staff. Diane knew from other teachers that he was quick to call whenever he thought that they were not providing sufficient challenges for his daughter. When James called Diane, the conversation began calmly enough but escalated quickly to an unpleasant pitch.

"Hello, Mrs. News, this is George James, Margie's father. I've heard about the start-up of the G&T program, and I wanted to make sure that Margie will be included in it."

"Mr. James, I'm glad that you're so interested in Margie's progress, and . . ."

"Progress? I'm not calling about her progress. My daughter is smart enough to be in the program, and I intend to see that she gets there."

"Go on."

James was only too happy to continue. "I know she's gifted, and she deserves a lot more than she's been getting in your class. If she's having any school problems, *you* have got to be the cause. How can you let her get away with such sloppy writing and careless spelling on her papers? Don't you ever take time to look at the assignments these kids turn in? I have to go over every single thing she's written in class—everything she's done in there! What kind of teacher lets kids do such work? It's not my job to be on her case every night, correcting her, seeing that she does her work neatly and properly. You should be setting those standards, and I'm warning you now, I'm giving you notice that I'm going to be watching your teaching very carefully. You have an obligation to teach my daughter well and to recommend her for G&T. If Margie isn't in it, you better have some good reasons why a bright black girl was excluded."

Diane hardly knew how to respond to George James's tirade. She muttered something about the doorbell ringing and hung up. Diane was both upset and angry as she replaced the receiver. She felt that James had practically threatened her. And she was angry that he hadn't given her a chance to tell him about the creative-writing assignments she gave. They allowed for inventing spelling and sloppiness in early drafts so that students could concentrate first on the creative process of writing stories and poems.

But Diane recognized that she could not discuss certain aspects of Margie's classroom performance with her father. How could she tell him that although Margie's test scores were at the 91st percentile, the girl was what the literature called a "concrete thinker?" When class discussions veered away from straight recall of text material, Margie would not participate; slouching low in her seat, she would rest her head on her desk as if exhausted. Diane tried to encourage Margie to think more analytically, but her responses always remained at the level of concrete thought. She never brought new insights to the group. She did not seem to be a prime candidate for the G&T program.

The obvious choices were Mark Sullivan, Seth Cohen, and Josh Arnold, all of whom scored in the 99th percentile on the ITBS; they were the only three in the class to do so. Their daily homework and quiz grades were equally high, their classwork was consistently excellent, and they were lively participants in class projects and discussions. But all three were white and male.

Diane thought about the other student she wanted to recommend. Stuart Johnson's offbeat humor and easygoing manner had won him many friends in the class. He was genuinely funny and could easily have become the class clown, but he never called out jokes or disrupted the class. Diane believed that he was truly gifted. She smiled as she remembered her original impressions of him.

Stuart was a 10-year-old slob. His lank, black hair was rarely combed. His clothes looked as if he dressed in the dark; everything was clean but rumpled and mismatched. Diane often had trouble reading Stuart's scrawled handwriting, but once she could decipher it, she found that his work was consistently accurate. His creative writing seemed beyond his years, and he always completed the bonus critical-thinking questions she included on worksheets.

When Diane began a new topic, Stuart was the student who made insightful connections to related material. Last week Diane introduced the topic of Eskimos in Canada. Stuart was the one to notice the closeness of Alaska to Siberia and to speculate about the existence of an ice bridge between the two regions.

Students enjoyed having Stuart in their group for class projects because he often provided a creative edge.

Stuart was new to the area, but he quickly became friends with Seth, Mark, and Josh. Diane would hear them cheerfully arguing with each other at lunch time, with Stuart often defending his more unusual views. His friends also loved challenging Stuart's math ability. Diane once overheard a problem the boys had given Stuart.

"C'mon, Stuart," said Josh. "You'll never get this one. What's 32 times 67—and no paper!"

Stuart paused for only a moment. "2144," he replied.

His friends quickly took out paper and pencils to check him.

"Tell us your trick," said Mark. "There's no way I can do that stuff in my head. Are you a pen pal of David Copperfield or something?"

Stuart grinned and shook his head. "I don't know how I do it. I can just see the answers." The boys were then off arguing about some new topic, and Diane walked away, amazed.

While Stuart's skills were outstanding, his test scores didn't reflect his ability. Diane had checked Stuart's records from his former school. His grades were just above average, and he scored in the 88th percentile on the standardized achievement test. Even so, there was no question in Diane's mind that Stuart was gifted.

Diane decided to ask Bob Garrett, the principal, for advice. Garrett was in his first year as principal of Talner Elementary School. He had been a teacher in the district for several years and then an assistant principal. Diane was the first teacher he hired, and she knew that he liked her teaching style so far. He seemed to be the appropriate person to talk to about her concerns.

"Mr. Garrett, I'm in a bind. I received the district memo about the gifted and talented program, and the limits on four students per classroom sound absolute. But I have five possible candidates and several questions about two of them."

"Who are the five?" he asked.

"Well, Mark Sullivan, Seth Cohen, and Josh Arnold are clear choices because of their scores and class performance. The other two are Margie James and Stuart Johnson. Their scores are fairly close, but there are some other issues that concern me."

Mr. Garrett said, "If those two seem about equal, I'd say that you really need to consider the issue of racial balance. All our programs, and especially this one, need to reflect the diversity of our student population."

"I realize that," said Diane. "But they are both black."

Mr. Garrett looked puzzled. "Stuart? Really?"

Diane nodded. "I know. I met Stuart's dad when he came to a parent conference. He's black."

Garrett shook his head. "Look, Diane, you've got a tough problem. You're a good teacher, and I certainly trust your judgement. I'll back you up on your decision, but at this point I can't tell you whom to pick. You know the kids, so it's your call."

Diane appreciated the vote of confidence, but her meeting with the principal hadn't been much help. While her background and experience should have made the decision process an easy one, she was faced with a set of unfair criteria, an angry parent, and two students who were competing for one slot. Diane again turned her thoughts to Margie. Using district criteria only, Margie should be her choice. But Margie did not show the brilliance and thinking skills that Stuart displayed, skills that flourish in a gifted and talented program. However, Margie was a girl. Perhaps in a more intimate setting, Margie's skills might develop. So much of Diane's energy had gone into the study of women's issues. How could she choose four boys from her class? And it would look as if she had chosen four white students, since no one seemed to know that Stuart Johnson was black. George James would be furious. Diane had picked up his implication that she was a racist, but she was so angry at his demands that it was just one more unreasonable piece of her conversation with him.

"Why can't the district's standards be more flexible?" Diane thought. "Why must I choose only four students?" Diane stared at the five names on her list, wondering what to tell Mr. Garrett tomorrow.

Melinda Grant

A first-year elementary school teacher with many innovative ideas is uncertain about her classroom activities because the teacher in the next classroom continually warns her that she will be held responsible for the students' end-of-year standardized test scores.

Melinda Grant sat down at Andrea's kitchen table and accepted the cup of coffee gratefully. It was a cold, wet day, and the warm kitchen and sharp aroma of coffee made Melinda feel good. She had been looking forward to this Thanksgiving break as a chance for professional reflection and for catching up with her friend and neighbor, Andrea Samson. Melinda had been teaching full-time at Conway Elementary School in Littleton since September, and the time demands of her new job prevented her from enjoying a long visit with Andrea until now.

"Mel, it's been so long! I feel like I never see you anymore." Andrea's welcoming smile erased the weeks since the friends had last spoken. "How many people did you have for dinner yesterday?"

"Ten!" replied Melinda. "And I didn't even start—I mean not even the shopping—until school was out on Wednesday afternoon. I can't believe how much time teaching takes." Melinda's smile belied the complaint in her words. "How about you? Did you feed a small army?"

"Just my family and my sister and her kids," answered Andrea. "But let's not talk about cooking. I want to hear all about your new career. Is it working out the way you expected?" Andrea passed Melinda the sugar and leaned forward expectantly. Melinda doctored her coffee and settled into her chair, pondering where to begin.

Melinda had entered her third-grade classroom sure of her methods and convinced about the kind of teacher she intended to be, but ten weeks of exposure to the way other teachers did things had made Melinda pause to reflect. She remained committed to her beliefs but had been looking forward to this discussion with her friend. As a parent, Andrea was familiar with the school district. Melinda had a family of her own, and she knew that Andrea shared most of her ideas about children, learning, and the role of schools. They had spent many Saturday mornings commiserating at this same table about their children's education, and now that her role had changed, Melinda needed some of Andrea's reassurance.

This change in her life began two years ago when Melinda, who had worked for twelve years as a part-time computer software designer, became dissatisfied with her position. Her company was acquired by a larger computer firm, and her job description was altered dramatically. She decided to change careers and returned to graduate school to become certified in elementary education. Melinda enjoyed being a student again and dealing with the theoretical problems of education, but after a year attending full time she was eager to put the theory into practice. She was delighted when Littleton offered her a teaching position. Melinda, her husband, and their daughter had lived in the community for the past nine years, and Melinda was familiar with many of the school district's personalities and philosophies, though the school in which she would be teaching was not the one her daughter attended.

Melinda spent most of August eagerly preparing for her first class. Knowing she wanted her classroom to be an interesting and exciting learning environment, she started to collect items she knew she would use: books, a fish tank, cushions, all kinds of art materials, even an old sand table rescued from a closing nursery school—"garage-sale material," her husband complained, only half kidding. Melinda justified the trouble she went to by asking herself, "How could I explain on the one line on Littleton's requisition form what a sand table would be used for?" She emptied her garage and brought everything to her classroom in the last week of August, and she and Shawna, her 11-year-old daughter, spent the week preparing the room for the beginning of school. At the end of the week, both agreed that the room looked great. Melinda valued Shawna's opinion and her input. After all, Shawna had experienced third grade more recently than Melinda had.

Her class was a normal one for Littleton: twenty-five students. Of the thirteen boys and twelve girls, ten were white students, eight black, five Hispanic, and two Asian. She found them an eager, active group of children, some intellectually more mature, some physically more mature, some emotionally more mature, and all with potential for success in school. That was Melinda's attitude toward education, formulated on her own but reinforced by her year of studying educational theory. She truly believed that every child could learn if motivated, challenged, and helped to develop his or her potential.

Melinda settled into her new position more easily than she ever imagined she would have. As it turned out, the children were more nervous and unsure of themselves than she was, and all her hard work in preparation, combined with her good sense and easy manner, made the job a pleasure. Melinda had strong ideas about how to approach her class. She wanted to focus on critical-thinking skills and to use an interdisciplinary approach to all the content subjects. She wanted to use lots of group work, especially cooperative learning groups, to channel the natural bent of 8-year-olds toward positive social activity. She also hoped to integrate artistic projects into the standard subject areas as much as she could. In her week of preparation she had arranged the room to accommodate her teaching strategy, with the desks forming groups of five students each, with tables for science and reading centers located at the periphery of the room, and with the sand table ready for a class project she was planning that would last for at least half the year. Melinda envisioned a classroom full of activity and movement, fun and learning.

On the first day of class, Melinda met Barbara Stratton, the third-grade teacher from the room next door, and quickly saw how differently two people could approach the same job. A friendly woman in her forties, Barbara had been teaching at Conway for almost twenty years, working mostly with the third grade. She was quick to offer her help and invited Melinda into her classroom at the end of the day. Barbara Stratton had arranged the desks in her room in four rows of six, with two desks placed several feet away from the others. "For the troublemakers," Barbara explained. "And, as usual, I have several of those," she chuckled. "I find this seating arrangement keeps them somewhat controlled." Melinda nodded, preferring not to get into a discussion of behavior management with a twenty-year veteran on her first day on the job. In that first meeting, Barbara seemed a curious mixture of tough and tender as she alternated between complaining about the bad behavior and low intelligence of her students and offering insightful ideas about who needed help and how to provide it. "All this in only six hours of observation," marveled Melinda to herself.

As the school year progressed, Melinda found that Barbara was always willing to extend help and advice; Barbara was happy to play the role of mentor as long as Melinda accepted the role of eager novice. She offered worksheets she used for basic math and language arts skills, suggested ideas for seatwork, and shared birds' eggs, hornets' nests, and other nature finds. Melinda appreciated Barbara's attention despite the fact that she and Barbara were as far apart as two teachers could be in regard to educational strategy. Shawna noticed it when she visited her mother's classroom in October. "You both teach third grade, but your rooms look so different. She has all those posters that kids hate, about good foods and good punctuation, and she hangs up those boring math tests, and only the ones with '100 percent' on them. Almost everything on your walls was made by your students, and your room is full of class projects. I love your room, especially the city of the future in the sand table. If I were in third grade, I'd want to be in your room. It looks like it would be more fun!"

Melinda accepted the praise even though she wasn't sure an 11-year-old's definition of fun would stand as an evaluation of teaching performance. Besides, she valued much of the advice Barbara Stratton so regularly dispensed. The day after Shawna had registered her performance appraisal, Barbara came into Melinda's room to share lunch with her. Between bites of tuna salad, Barbara asked, "Have you begun organizing your practice work for the Iowa test yet? I know it seems a long way off, but you need to get your kids ready. So much depends on their scores. You get measured right along with the children. I have some great workbooks you can borrow to begin making copies for practice for the class."

"Barbara, the test is months away. We're doing so many things in class right now. I'm starting a writing workshop, and the students will begin making animal habitats next week. I think I'll dampen their enthusiasm if I introduce workbook drills. They'll get the skills some other way. I'm sure my class will do OK on the test."

"I hate to keep reminding you that you're new at this, Melinda, but there are parents out there who will measure *your* ability, not their children's, by how well the students score on standardized tests. Your job is to teach these children how to get the best scores they can. It will make them look good, and it will certainly help your position."

"But the kids need so much more, and school can give them so much more. The parents must know that the kind of work their kids bring home now is as important as standardized test scores."

Barbara smiled and patted Melinda's hand. "I'm only telling you this for your own good. Children need to master basic skills before they deserve special projects. Every year they give me the dullest students. The district claims it doesn't track at this age, but every year I get the worst kids. I spend all my time on skills with them—drill, drill, drill. Sometimes I get depressed because it's not much fun, for me or for them, but my students always have the highest scores in the entire district. If I let them spend their time building projects and drawing pictures and writing stories, they will score poorly on the Iowas. And I know my success as a teacher here depends on my students' scores on that test."

Melinda nodded her agreement and changed the subject. Later that week she began to do some checking. Barbara had not boasted idly. Her classes were, in fact, consistently among the highest in the district on the Iowa tests. And Barbara's class of third-graders this year did seem to have an overabundance of students with problems, at least in comparison to Melinda's class. Barbara regularly told her stories of the children's problems, both academic and behavioral, which Melinda was sure she wouldn't know how to handle. "A value-added comparison of teachers would make Barbara Stratton a candidate for 'Teacher of the Year,'" thought Melinda.

As she finished telling Andrea about her classroom and about the concerns that Barbara raised, Melinda leaned back in her chair and concluded, "So I can't argue with the results she gets, but I just can't bring myself to teach that way." It had taken Melinda an hour to summarize her situation for her friend, sharing her doubts about the efficacy of Barbara Stratton's approach and her own disdain for standardized tests. "I know my class learns basic skills through children's literature, creative writing, math projects, even activities like drawing pictures, creating masks, and building futuristic cities. Since I'm not drilling the students directly, as Barbara does, they probably won't show dramatic test scores, but the learning will last."

Melinda leaned forward again and spoke emphatically, confident that Andrea would be sympathetic to her position. "They'll be more critical and more creative thinkers; they'll be able to use their whole brains; they'll be able to see more around them; they'll be better citizens; they'll know how to work cooperatively. Surely district administrators and parents must know that knowledge can't be measured just by standardized tests."

Melinda ended her speech with her hands open and extended, both to emphasize her point and to welcome Andrea's support. In spite of her confident delivery, Melinda was anxious for moral support from her friend.

But Andrea let a moment pass before replying, and while her tone was kind, her response was devastating. "Don't be naive about this school district, Mel. Littleton is a small city with some urban problems and a middle class that's worrying about becoming the minority. If we want to keep a strong middle class here and encourage other families like us to move in, we've got to maintain high test scores at all levels. You read the local paper. The test scores of each district in the county and of each school in each district are published every year. The school board receives tremendous pressure from local citizens to keep those scores high. People who own their own homes are particularly strident on this issue. You know that. All anyone talks about is property values in Littleton. And even though the papers don't publish individual class scores, everyone in the school knows which teachers' classes score the highest and which the lowest. Even parents know! I think your classroom sounds terrific, Mel, but you better cover all the bases. I hate to say this to you, but I think Barbara Stratton is right."

Leigh Scott

A high school social studies teacher gives a higher-than-earned report-card grade to a mainstreamed student, on the basis of the boy's effort, and is confronted by another student with identical test grades who received a lower report-card grade.

Leigh Scott felt the flush slowly leave her face as she watched Aaron Washington leave the classroom, slamming the door behind him. It was the end of the second grading cycle; students had received their report cards the day before. Leigh had just taken off her coat and was on her way to the teachers' room to get a cup of coffee before the bell rang when Aaron came into the room.

He began, "We got to talk about my American government grade." It was clear that he was angry.

Leigh moved to her desk and responded, "Hi, Aaron. What's up? You're upset about your grade?"

"You gave me a D."

"You did D work."

"So did Dale, and he got a C." Aaron was leaning over the desk toward Leigh.

"Aaron, this is not a good time to talk about this. The bell is going to ring in a few minutes. Why don't you see me after school this afternoon."

Aaron shook his head at her suggestion. "I have practice after school. We have to talk now."

Now it was Leigh's turn to shake her head. "This is not a good time; I have to get ready for homeroom. Besides, there's not really anything to talk about."

Aaron straightened up, took a couple of steps back from the desk, and said, "You gave a white kid who got the same grades I did a C, and you gave me a D. I even did more homework than Dale. I say we *do* have something to talk about."

Leigh capitulated. "Come in tomorrow morning at 7:30, and we'll talk before homeroom period."

Aaron nodded, strode out of the room without another word, and let the door slam as he left.

Leigh had been teaching social studies at Littleton High School for eleven years, and this was the first time a student accused her of racial bias. Students sometimes complained about their grades, and Leigh was always willing to

147

reconsider a grade. But she never had a student suggest she was biased. Leigh had spent her entire teaching career at Littleton, so she had been teaching classes that were mixed racially and ethnically for a long time. She considered herself color blind when it came to assigning grades.

At Littleton High School, students were placed into one of four academic tracks: honors, above average, average, and remedial. Teachers were responsible for five classes a day, with the honors classes typically assigned to senior faculty. Newer faculty taught mostly average and remedial sections. Leigh taught a senior-level honors American history course, two freshman above-average sections of world history, and two sophomore average-level sections of American government.

Leigh graded her two sophomore American government sections on the following requirements each cycle:

- Tests (usually three or four, depending on the material)
- Homework (collected three times a week)
- A project
- Participation in class discussions based on the textbook readings

The textbook was written on an eighth-grade reading level. Leigh's tests were a combination of vocabulary, multiple-choice, and short-answer items. Leigh didn't require that students in the average sections answer essay questions. Students selected projects from among several choices: writing papers, constructing something appropriate to the topic, making a presentation to the class, or writing book reports on pertinent readings.

During homeroom period, Leigh consulted her grade book and confirmed that Aaron's information was accurate. Neither he nor Dale had done particularly well this grading cycle. Both had received mostly D grades, with an occasional C. Neither participated in class discussions unless called on. However, she knew that she had given Dale the higher grade because of his effort, not because of his color. Dale was a learning disabled student mainstreamed into Leigh's class.

Typically, a mainstreamed student would be placed in a remedial section, but Dale's case was an exception. He was in an average-level class because his resource room teacher, Meg Dament, requested the placement, feeling that Dale needed a more academic environment and a higher-achieving peer group than he would have had in a remedial section. Meg and Leigh had known each other since Leigh came to Littleton. Leigh admired Meg's dedication and her tenacity on behalf of her students. It was clear that Meg cared deeply about the students she served and wanted them to have whatever educational normality she could engineer for them. Meg was able to mainstream her "best" students into average-level, not remedial, classes. She actively sought teachers who would be responsive to her students' needs and to their efforts. It was not easy to convince high school teachers to work with classified students, but of the four resource room teachers in the high school, it was Meg who made the most regular class placements.

When Meg requested Leigh as Dale's teacher, Leigh understood that Dale was not a very good reader and that he would not volunteer in class. Leigh and Meg spoke regularly about Dale's progress, as well as the classroom requirements. Meg helped Dale prepare for Leigh's class, and he was showing real improvement since the first cycle, when his grade had been a low D.

Additionally, Dale's attitude in class was positive. He had learned to exhibit "teacher-pleasing behaviors": He looked attentive, he tried to take notes, he almost always carried his textbook and notebook and a pencil, and he never disrupted the class. Aaron had a different style: He would put his head on his desk during class discussions, he seldom brought materials to class, and he often talked to friends while Leigh was lecturing.

Nevertheless, their grades during the cycle were nearly identical, and Aaron was demanding an explanation. Leigh drove home that day wondering what she would tell Aaron during their appointment the following morning. Aaron's anger, coupled with his charge of racism, exacerbated her anxiety about their meeting. She also knew that she would have to figure out what she might do to prevent this from happening in the future, since she anticipated that she would continue to have mainstreamed students in her classes and she believed they should be rewarded for effort and improvement.

Anita Underwood*

An experienced and enthusiastic third-grade teacher describes in detail her plans and her activities for the first day of class for the new school year and shares her sense of excitement and her concerns.

A week ago I had carefully addressed postcards to unknown names announcing that I would be their third-grade teacher for the new school year. Most of the children's names were unfamiliar to me, an understandable situation since Roosevelt Elementary School in Littleton enrolled six classes of third graders. As I waited now to see the faces of the children in my class, a surge of emotions raced through my body—eagerness for the journey together to begin, sadness that this was not the previous class that I had so adored, fear that too many would lack basic skills, and concern that there would not be enough of me to go around. I also was filled with hope that we would become a family, a community of caring, sharing learners by the end of the year. I glanced around my room one more time, cheered by the brightly colored posters, the activity centers, the blank spaces soon to be filled with children's work. Although I was starting my twenty-second year of teaching and my eighth year as a third-grade teacher in Littleton, I still felt the nervous anticipation of a new school year.

It was now 8:40, time to begin. No bell rang but a soft roar had begun and grown to a crescendo as the halls filled with children's voices. I stood at the door of my room and soon Timmy Elliott stood before me, clutching his postcard.

"I'm Timmy," he announced.

"I'm Mrs. Underwood." I replied. "Welcome to Room 311. Choose a desk that fits, put your school supplies away, find a locker you can reach, and then check out the room. I'm glad you're here, Timmy." He looked at me, gave a nervous smile, and some of the apprehension eased from his face.

I greeted twenty-six more children and reassured the parents who accompanied many of them. Some of the parents were as curious as the children and wanted to see what the teacher looked like. Others came to say hello or to let me know that they were interested in their child's education. I understood that

*Developed by Mary Endorf, Augsburg College.

it took an act of trust to turn their children over to me. I hoped that I would live up to that trust.

Getting acquainted on the first day is a special time, one that can begin to nurture confidence or cause tightness, fear, and anxiety. It seemed to me that children would be comforted to know that the teacher was once in third grade too, so I began with a personal story from my third-grade experience and passed about a picture of myself at their age. Pictures of my family and more memories followed. While they sized me up I did the same. "My name is Anita," I told them. It helped them to know that I, too, have a name.

I did some quick counts as I introduced myself and heard from them. My observations told me that there were thirteen girls and fourteen boys and fourteen children of color—five Asian-Americans, seven African-Americans, and two Latino children. It's difficult to judge socioeconomic status on the first day of school. Everyone is clean, pressed, and polished like the entryway tiles they walked across. All of their possessions are new. A magnet school, Roosevelt draws students from elegant, historic mansions lining Summit Avenue and graffiti-covered projects fronting Selby Avenue. Those are the extremes. The rest of the children come from what is left of the middle-class families in the community. I know from reading the local papers that there are many single parents raising children here in addition to families who have immigrated from all around the world.

The thing that makes the first day of school wonderful is that it is the only day of the year when all the children feel equal. I did not yet know where the rough spots would be, which stars were shining, which just beginning to twinkle, and which as yet had not begun to glow. On the first day they were all the same, and in a carefully constructed way I planned to take a first look at their learning needs.

We continued with the business of getting acquainted and comfortable. Susan wondered why I hadn't passed out books yet. This was a great question; it gave me an opening for the speech that described the philosophy that would guide our learning this year. "This is going to be a literature-based classroom. What that means is that we will do all of our learning from 'real' materials rather than textbooks. We will read a variety of literature during the year: action, nonaction, poetry, magazines and some things from materials you will choose. You will have many choices in what and how you learn."

Susan smiled slightly. "Sounds good to me. Is it legal?"

"I hope so," I replied. Those that got it giggled, the rest played and squirmed restlessly. I put the philosophy into action by introducing a story called *Never Spit on Your Shoes*. We read and laughed our way through the story, with me pausing at different points to get their reactions and ideas. Everyone was smiling when the story ended, and I felt we'd made a good start.

We took a short break for a snack, and then I passed out note cards. "Please write down three questions that you would like to ask me. You may ask anything that interests you, and I will answer the questions honestly. Spell the words that you know correctly and circle the ones you are not sure of. Be sure to put your name on the upper right-hand corner of the card."

The cards told me at a glance many things about my new class. Immediately it was clear that there was a huge range of ability. Some students appeared to write in a code that I could not decipher, and they circled nothing. Billy, Joseph, Shamika, Timmy, and Anna wrote sophisticated sentences with few circled words. Toni told me she couldn't think of anything to ask.

The handwriting was as varied as the skills. Some children were still struggling to print; others attempted cursive. One student, Barry, ignored the whole thing and worked silently on the drawing he had begun as soon as he had found his seat. He ignored my request to join us. I told the students I would answer the questions on the cards after lunch, and we moved on to another activity.

I gave them oral and visual instructions for the construction of an eight-page book that would be titled *The Me Book.* This project allowed the children to demonstrate many skills and provided me with information about their cognitive development, their writing, their fine-motor skills and artistic interpretation, their ability to understand a task and follow directions, their neatness and sense of order, and their confidence level. Each student began to create the booklet by folding a large sheet of drawing paper. A few were able to accomplish the task as presented, but most needed help. Several required constant reinforcement, asking at each step, "Is this right?"

With the folding completed I listed the title and page-by-page information on the board. A hush fell over the room as the class got down to work. A sudden volley of questions erupted as the students realized they had to make some decisions on their own. "Should I write everything first?"

"Do you want me to put a picture on the front?"

"Do you care how much I write?"

"What if I can't draw my mom?"

"What should I do first, write or draw?"

"I've never seen my dad but I know I have one. Should I put him in too?"

"This is your book, and I would like you to decide what is important to you and surprise me," I told them. Again quiet prevailed as new crayons were carefully opened, long pencils cradled correctly for a while, and minds busily created masterpieces that would surely please me.

I wandered about the room observing. Mai Lin, Xiong, and Leah hadn't started. Barry joined us and was putting lavish detail into the writing of his name. Tomas was still fussing over what it was I wanted him to do. Eddie was having a great time drawing rappers in Cris Cross clothing. Susan muttered something about hating to draw and continued to write. Anna had many drawings of her family and had written several sentences describing them. Drew was still reading the book, *How Things Work,* that he found at the beginning of the day and hadn't heard a word regarding this assignment. Jimmy was doing the tasks as asked but in microscopic scale, and Elliott, who hadn't started either, tugged at my sleeve and asked, "How do you like my new school clothes my daddy bought for me?"

The next day the children would finish their books and share them with each other. Some would read with strong confidence; others would hand theirs to me to read; some would have only pictures to share because they have not yet learned to read and cannot write. The small books will be the first entry into their assessment portfolios.

We cleaned up from this project as lunchtime neared. Again, I observed the students as they wound down this activity. Some stopped as soon as I told them it was getting close to lunch time, mid-word, mid-sentence, mid-drawing. Others moaned, unwilling to break off their work. A few finished the part they were working on, neatly folded their papers, and gently laid their materials in their desks. I reminded students to take care of their pencils and crayons since they will be responsible for keeping their own materials. Some students ignored this injunction—crayons and pencils were left where they were dropped or fell.

The afternoon of the first day went by swiftly. The children returned from lunch and playground time with an abundance of energy, so we did a "meeting and greeting" activity that helped us remember each other's names and shifted from moving around the room to sitting at desks. When everyone was seated, I began to answer the questions on their cards. At lunch, I had sorted the questions into those about school, those about my personal life, and general questions. I answered the school questions first and asked for others that these might have raised. Then I responded to the personal ones, asking the students for like information about themselves. We talked about our animals, brothers and sisters, favorite foods and television programs, vacation experiences. Finally, I answered the more general questions—explaining that some of the topics raised by these questions would be the subject of science, social studies, or reading lessons. We talked about how to gather information, discover new ideas, share our questions, listen to other people's views.

Our final first-day activity was a math game. In the five hours the children had been with me, I had begun to observe and note, formally and informally, their social interactions and language skills. Before the day was over, I wanted to get a sense of how they used numbers, solved problems, thought mathematically. One of the ongoing activities this year would be a trip around the world. Starting in Littleton, we will span the globe, returning "home" in June. We will do reading, writing, science, social studies, and math activities as part of our travels, and I introduced this project by hanging a large map of the world, finding Littleton, and asking students where they would want to go. We listed many places and took some straw votes to identify the most popular choices. Then students calculated distances between different locations. I'd prepared a sheet that gave the miles from Littleton to places that have proved popular in the past. As well, travel guides that included some information they might need were available.

The discussion had been lively, and I noticed that all the students joined in but Elliott and Barry. Drew had put away *How Things Work* to become an active participant, and he immediately went to work on the problems I had assigned. As earlier, I noticed that some students couldn't seem to get started without a lot of support and reinforcement, while others eagerly "jumped in," anxious to do the task I presented. With fifteen minutes left until dismissal, I collected the papers, and we all came together in a circle to talk about our first day.

Everyone who wanted to speak was to say one positive thing that happened during the day. I began, reporting that it was a good day for me because I learned so many of their names, and I heard their laughter many times. Many students volunteered and shared observations about meeting new friends and seeing old ones. Others spoke about different classroom activities, lunch, playground, the books and magazines. We ran out of time before we ran out of speakers. As noise filled the halls again, students gathered up their backpacks and lunch boxes and lined up for the trip home. I again stood in the doorway, saying goodbye, watching who left with whom, who forgot things, who seemed to know just what to do.

When the last student left, I sat at the desk and thought about them. After this first day, what conclusions could I draw? What did I know? How would this information guide me? What would we do tomorrow?

PART FIVE

Mainstreaming

Allison Cohen

A resource room teacher opens a resource room at an elementary school that has never had any special education classrooms. She believes the teachers are colluding to make the mainstreaming program fail.

No one was sure when the teachers at the Bidwell Elementary School in the Lumberton school district began to refer to themselves as "the old biddies," but the name had stuck, and a short time after Allison Cohen began teaching in the new resource room in Bidwell, she came to the conclusion that the name was appropriate.

The Lumberton school district, located in a suburban area of a large northeastern state, was created many years ago by merging the school districts of seven neighboring townships for purposes of improving the school services they could offer to the children residing in the townships. Currently serving almost 11,000 children in kindergarten through grade 12 with sixteen elementary schools, four middle schools, and three high schools, Lumberton employed 1200 teachers and staff and 60 school administrators.

Bidwell School was different from all the other elementary schools in Lumberton in a number of ways. First, it was the smallest school in the district. There were only two classes at each grade level, with a total of thirteen teachers in the building. (One kindergarten teacher taught both the morning and the afternoon kindergarten sessions.) Because of its size, there had been no full-time special teachers at the school. Art, music, physical education, remedial reading, and computer teachers visited the school weekly, but the regular staff consisted of only the thirteen classroom teachers and the principal.

All thirteen teachers were women, and all had been there for a long time. The "newest" teacher, Theresa Conti, began teaching there fourteen years ago. Mary Edgerly, the principal, had been a Bidwell teacher for twenty-two years prior to her appointment to the principal's position four years ago. The current staff averaged twenty-one years of service at the school, with Margaret Antonelli holding the longevity record—thirty-three years of consecutive teaching at Bidwell.

The teachers' years together and their ability to work as a team accounted for another difference at Bidwell. The teachers were very powerful. For example, there had never been a special education classroom in the building. Over the years, Bidwell principals had successfully argued that it made more sense to bus the few special education students from Bidwell to a neighboring school than to bus many special education students to Bidwell's small setting.

The teachers' power was also seen in the fact that in the past fourteen years none of Bidwell's teachers had been transferred to another school in the district. Bidwell was the only school in Lumberton that had not had recent staff changes. The teachers remained exempt from staff shifts even when Bidwell's enrollment declined in the early 1980s and some classes fell to fewer than fifteen students. Recently, school enrollments had increased, and there were now between twenty-two and twenty-five students in each class.

Some people in the district attributed the power of the Bidwell faculty to Margaret Antonelli. Her family had lived in Lumberton for years, and she was said to be "connected" to local politicians and other powerful people in the community. Margaret, who had never married, still lived in the house where she had been raised. Until recently, she had cared for her aging mother, who died this past spring.

There were other people on the Bidwell faculty with strong connections in the community. The principal was the sister-in-law of the superintendent of schools, and two of the teachers were related to members of the school board. A fourth teacher was married to the scion of one of the wealthiest families in the community.

The most recent challenge to the status quo at Bidwell occurred two years ago when Ruth Greenburg, the director of special education, tried to start a resource room in the building as part of a pilot mainstreaming program. Until then, all mildly handicapped elementary school students in the district had been served in self-contained special education classrooms. When Ruth Greenburg was promoted to the position of director of special education, she initiated resource room programs in the district. At first, as the services to mildly handicapped elementary school students in Lumberton began to change, Mary Edgerly was able to argue successfully that Bidwell was unprepared to test a new program since the teachers had no experience with special education students. But even as Mary won that battle, she knew that a resource room would soon come to her building. Ruth Greenburg had been responsible for changing the special education program in such a way that district policy now called for a resource room in each elementary building. For two years, Ruth had held inservice meetings for all elementary school teachers to prepare them for mainstreaming.

As Mary had anticipated, two years later the resource room became a reality, and Allison Cohen was the teacher assigned to the class. When Allison arrived at Bidwell, she knew little of its history. She had been hired to teach in Lumberton immediately after she graduated from the state university with a B.S. in elementary and special education. Two years before, after teaching in a self-contained learning disabilities classroom for five years, she was asked to move to a resource room as part of the pilot program the district was establishing to mainstream many of its special education students. She found the resource room program stimulating, and she knew that her classroom was seen as a model by other teachers. She also knew from attending meetings with other resource room teachers that her relationships with the teachers in her building were better than most.

Now 28, she was married and had a 3-year-old child. A bright, feisty red-head who managed to balance her work and home life with humor and high spirits, she knew that Ruth Greenburg had selected her for this assignment because of her upbeat personality and success in her first resource room assignment. Other than that, she got little information from Ruth about the Bidwell situation.

When school started in September, she found eleven children on her class roll. These were all former Bidwell School students who had been served in special education classes in other elementary schools and who were being returned to Bidwell to enter their assigned grade and receive resource room support. These students had been selected by the Committee on Special Education (CSE) as the most likely to be successfully mainstreamed from among all the children in self-contained classes whose home school was Bidwell. It was expected that Allison's class would be completed as other Bidwell students were returned to their home school and as newly eligible students were scheduled for the resource room instead of being sent to a self-contained class in another school.

Allison began the school year by meeting personally with each of the seven teachers who had a resource room student and talking about the role that she and the resource room might play in helping both the child and the teacher. The teachers were very gracious and listened to Allison with interest. They didn't seem to have any questions or objections, and Allison told her husband that she felt that they probably were going to serve the returning students well, given their years of experience.

But on the second day of school, June Jamison, one of the third-grade teachers, came to Allison to request additional resource room time for Seth, the mainstreamed student in her classroom. As Allison tried to explain that Seth was expected to spend most of his day in the regular class, June nodded and with a smile said, "Yes, dear, and you are quite right to try to follow policy. But don't you think your first responsibility is to the child? Seth so needs your help."

Allison agreed to bring Seth to the resource room for an additional half hour each day and told June that she would check with her at the end of the week to see how Seth was doing. June responded, "I'll be happy to talk with you then."

The following day, Anna Richards, the other third-grade teacher, came to see Allison. "As you know," she began, "I have two resource room students in my class. Third grade is a very difficult year, and neither of these children is able to keep up with the class. They seem very discouraged, and I'm worried about them."

Allison responded, "Perhaps I could observe the children in your class and see how they are doing."

"Oh, no. I'm sure that would upset them. I think they need your help in your classroom." Allison noticed that Anna emphasized "your classroom."

When Allison said she would see the two children for an additional half hour each day, Anna responded, "Half an hour! That won't be long enough. These students need help in reading, arithmetic, and spelling. I was thinking of two more hours a day."

Allison tried to reason with the teacher. "Miss Richards, the whole idea of mainstreaming is for the children to be with other third-graders in your classroom. I really shouldn't see them for two more hours a day."

The two teachers finally agreed that the students would spend an additional hour a day in the resource room. As Anna left the classroom, Allison felt that the worst was over, since third-grade teachers throughout the district were the most concerned about mainstreaming as a result of a recently instituted state Minimum Basic Skills Test, which was given in third, seventh, and eleventh grades.

She couldn't have been more wrong. By the end of the second week of school, she had been visited by four more teachers, each of whom came to request more time in the resource room for her mainstreamed students. Without showing anger or impatience, they all told Allison virtually the same story: The students needed more help than they could give; therefore Allison would have to do something.

Allison decided to try to work with the teachers by suggesting the sort of simple classroom accommodations that had helped the teachers in her previous school. When June told her that Seth could not follow oral directions, Allison suggested that June write the directions on the chalkboard.

June responded, "Well, of course I've tried that, but it just did not help a bit. You know, my dear, you have only five children at a time. Until you've had experience with large groups of children, you really can't imagine what might work in a classroom like mine."

Allison then tried to observe her students in their regular classes. She first approached Margaret Antonelli, figuring that if she could win her over, the rest of the faculty would be pushovers.

"Miss Antonelli," Allison tried to be winning. "Jeff has said the nicest things about your classroom. Since other students are having some problems, I'd like to watch him for a while in your room to see if I can figure out what special things you are doing."

Margaret looked at Allison without smiling. "I really don't think that's a good idea. It would make Jeff and the other children uncomfortable for you to be there."

Another time, Allison had to blink back tears of frustration when a teacher responded to her suggestion that she visit the teacher's classroom by saying, "Perhaps you could run some copies of my worksheets or correct some student work if you are looking for things to do."

And if she went into a classroom without an invitation, the teacher would stop the lesson, speak politely with Allison, and not resume the lesson until Allison left the room.

When Allison tried to discuss the problem with Mary Edgerly, the principal spoke with her in an even tone. "I think you should know that the teachers at Bidwell are the best in the district. I'm sure that every decision they make is in the best interest of the pupils." Allison explained that she respected the teachers but that they were fighting her efforts to mainstream the students. Mary seemed annoyed and responded, "When you have had as much experience with children as these teachers, then you'll understand."

Allison found herself showing her frustration. "But the resource room isn't working!" she told Mary in a louder-than-usual tone.

Mary seemed to sense her distress and responded, "The teachers are very happy with the resource room. The children are getting along well, considering, and I think you should just keep on helping them. If that means spending more time with them in the resource room, then you should do that without getting all upset."

Mary ended the conversation by putting her arm around Allison's shoulder and saying, "In fact, I just saw Ruth Greenburg at a meeting and told her what a wonderful job you are doing. I told Ruth I owed her an apology for resisting the resource room, since it's working out better than I could have imagined. And I made it clear that you are the reason we are so happy with the program. I really think you just need to have a little more confidence in yourself."

"Talk about damning with faint praise," Allison thought to herself. She knew that the resource room was not working and that she was not doing her job. She still had only eleven children in her class, and she was seeing each child for at least three hours a day. She was not working with the teachers, and most of her time in the resource room was spent teaching developmental reading, language arts, and math, since the students were missing instruction in those areas by being in the resource room instead of their regular classrooms.

Allison felt that the Bidwell teachers had entered into a conspiracy against her while maintaining a surface cordiality and friendliness. The first time she mentioned that feeling to her husband, he laughed and said, "The old biddies in a conspiracy? Allie, you've got to be kidding."

But Allison wasn't kidding. She really had come to think of the Bidwell teachers as evil. She no longer believed that it was a coincidence that their responses to her and the children were so alike. She was convinced that they were trying to prevent the resource room from succeeding.

Beyond that, she felt that Mary had finessed her by lavishly complimenting her to Ruth Greenburg. If she went to Ruth with her problems, Ruth would probably think she was crazy. There was no one in the building with whom she could talk. She needed an ally who knew what it was *really* like in that school and who could give her advice. She did not know where to turn.

Lynn Collier

An experienced resource room teacher is confronted by a frustrated classroom teacher who wants an emotionally disturbed student who has outbursts in his classroom to be removed.

Lynn Collier drew a deep breath as she listened to Alan Williams complain. "You've got to do something about her," Alan pleaded, almost plaintively. "Tara's behavior is making it impossible for me to control my class. That's never happened to me in fifteen years of teaching. It's only October, and I'm already dreading the rest of this year."

Although this was her first year as a resource room teacher, Lynn knew about Tara Atkinson. She had first met Tara four years before, when Tara was a second grader in Lynn's self-contained special education class at Willow Street School in Littleton. Lynn remembered that first year with Tara very well. The summer had left her refreshed and enthusiastic about the coming school year, and for the first time she was to have two girls in her special education class. The eight children ranged in age from 7 to 9. Most were of average intelligence, but their academic progress had been impeded by their emotional outbursts. No one in the class was reading beyond the first-grade level.

Lynn had carefully read all the background material on Tara provided by the Committee on Special Education (CSE). Tara's parents had been in their forties when she was born. She had a half-brother and a half-sister, both in their twenties. She had been referred for special education services in October of her kindergarten year because of her severe emotional outbursts, her refusal to complete simple assignments, and her withdrawal from peers. Psychological testing indicated that her IQ was in the above-average range. However, her academic performance was considerably below average. She was found to have serious emotional problems and was placed in a self-contained class for disturbed students. The latest CSE report said that Tara's mother had been hospitalized several times due to mental illness. The mother was said to have suffered two nervous breakdowns. Tara had witnessed several episodes in which her mother exhibited aberrant behavior.

At Lynn's first meeting with the girl, Tara seemed sweet and slightly shy. An attractive child with brown hair and big eyes, Tara appeared unsure of herself and uncomfortable in the first few weeks of school. Eventually, partly due to Lynn's subtle encouragement, Tara began to interact with Madeline, the other little girl in the class. She and Madeline began to eat lunch together and stay close by each other on the playground, avoiding contact with the other students. They did not participate in the organized games, even when encouraged by students or teachers.

Tara progressed quickly in academic tasks. It seemed to Lynn that the more comfortable Tara felt in the class, the more her reading and math skills improved. Her behavior, however, continued to be erratic. Some days Tara would have outbursts in class, acting particularly stubborn or refusing to do her work. She would usually comment that she had a bad night at home and was tired. Lynn tried to get Tara to express her feelings, but the child told Lynn that things that happened at home were "private business." Tara did occasionally make comments, albeit under her breath, about her mother, saying that her mother was mixed up and that she did not have to listen to her.

At other times, Tara's outbursts centered around Madeline, her new friend. Tara would make cruel comments about Madeline's weight, or her clothes, or her glasses. Madeline never defended herself against Tara's remarks, although Lynn knew she was hurt. When Lynn intervened in Tara's verbal assaults on Madeline, Tara would run from the room, screaming that she wanted to be left alone and that she hated everyone. Once she calmed down and returned to the class, she would be friendly to Madeline, but she seldom, if ever, apologized.

By December of that year, Tara's outbursts had begun to subside and her reading skills were improving dramatically. Lynn began to consider mainstreaming Tara in a second-grade class for reading after the Christmas holidays. The CSE and Tara's parents agreed that it was a good idea, and the team approached Amy London, who was considered to be an excellent second-grade teacher. Amy agreed to accept Tara into her class and met several times with Lynn to discuss how to mainstream Tara successfully.

From the moment it was mentioned to her, Tara was nervous about going to the second-grade reading class. Her first two weeks there were not successful. She responded only to direct questions, never participated willingly, and did not interact with the other students. She did not want to talk about her reading class with Lynn, and Lynn did not press her to discuss it. After two weeks, Tara refused to go to the reading class, explaining only that she hated the class and the students. Lynn insisted that Tara continue to go and began to walk her to the class, even though Tara protested. Tara's behavior in Lynn's class worsened, with most of her negative behaviors directed toward Madeline, and even her reading skills seemed to deteriorate. When pressed, she finally told Lynn that the other students made fun of her because she was in a special class and rode a special bus to school. She said the other students pointed at her and giggled.

Lynn and Amy both felt that mainstreaming Tara was too important to give up so quickly, and they decided to try several modifications to help her feel more at home in the mainstreamed classroom. First, Amy identified a popular second-grade student as Tara's buddy. This student sat next to her and helped her with anything she didn't understand. At the same time, Tara and Madeline began to eat lunch with the second graders. Tara's buddy sat with them and helped them "integrate" into the group.

Lynn began to spend some time in the second-grade class, teaching a lesson or working with students. This helped relieve some of the negative attitudes toward Lynn's class. Finally, Amy taught a unit emphasizing differences to sensitize her students to other people's feelings and show how all students are "different."

Though Tara never spoke about the second-grade class and often had to be urged to go to Amy's classroom, Lynn's and Amy's work seemed to have paid off, as Tara relaxed more in Amy's class and her outbursts in Lynn's class abated. In the spring of that year, during Tara's annual reevaluation, the CSE asked Lynn about moving Tara back to her home school, since special education services were now available there. Tara's parents had requested the change so that she would not have to ride the bus to school. Lynn agreed and met with Tara's new teacher to discuss strategies for mainstreaming her for reading with one of the third-grade classes in her new school. Only later did Lynn discover that Tara had been mainstreamed at first, but her behavior problems had resurfaced and the mainstreaming attempts quickly were discontinued. Tara spent the next three years in a self-contained class for emotionally disturbed students.

At the end of her fifth-grade year, Tara's parents requested that she be reassigned to the Willow Street School and to Lynn's class. When the CSE approached Lynn, they explained that Tara's parents believed that Tara's most successful school experience had been the year she was in Lynn's class. The CSE had reevaluated Tara and recommended she be placed in a regular sixth-grade class taught by Alan Williams, with two periods a day in the resource room. This was ideal, since Lynn had been assigned, at her request, to the new resource room at Willow Avenue. The CSE reasoned that with a sensitive sixth-grade teacher and a resource room teacher who knew Tara and who would work in collaboration with the sixth-grade teacher, Tara might have enough support to be successful in regular education and thus be better prepared for middle school the following year.

Lynn and Alan Williams had taught together at Willow Avenue School for seven years. Alan had been an elementary school teacher for fifteen years, all of them in Littleton. In addition to his classroom experience, Alan directed the class play for the high school and for the past nine summers had been a teacher in the district's summer camp program, designed for elementary-level special education students—those classified learning disabled, emotionally disturbed, and mentally retarded. Alan's sixth-grade class contained twenty-two children, four of whom were classified learning disabled and one, Tara, emotionally disturbed.

According to Alan, the difficulties with Tara began early in the school year. At first, Tara seemed a model student, quiet, a little shy. She did not interact much with the other students, but she completed all of her assignments and seemed to be keeping up. One day, though, after a particularly lengthy social studies lesson, Tara suddenly erupted. Jumping up from her seat and shouting obscenities at no one in particular, she ran from the room. "I had no idea why," Alan said. "I sent my aide to look for Tara. She found her in the hall, very calm, not at all upset."

"I had read all about Tara's history in her school records," Alan continued, "but I had no warning her behavior could be so explosive."

"Have you talked to Tara about the incident?" Lynn asked, feeling sympathy for both teacher and student.

"Sure, but she didn't want to discuss it. She promised me it wouldn't happen again. Her word wasn't worth much. At least four times in the last two weeks, she's done the same thing. Every time she goes off, I feel my control of the rest of the class slipping. They see that I can't handle Tara. It won't be long before I have more than one behavior problem."

"Why didn't you come to me when this first happened?" Lynn asked. "This is the first I've heard about any problems. Tara hasn't mentioned anything, and neither have any of your other resource room students." In fact, Lynn had been amazed at how smoothly the resource room experiment had been going and how much Tara had grown up since she had last seen her three years before.

"I thought I could handle it," Alan answered. "I've worked with plenty of kids with handicaps. You should see the kids in the summer camp where I teach. They really have problems, and they are all evident the first day. I've never seen one like this, though. I just can't get through to her. And the thing that scares me is that the other mainstreamed kids are likely to take their cues from Tara. I think I can work with them. They seem to be making progress. But unless you do something about Tara, and quick, she's going to ruin it for everyone—me included."

Laura Conway

A resource room teacher is surprised and saddened to discover that one of her favorite sixth-grade students hates the resource room and wants to stop coming.

Laura Conway read Mike Abbott's autobiography one more time:

MY LIFE

Hi. I'm Mike and I'm 13 years old and in sixth grade at Washington Elementary School in Littleton. I am the youngest of three boys in my family. There are no girls except for my mother, who is 41. Even our dogs are males. We have two golden retrievers, Jesse and Strom. My father named them for two Republican senators.

My brothers are Jim (he used to be called Jimmy but he lost the ending of his name when he went to college) who is a sophomore at State College and Paul who is a senior at Littleton High School.

What I like best are the Philadelphia Phillies, MTV, and almost all food that is not green and creamy. What I like worst are school, especially the resource room (sorry, Mrs. Conway), having to do chores, especially raking leaves and shoveling snow, and getting up early.

My father is the manager of a clothing store in the mall and my mother is a math teacher at the middle school. When I was born I had a full head of black hair and I weighed 8 pounds, 8 ounces. I still have black hair and brown eyes and I now weigh 104 pounds. Since I'm 5′4″ you can guess that I am very skinny. I eat all the time but it doesn't help. I guess that's OK because I get to eat as much as I want, which is good.

I started school when I was five and I spent one year in kindergarten and two years in first grade. In second grade I went to a special class all day. I did that for two years and in fourth grade I went to regular fourth grade and also to the resource room. I hate the resource room because I feel dumb to have to go there. The good thing is Mrs. Conway who is really nice and takes lots of time to explain things and the computer where I do lots of cool things. The rest is terrible, like the other kids and the dumb things you have to do there. I always have to leave my real class when good things are going on, like science and art.

Sixth grade isn't too bad, except for math which is very hard and geography which is very boring.

When I grow up I would like to produce rock videos or be in television production. I'd really like to be on TV but I am probably too funny looking to be in front of the camera.

Laura Conway pensively folded the cover back over Mike Abbott's work and reflected upon her own. Laura prided herself on creating a classroom that was good for students. Since she began teaching in the resource room for learning disabled students nine years ago, she had tried to select activities that enabled students to experience success. She had helped them meet the requirements of their regular classes, knowing that the support she offered gave students a positive alternative to their regular classes, where they were typically the slowest students, subjected to the teasing of their classmates and to veiled annoyance from teachers. She also knew, both from student reports and from teacher talk in the lounge or at meetings, that the teachers' annoyance was not always well hidden.

Laura believed her students liked the resource room. They often requested extra time with her, and some were upset when they had to leave. She introduced them to tools and techniques not otherwise available, such as the word processing program Mike had used to edit and spell-check this very draft. Mike had learned to use the personal computer in her room; in fact, he spent most of his ninety minutes with her each day using it for writing, for practice activities in math, and for computer games.

Laura liked Mike. He was an attractive child, with a sense of humor and good interpersonal skills. He was also one of her success stories. When Mike came to the resource room three years earlier, he had already spent two years in a self-contained class for learning disabled students. He did not have many academic skills, and he was very shy. In the three years that Laura had been his resource room teacher, he had made remarkable strides. Laura knew that his success in sixth grade was due in large measure to her support of him. Left on his own, Mike would turn in sloppy work, if he turned it in at all. He would not be so well organized and he would soon be very frustrated trying to meet the demands of sixth grade. Laura also knew that Mike's sixth-grade teacher was not terribly patient. She would not tolerate Mike's poor work habits. Without the help that the resource room offered, Mike would be in real trouble.

But how could she tell Mike that? *Should* she tell him? Laura felt as if she were the only teacher in the building who understood Mike, and now he wanted to be cut loose from her protective support. The thought of casting him adrift worried her. She picked up his autobiography once again.

Joan Martin, Marilyn Coe, Warren Groves

A classroom teacher, a special education teacher, and an elementary school principal hold different views about mainstreaming a boy with poor reading skills into a fourth-grade social studies class.

Joan Martin looked out on her empty fourth-grade classroom and rubbed her temples. She walked over to Donald's desk, ran her hand over its scarred top, and squeezed her bulky frame into the seat. Despite her concerns, she smiled to herself, realizing she had sat down at Donald's desk hoping to understand him better by putting herself into his physical place in her room. She was looking for a solution to what she had come to think of as "the Donald thing."

Joan had been teaching elementary school in Littleton for fourteen years, and this fall she began her sixth year teaching fourth grade at Roosevelt Elementary School. Now approaching 45, she was distressed to find herself with a problem that she could not resolve, a problem for which her experience and skills had not prepared her.

The previous spring the Committee on Special Education (CSE), principal Warren Groves, and special education teacher Marilyn Coe approached Joan and asked her to mainstream three special education students into her social studies class during the upcoming school year. She agreed without much hesitation. She was flattered that they had chosen her from among the five fourth-grade teachers in her building, and she believed at the time that she needed and could handle the challenge of these students. Sitting at Donald's desk, she wondered how she could have so seriously misjudged her own situation.

Joan completed her teacher preparation program at a small private college in New York more than twenty years ago. She taught for the two years following her college graduation and then left teaching to marry and raise a family. She returned to the classroom when her youngest children (twin sons, now juniors in college) entered first grade.

Since her return to teaching, Joan had been working in a system in which students with serious learning problems were served in special classes. Therefore, her classroom problems were limited to an occasional outburst of frustration or anger or to the prepubescent silliness associated with 9- and 10-year-olds. One of the reasons she enjoyed teaching in Littleton was the quality of the support services available to students with real needs. Joan's feeling was that these services enabled her to be more effective with the students assigned to her classroom. Over the years she earned a reputation in the district for being a creative, demanding teacher who was able to challenge her students successfully. Parents of gifted fourth-graders often requested her, feeling she would enrich their child's curriculum.

For Joan, fourth grade had become somewhat boring, and she was considering asking for a change of level. When she was approached to mainstream the special students, she readily agreed, partly to have a new challenge in her teaching. While two of the mainstreamed students, Barry Frederick and Michael Neafe, were not presenting many problems, Donald Garcia was proving to be more of a challenge than she anticipated.

Donald was a learning disabled (LD) student who had spent most of his school years in a self-contained classroom for students with learning disabilities. Joan knew that he, Barry, and Michael were being mainstreamed for the first time and that Donald was the least skilled of the three. She had been "briefed" about the students by the CSE and Marilyn Coe at a meeting the previous June, just before school ended for the summer.

Aware that the students might feel a little awkward in her class, Joan made sure each had a desk "right in the middle of the action" and that their desks were nearer to the other students than to each other. She welcomed them warmly when they started and then tried not to treat them any differently than she treated her other students.

However, it was clear almost immediately that the three students, particularly Donald, were very different. All of them seemed to need more attention than the typical fourth grader. None of them was very outgoing in the class, and they were hesitant about their work, asking many questions and regularly seeking reassurance that they had the correct answers or were doing the right task. Donald took much longer than the other two to complete any in-class assignment, and he never volunteered to read in class.

When Joan gave her first surprise quiz, something she did regularly to keep the students on their toes and actively involved in the daily assignments, Donald was unable to answer any of the questions. While Barry and Michael did poorly on the quiz (as Joan had anticipated), they tried to answer the questions and showed some evidence of preparation. Joan was so startled by Donald's blank paper that she went to see Marilyn Coe to discuss his quiz.

Marilyn explained, "Donald probably couldn't read your test. You know that he reads on the first-grade level."

Joan reacted immediately. "He shouldn't be in fourth grade if he can't read the work! I just can't imagine how a child that poor in reading can stay in my class."

It was clear to Joan that her reaction troubled Marilyn, who responded to Joan in a very soft voice. "Yes, Donald can't read very well. But he's a very nice little boy who has been isolated from his peers for a long time. If he doesn't have an opportunity soon to get to know kids his age, he'll start middle school isolated and probably acting inappropriately. And you must be making some progress with him. He actually has begun doing some things with other kids that he didn't do before he went into your class. I saw him on the playground with a bunch of your students, and he talks about your class and his new friends a lot when he's in my room."

Joan quickly retreated from her hard-line position. She nodded at Marilyn and said, "OK. I'll try to help him with the content. And I won't give any surprise quizzes without warning you."

For the next few weeks Joan observed Donald closely in her class. He contributed in class discussions if she called on him, and he participated in small-group activities. (In the first marking period the students were creating murals depicting the growth of the American colonies.) However, she also noticed that he did none of the reading or writing activities, nor did the other students ever ask him to contribute to the academic aspects of his group's project. When it came time to reorganize work groups, no group actively chose Donald, and Joan had to ask one of the students to include him. The student did so willingly, mentioning that Donald was a nice kid but not too smart. The only appropriate work he turned in was done with Marilyn Coe's help. He continued to fail Joan's tests.

Joan often described her teaching by saying that she believed her students' reach should exceed their grasp and that she continually asked more and more from her students. They knew and expected that from her and were even disappointed if one of her assignments turned out to be "easy." But Donald was unable to achieve even her simplest goals. To ask more from him would mean increasing his frustration level. Yet she couldn't decrease her expectations for the class as a whole or for the small groups. And if she created individual assignments for him, she would be defeating the purposes of mainstreaming by setting him up as different and less able. As the days passed, she came to believe that Donald did not belong in her class. She felt strongly that mainstreaming was not good for students if they ended up hating the class and school or if they felt "dumb" as a result of the mainstreaming. Though he did not seem to be unhappy in the class, Joan suspected that Donald was feeling that way. Given her classroom requirements, it was clear that Donald was failing social studies and that Joan would have no choice but to give him an F for the marking period. It wasn't that Joan thought Donald was a failure; he just could not meet the reading and writing demands of her class.

Feeling frustrated and angry that she had brought this on herself, Joan met with Warren Groves for some advice. Warren had been her principal for nine years, and they liked and respected each other. His response was straightforward: He told Joan that if Donald could not do the work, he did not belong in her class. Warren volunteered to make that position clear to Marilyn and the CSE, but Joan felt that was her responsibility. She arranged to meet the next day with Marilyn to discuss returning Donald to the LD classroom. Although she had been meeting with Marilyn regularly and knew this would come as no surprise, Joan was feeling terrible about making this request. She understood why Marilyn felt Donald needed to be mainstreamed and she appreciated that Marilyn had chosen her as the teacher to accomplish this. She also knew that Marilyn had a lot riding on Donald's success and that this would be a blow to her mainstreaming efforts in the school.

Joan sighed and got up from Donald's seat. She returned to her desk and packed her briefcase with work to take home. She knew that even though there were no papers in her bag to indicate it, most of her thoughts that evening would center on Donald and her meeting with Marilyn the following day.

• • •

Marilyn Coe sat in her classroom thinking about tomorrow morning's meeting with Joan Martin. She realized that she might have blundered when she decided to mainstream Donald Garcia into Joan Martin's fourth-grade social studies class this fall. Marilyn knew that Joan was upset by Donald's poor reading skills and that, despite his efforts, Joan was going to give him a failing grade. At the moment, however, Marilyn felt that it was she who had failed, and now she was wondering if there was anything she could do to remedy the situation. She didn't have much time to figure out a solution: She and Joan were meeting in the morning, and it looked like the only option Joan would offer would be for Marilyn to remove Donald from her class. Otherwise, Joan would have to give him a failing grade in social studies for the first marking period.

Marilyn understood many of Joan's reactions because she had spent nine years as an elementary school teacher before beginning a new career in special education. Now 39, she had "retired" from teaching for several years to raise her children and had spent three years tutoring remedial students before returning to a local university to complete a master's degree and become certified in special education.

She was remembering just now the excitement she felt last January as she approached her return to full-time teaching after accepting a midyear position in a self-contained LD classroom in the Littleton school district. With some trepidation, but also with lots of excitement, Marilyn started her new assignment.

Marilyn found herself in a medium-size elementary school supervised by Warren Groves, a very professional principal, and staffed by conscientious, hardworking teachers. Marilyn's class was one of two self-contained learning disabilities classes in the building. There was also an LD resource room in the school. Because there were two types of LD classes in the building, many teachers thought the children in the two self-contained classes were too difficult to mainstream.

Marilyn tried to set up a classroom that was visually appealing and educationally interesting and stimulating. She was determined to find success in her new position. By March, Marilyn felt that the class was doing well and that things were going smoothly. The students, all boys ranging in age from 6 to 9, settled into a consistent routine and seemed happy in the structured classroom environment Marilyn had created.

When Marilyn took over the class, she was surprised to learn that none of the boys was mainstreamed into any regular education classes. In May, as Marilyn prepared to meet with the CSE to make recommendations for the following school year for her students, she wanted to suggest that several of her students be mainstreamed into some academic subjects. However, Marilyn found herself hesitating, since she had so little experience with this type of decision. The CSE was available to guide her but felt the final decision to mainstream should be left to her. As she tried to make up her mind, Marilyn was feeling the double handicap of her inexperience in special education and her brief time in the school.

When she turned to the principal for guidance, Warren Groves offered his views on mainstreaming but avoided the actual decision. He told Marilyn that he did not know enough to make appropriate recommendations; he felt that was her job, in cooperation with the CSE. However, he did tell her that he believed that students should be mainstreamed primarily for reading and math and only when success could almost be guaranteed so that the children would not have to deal with more failure. The CSE's attitude was that more mainstreaming should be attempted in all areas; it felt that too many children were placed in self-contained classes in the district. When Marilyn asked why so little mainstreaming had occurred with her students, the CSE explained that it didn't want to take a position that the principal might not support unless it had a strong special education teacher behind the mainstreaming effort.

After spending a lot of time going over student records and talking with anyone who might help her, Marilyn decided to mainstream two of her students for math. Both boys had developed enough competence in the subject area to be successful in the regular class, particularly if she provided a little additional help in her classroom.

Marilyn also decided to mainstream the three oldest boys in the class, Barry, Michael, and Donald, into the fourth-grade social studies class even though one of them, Donald, was very weak in reading skills. Her rationale was based on three premises. First, in three years these students would start middle school, and it seemed that the present time was not too soon to begin preparing them for the demands they would face there. Second, Marilyn felt that she "cheated" her students in the areas of science and social studies, since reading, math, and language arts took up the largest part of each school day in her class. Third, all three boys were shy children who had spent most of their school years apart from their same-age peers. Marilyn felt they needed more time with other 9-year-olds, who could serve as models.

All her recommendations were agreed to by the CSE and the principal. They suggested that she closely monitor the students mainstreamed into social studies. Warren paid particular attention to Donald's case when she presented her ideas to him. That reinforced for Marilyn that the principal was "tuned in," since Donald had been her greatest concern.

Donald, a 9-year-old, had spent two years in the self-contained LD class. He was an only child, living with his mother and father. Donald's original psychological report confirmed his academic deficits and described him as "immature, with a short attention span." There were no reported health, financial, marital, interpersonal, housing, or community problems; nor were any significant birth, medical, or developmental difficulties reported.

The CSE report noted that Donald's mother, whose native language was Spanish, spoke English with some difficulty. Donald understood but did not speak Spanish. Donald's father reported that he had experienced difficulty reading when he was in school. The parents had always been supportive of the CSE decisions and welcomed help for Donald.

The main drawbacks for mainstreaming Donald were his primer reading level and his shyness and low self-esteem. However, Marilyn knew that despite his reading difficulties, Donald was able to understand concepts presented at his age and grade level and had very good listening comprehension skills. He was aware of current events, and he would bring a wide range of educational and cultural experiences to the class. He had traveled to South America with his parents several times and could relate those trips to other experiences. Yet Marilyn knew that Donald did not fit Warren's "model" for mainstreaming.

Joan Martin, the fourth-grade teacher whose class Donald would join for social studies, had a reputation for creativity and flexibility, but she was known for teaching to the upper levels of her class and holding high expectations for all her students. She was selected on the basis of Warren's recommendation and a meeting with the CSE at which the committee recognized that she was willing to accept all three of Marilyn's fourth-grade students.

In September, Joan welcomed the three self-contained LD students warmly, giving each his own desk and materials. The students were so enthusiastic about attending the fourth-grade class that Marilyn began to relax about her decision.

Her sense of comfort was short-lived, however. At the end of the third week of school, Joan came to see Marilyn to discuss Donald. She showed Marilyn the results of the first social studies quiz, given as a surprise to make sure all the students were keeping up with the reading. Donald had not responded to any of the questions. When Marilyn reminded Joan of Donald's reading level and explained that he probably could not read the test questions, Joan reacted strongly. "He shouldn't be in fourth grade if he can't read the work. I just can't imagine how a child that poor in reading can stay in my class."

Marilyn was shocked by the strength of Joan's response. She decided to try to focus on Donald's needs, not his weaknesses, as she answered Joan. "Yes, Donald can't read very well. But he's a very nice little boy who has been isolated from his peers for a long time."

Marilyn went on to explain Donald's social needs for being in the class, and she discussed how important it was to prepare classified students for their next educational level. She also told Joan that she had noticed that Donald was now involved with other fourth-grade students on the playground. Marilyn concluded, "He talks about your class and his new friends a lot when he's in my room."

Marilyn realized her explanation had made an impact when Joan responded by agreeing to keep Donald in her class and to try to help him with the content. Joan observed that his contributions to class discussions were very appropriate and said she would watch him in class to see if he made any progress.

After the meeting with Joan, Marilyn began to work with Donald in her class on his social studies assignments. She knew that the best solution would be for Donald to learn to read the social studies material, but Marilyn also knew that she would not be able to bring him to grade-level reading. She continued to meet with Joan to talk about Donald's progress and to see if Joan would consider changing her grading procedures to accommodate Donald's needs. Marilyn knew that she had to go slowly, since she was an untenured teacher and it was not her role to tell other, more experienced teachers how to handle their classes. She did not feel that she was making much progress with Joan, since Joan kept talking about Donald's failing grades.

Marilyn decided to talk with the principal and the CSE to see if they could help her find a solution to the problem. It was clear to Marilyn that Joan was not comfortable making an exception to her strict grading policies for Donald.

When Marilyn met with Warren, she felt she was receiving mixed messages. On the one hand, the principal told her that she, not he, was the expert in special education and mainstreaming. Yet he reminded her that he believed that students who could not be successful in meeting the teacher's demands should not be mainstreamed.

On the other hand, the CSE supported Marilyn's decision to keep Donald in fourth-grade social studies, since the committee had also noticed the difference in his social interactions. The CSE was willing to meet with Joan to support Marilyn's position.

Marilyn appreciated the support of the CSE but did not think that it would affect Joan's position on her grading policy. As long as Donald had to meet Joan's standards, he was bound to fail, and Marilyn felt she would appear stubborn if she insisted that he remain in the class even though he would fail. It seemed to her that Joan's grading system was the key to solving the problem. However, Marilyn did not know how to convince Joan to alter the system.

• • •

Warren Groves watched Joan Martin leave his office; as the door closed behind her, he sat down heavily in his chair and sighed aloud. In the past week two of his strongest teachers had come to him to discuss the same child, Donald Garcia. It was clear to him that these two caring, sensitive teachers were on a collision course over the best setting for Donald. Warren knew that one of his responsibilities as the principal would be to mediate if they could not reach an amicable, appropriate solution.

Warren tended to trust his teachers and preferred to let them make their own decisions. He typically offered an opinion that would not tie a teacher's hands and then suggested that the teacher was the front-line expert. He only took a firm stand when he saw that a teacher's decision would lead to a real problem or when there was a conflict that the parties were unable to resolve without his intervention. The problem with Donald seemed to be leading him to the latter situation.

As Warren retraced the events that led to his meeting with Joan today, he reminded himself that he could have prevented this entire situation last May if he had told Marilyn Coe then that Donald was not an appropriate candidate for mainstreaming. When Marilyn and the CSE met with him to discuss mainstreaming some of the students from Marilyn's self-contained LD classroom, it was obvious that Donald did not have the reading skills necessary to deal successfully with a fourth-grade social studies text. But Marilyn made a strong case for social mainstreaming for this student, a case that Warren knew made sense as a long-term solution to Donald's problems. As long as Donald remained in the self-contained setting, he would not have the opportunity to make friends with the nonclassified students, nor would he have those students as models for the behaviors that preadolescents needed to learn.

Warren went along with Marilyn for a second reason. In addition to believing that her social mainstreaming argument was a good one, Warren wanted

Marilyn to know that she could have the opportunity to implement her policies without having to fight for each one. Although she was a new teacher, she had the potential to be one of the strongest teachers in his building. Warren knew that if he encouraged and supported her, she would gain the confidence needed to emerge as a leader within the school. Since he believed that strong teachers were an asset to a school, he wanted to help Marilyn try to implement her ideas.

He suggested that Joan Martin be the teacher who mainstreamed the three fourth-grade students because he wanted Joan to have a new challenge. Joan was one of those teachers whose classroom could make any principal look good, and Warren appreciated her skills. He knew, however, that she was easily bored and that he did not have another opening in his school for her. He feared that Joan would leave his school for a more interesting classroom if he could not provide one for her. He hoped that she would rise to the challenge of these hard-to-teach students and, in doing so, find sufficient reason for remaining in his school.

But now Warren had the feeling that his plans had backfired. Although he had warned Marilyn that mainstreaming Donald could prove to be a difficult undertaking, Marilyn had not taken that warning seriously enough. She should have better prepared both Donald and Joan for their mainstreaming roles. Was it too late to help her save her plan and keep Donald in a regular fourth-grade social studies class?

Additionally, he should have given Joan more incentive to guarantee that the mainstreaming of these students would be successful. He wondered if it was too late to do that now. Would Joan be willing to rethink her position about grading just days before the report period ended?

Warren knew that the two teachers were meeting the following day. He called to his secretary and asked her to find out when their meeting was scheduled. He realized he was about to spend the remainder of the day trying to come up with an idea that would help them resolve their conflict over Donald. His plan would have to meet two goals: It would have to be in Donald's best interest, and it would have to allow both Joan and Marilyn to save face and leave the meeting feeling that their professional beliefs had not been compromised. Warren was not sure he could accomplish that. He sighed again. It was days like this that made Warren wonder why he had not gone into his father's insurance business.

Cassie Stern

An experienced LD teacher is assigned responsibility for a new resource room at an elementary school and finds her most serious problem to be how to handle a particularly difficult child newly referred for services as learning disabled. His regular fourth-grade teacher seems unable to cope with his problems, and Cassie fears he will be passed on to fifth grade where the teachers are resistant to mainstreaming.

Cassie Stern, the resource room teacher at Kennedy Elementary School in Littleton, stared at the end-of-year grade report of Michael Dean, one of her fourth-grade resource room students. Normally Cassie would interpret a recommendation for passing to the fifth grade as a triumph for one of her mainstreamed students, but with Michael she wasn't so sure. In fact, Michael's behavior problems were so serious now that she was certain the promotion to fifth grade was a mistake. As she thought about Michael, she reminded herself of when he had first come to her attention.

Cassie had assumed responsibility for the new resource room at Kennedy the previous year after spending three years teaching LD students in a self-contained classroom at Kennedy. She had looked forward to her new job and one of the benefits that came with the resource room—working with regular classroom teachers. Her goal was to foster positive relationships with these teachers by being as approachable, nonjudgmental, and constructive as possible. She knew that establishing a cooperative relationship with the other teachers was crucial to the success of the resource room concept.

Since this was the first year a resource room had been in place at Kennedy, most of the students had been in self-contained special education classrooms in prior years. Cassie was careful to attend to any adjustment problems the students might display as they were mainstreamed with resource room support. She anticipated that many of the regular classroom teachers would be reluctant to have classified students in their rooms, and she had designed an orientation and consultation plan to address their concerns and establish a strong reputation for her services.

As the year progressed, Cassie sensed that the teachers were becoming comfortable with the LD students in their classes. They seemed to be making every effort to treat them in the same way they treated all their other students. While there were some problems, particularly with a group of fifth-grade teachers who were not sure why the district had decided to change its policies, generally Cassie felt that the teachers were giving mainstreaming a fair chance in her school. And some of them, like Barbara Loft, occasionally approached Cassie for assistance with their regular classroom students.

Cassie encouraged this consultation. Indeed, when the district director of special education offered Cassie the job that summer, he had emphasized the role she was to play in analyzing referrals for special education services from the general student population. The resource room now represented exactly that: a new resource to serve teachers and students at Kennedy in creative ways not previously possible.

So, when Barbara Loft approached her about Michael Dean, Cassie listened carefully despite recognizing the litany she had heard so often from the regular classroom teachers at Kennedy.

"Michael constantly demands my attention. He keeps asking unnecessary questions about all of his work."

"How do you know his questions are unnecessary?"

"Well, he can do grade-level work. I've seen that. But he almost never completes his assignments. And, no matter how much help I give him, his work is really disorganized." Barbara Loft looked at Cassie with an expression of honest helplessness. "He's driving me crazy with all the questions!"

Cassie nodded sympathetically. "What else should I know about him?" Barbara handed her a folder, and Cassie opened it. "Let's see. Michael James Dean, eight years old. I see that he just moved into the district this year."

Barbara didn't skip a beat. "Right, and he hasn't made one friend in four months. He's alienated all of the kids in my class."

"What does he do?"

"Exactly what he does with me. He annoys them with his inappropriate comments and questions. He seems to say the most outrageous things in order to get attention. But it works just the opposite. Everyone avoids him."

Cassie nodded. "May I observe him in your class tomorrow morning?"

"By all means. I'll take any suggestions you can give me."

The following day Cassie spent some time in Barbara's classroom, observing Michael. In spite of her initial skepticism, she quickly confirmed Barbara's reports about his demand for attention and his alienation from the other students. Cassie was concerned enough to inform the Child Study Team (CST) of the situation. The team met several weeks later, after gathering more information, to share their findings about Michael.

Janis Johnson, the school social worker, reported first. "Michael is an only child. His mother is a nurse who works part-time, and his father manages a food store. It seems that he's close to the mother but doesn't get along well with his father."

"Who told you that?" asked Ellen Simmons, the school psychologist, who chaired the committee.

"The mother. She said that Michael can be disrespectful and that his father's not a good disciplinarian. According to Mrs. Dean, the father doesn't know how to handle him. When he misbehaves, he just begs him to act right. But it seemed to me that the mother was overprotective and let Michael have his own way, even if the father disagreed."

"Why do you think she overprotects him?" interjected Cassie.

"You know how big that kid is?"

Cassie nodded. "He's really overweight," she agreed.

"Well, so is the mother," replied Janis. "She told me that last summer Michael went to Weight Watchers camp and lost nearly thirty pounds. But he's put it all back on. The mother gives in to him when he wants something to eat. She told me she can't stand to let him go hungry."

"No siblings. How about other social relationships?" asked Ellen.

"According to the mother, most of his friends in the neighborhood are kids two to three years younger than Michael. I don't think the mother likes this. She described Michael as silly and immature. Then she told me that he can't make friends because he won't fight. She says he's a scapegoat because he tries to follow his parents' advice to 'talk things out.'"

Ellen Simmons then shared her psychological evaluation. "Michael has average intelligence but erratic subtest scores. There is no consistency in his scores. For example, his comprehension subtest is thirteen, way above average. But his reasoning score is eight, below average. Usually comprehension and reasoning scores are close."

Cassie had also done some diagnostic work with Michael. "Ellen, I found that he was willing to attempt all of the tasks I gave him, but his work was terribly haphazard. He needed constant direction."

"My experience exactly," Ellen said. "What were his scores?"

"Just about on grade level on everything, if I pushed and prodded. He'd try something and then say he couldn't do it anymore. If I encouraged him, he'd keep going."

The CST turned its findings over to the district Committee on Special Education, that completed the assessment and decided that Michael was eligible for services as learning disabled. Their final report stated that Michael "had significant perceptual difficulties in the areas of visual motor integration and short-term auditory memory."

Michael's support services were to begin with the start of his fourth-grade year. He was assigned to Cassie's resource room and to the regular fourth-grade class taught by Martha Davis. Mrs. Davis had just returned to teaching after a medical leave and seemed to Cassie to have little sense of how to structure a fourth-grade classroom. Cassie was especially concerned that Martha was very lenient and established few class rules.

By the end of September, Cassie felt she should consult with the school psychologist. "I think this is a bad setting for Michael. He needs much more structure."

"What are the indications?" Ellen asked.

"For one thing, he still has no friends. The other kids make fun of him, and Mrs. Davis is ineffective in stopping them. Now he's taken to trying to make friends by acting like a class clown."

"What does he do?"

"Well, he comes to school dressed in ridiculous outfits."

"Like what?"

"Oh, he'll wear wildly colored Bermuda shorts and large hats. He's been carrying a Cabbage Patch doll to school and taking it everywhere, even to the bathroom and the playground."

"What have you tried?"

"For one thing, I've tried to talk to Martha Davis. I suggested that she organize Michael's work by setting some goals with him. I gave her some specific ideas, but she hasn't tried anything. She just lets him behave like a fool, and she ignores the other students' responses. One time the other kids put a sign on Michael's back that said 'Kick me,' and even though he knew what it said, Michael wore that sign all day long. Martha didn't stop it."

"What are you doing in the resource room?"

"I'm working on language arts with him, but I'm also trying to teach him some social behaviors. I've talked to him about his clothes and about the doll."

"Has that helped?"

"You know, at first I thought it was working. After one of our discussions, Michael would actually change a behavior. For instance, he stopped carrying the doll and for a couple of days he dressed like a typical fourth grader. But then he'd start doing something equally inappropriate."

Ellen raised her eyebrows in silent curiosity, encouraging Cassie to continue.

"A few days after our discussion about his clothes, he began wearing a hat with elephant ears. He simply traded one outlandish piece of clothing for another."

"Have you been in touch with the family?"

"I really think the mother is part of the problem," Cassie sighed.

"Because of the clothes?"

"Partly. But she walks him to school . . . all the way to his classroom, holding his hand! The kids make fun of her, too. When I spoke to her, she said, 'Michael's Michael.' She's no help at all."

Ellen looked up from her notetaking. "I think we should try some in-school counseling. I'll make the arrangements and keep you posted."

Three weeks later, Cassie and Ellen met again, this time at Ellen's request. "In-school couseling isn't going to work," Ellen announced with an air of resignation. "After a couple of sessions, the counselor told me that she can't help Michael by himself. She thinks that his problems are too linked to his family's problems for her to be effective."

Cassie shook her head. "Now what?"

"I don't know. I called the mother and suggested family therapy. She flatly refused—wouldn't hear of it."

"Did she say why?"

"Sort of. She said there was nothing wrong with Michael that time wouldn't take care of. She said that everyone was taking all of this too seriously. Get this. The father wants to move the family where no one knows Michael, and Mrs. Dean told me that he's making too much of Michael's behavior. Sorry, Cassie. Looks like Michael's best shot is going to come from you and the resource room. We can't force the parents into therapy."

By the end of the school year, Cassie's frustrations had grown to the point that she felt overwhelmed by Michael and his problems. She was surprised by how much time trying to handle one child with a major problem could take. She felt that she was neglecting her other students and that her consulting time had fallen off dramatically. She had made no progress with Michael, either in academics or in his social skills. And now Martha Davis was passing him on to fifth grade without any thought, and that was going to be a real problem. There wasn't one fifth-grade teacher who would put up with Michael's classroom shenanigans. The three fifth-grade teachers were the most resistant in the building to mainstreaming and to Cassie's consultative help. She feared that Michael would spend less and less time in a regular classroom next year, perhaps even be removed, an action she was sure would make his situation even worse.

PART SIX

Student-Teaching Issues

Patricia Barnes

A student teacher who enters teaching after a career in the private sector finds herself unsure of her decision to change careers when she does not find immediate gratification in teaching.

Patty Barnes pushed her half-empty soup bowl toward the center of the cafeteria table. "I had the soup for my cold, but I think I should have had the fish for my brain." She rolled her eyes in self-deprecation and smiled at Evelyn Price, the other "mature" student teacher at Roosevelt Elementary School in Littleton. "Nobody told me that being perpetually sick was a characteristic of student teaching."

Evelyn nodded sympathetically. "Nobody prepares you for anything about student teaching, do they? But you seem really down. What's going on?"

"Evy, I am *so* tired. I just want to drop into bed every night by eight o'clock. But last night I *had* to make a decision about my observation lesson. I drank coffee and forced myself to think of an idea."

"What do you mean, forced yourself? You can't just turn on creative juices like that."

"I had no choice! I'm being observed on Monday! I've been completely panicked about this observation, and nothing's clicking. You know, when I worked for IBM, ideas would just fall into place—if I was running a meeting or needed an angle on an employee interview . . . " Patty's voice trailed off as she thought back to her seven years in corporate America. "But in this job nothing comes naturally. I feel like I'm always swimming upstream."

"So you just sat down and ordered yourself to think of something, right?" Evelyn tried to tease her friend out of her depression.

"Yes, I really did. Last night I said to myself, 'If I haven't thought of an idea by nine o'clock, I'll just stop everything and concentrate until I think of something.' So that's what I did. I hadn't had a brainstorm by nine, so I sat on the floor and spread all of my animal books on the rug and stared at them."

"Did it work? Did you have a brilliant idea?"

"Well, not until the next morning . . . brushing my teeth." At this Patty managed a little chuckle, at least. "I'm not really happy with it, but I'm out of runway—it will have to do."

"Tell me—what is it?" Evelyn also brought a business background to teaching. She typically displayed a demand for answers and action, and Patty liked that.

"I'm going to do a lesson in a riddle format, like 'I can meow, I am a blank.' It ties in the animal unit I've been working on with the kids, and I'll incorporate their sight words." She blew her nose and looked at Evelyn hopefully. "What do you think?"

"Sounds good to me. Where has Shelly been through all this angst? Hasn't she been any help?"

Shelly Johnson, Patty's cooperating teacher, was an experienced first-grade teacher whose classroom of twenty-four students was a busy, buzzing, consuming place. "Yes, she thought that since I had been doing animals I could incorporate that and the sight words into a big book. She even suggested one like *Brown Bear, Brown Bear, What Do You See?*"

"So why don't you use that? I know that book—the repetition in it is great for first-graders." Evelyn began to gather her dishes onto a tray while she tried to help Patty gather her thoughts.

"Yeah, I may close with it." Patty sighed deeply, sure that Evelyn's enthusiasm for the book meant she hated the riddle idea. "There is so little concrete feedback in this job," Patty thought to herself. "Nobody tells you just what they think, and the kids don't run up to you with, 'Hey, nice lesson, I really learned something, Teach!' At least at work I knew when something worked or when it didn't. I'd do a sales promotion, and people would *order* something. A signature on a contract is about as authentic an assessment as you can get! And I got lots of them."

"Hey, where are you?" Evelyn had apparently said something else, which Patty had missed while lost in thought.

"I'm sorry. Just feeling sorry for myself. What did you say?"

"I thought you'd been observed already. Fredricks saw me the second week of school."

"Me, too. But he came during morning routine. I took attendance and lunch count while the kids were doing their morning paper. Then I gathered them to the rug for morning board, calendar, and weather. So this time he said he wanted to see me do some teaching."

"Well, I think it will go fine. Just don't go crazy all weekend." Evelyn held open the door to the lunchroom. "Listen, Pat, you've got to get some rest. Schools are germ factories, and if you let yourself get run-down you'll be sick all semester."

"Too late for that advice!" Patty smiled ruefully. "I still have to prep the kids for the lesson, type up my lesson plan, and prepare the materials for this lesson, on top of preparing the other lesson plans that Fredricks won't be seeing." Patty rattled off this list so quickly that she ran out of breath and started coughing.

"Should I call you or leave you alone?" asked Evelyn as she walked away toward her class.

Patty thought her friend seemed a little impatient to get away. "I'm probably whining," she castigated herself. Patty put on her sales manager's smile and replied, "Nah, I'll be all right. I'll see you for lunch Monday and let you know how it went."

• • •

"So you must have been terrific! How did it go?" Evelyn nearly pounced on Patty when they met in the cafeteria three days later.

"It was OK." Patty smiled brightly enough and picked up a tray.

"OK! After all the agony you were going through on Friday? That's a little anticlimactic, don't you think?"

Evelyn was in a joking mood and Patty knew she just didn't understand what was really bothering her. "I'm not even sure I understand it," she thought.

"I think I did all right," Patty said aloud. "Let me think about it . . . it was only an hour ago." Patty paid for her meal as she spoke and headed for a table by the window, thinking again how spartan and crude this facility was compared to the amenities at IBM.

Evelyn was on her heels. "Where was Fredricks? Didn't he give you any feedback?" Evelyn reached for the salt shaker and began to pour salt all over everything.

"Sure. But he was more interested in how I maintained the children's attention—classroom management stuff. Oh, yes, he complimented my personal interactions with the kids and had some suggestions about diction and the language I used." Patty shrugged and held her hand out for the salt.

"He didn't have anything to say about the lesson idea itself? After you worked so hard on it?"

Evelyn's words opened the floodgate. "Yeah, I did work hard, Evy—I was up until eleven Friday night, and I worried about it all day Saturday while I was at the grocery store and the cleaners and over at my sister's, and I worked on it all day Sunday until almost midnight. I had to figure out all the details. My big book read 'I can bark, I am a blank; I can meow, I am a blank'; et cetera, et cetera. But I had to figure it out structurally. You know, should I fold the pages so that the answer isn't revealed until the children guess? Can a laminated book fold easily? If I prewrote the riddle chart, I'd only have to fill in the blanks during the lesson. If I took the time to write the whole sentence for every riddle, the kids would get bored. But then I worried that if it was all prewritten the kids wouldn't really have contributed much, and it would look too slick. Then I had the book half made, and I realized that I'd better prepare the book so when the kids drew their animals they wouldn't color where I planned to write the riddle. Then I had to come up with a catchy opening and type it up, and then I wanted to practice in front of the mirror, but I fell asleep."

"Practice in front of a mirror!" The best Evelyn could do was react to the final words of this stream-of-consciousness report. Patty saw her try, without much success, to stifle laughter. "You are making yourself crazy! You practiced in front of a mirror?" Evelyn's mirth changed to incredulity as she saw how troubled Patty seemed.

"Well, I always did that when I was going to speak at a business function, and they had us do it in sales school when we were first practicing sales calls. I thought it might help." Patty's sheepish feeling was almost a relief. At least she could identify it. "Pretty stupid, huh?"

"No, it is not stupid, just unnecessary. You cannot go through this for every lesson you teach, Patty. You're killing yourself."

Patty suddenly sneezed, as if to underscore Evelyn's point. "I know," she murmured, wiping her nose. "I don't know why this is so difficult for me. Everything has generally come pretty easy for me . . . college, my first career, graduate school. I'm not used to this feeling that everything is a constant struggle and that I never know how well I'm doing."

"Do you mean that they *told* you at IBM how you were doing?"

"Sure. You had annual reviews, and your salary and bonuses were tied to them. And I kept getting promoted, and that carried a strong message. I knew what was expected and how to do it."

"So remind me why you left."

Patty started to laugh, finally. "Because I wasn't accomplishing anything. I was getting lots of rewards, but the work seemed empty. I thought teaching would be fulfilling. That sounds so trite, but that's how I felt."

Patty stood up and left the table. In a few minutes she returned with a cup of tea. She stirred the steaming drink. When she spoke she sounded terribly sad. "Evy, I really wanted to be a teacher. I gave up a lot to do this. But I'm not sure now. I don't know if I can do it."

Steve Chandler

A student teacher placed in a second-grade class substitutes for his cooperating teacher when her father dies. He decides to discuss the death with the class. One child reacts to the discussion by disrupting the class so seriously that Steve must send him to the principal's office. He then has an unsatisfactory meeting with the child's angry mother after school.

The phone rang. "Who could it be at this hour?" thought Steve Chandler as he lifted the receiver. It was 7:00 A.M. on a Monday morning in late February, and Steve was about to leave his house for Roosevelt Elementary School in Littleton, where he had been student teaching since January.

"Hello," he said as he picked up the phone.

"Steve? This is Vicky. I have some terrible news." Vicky Falk was Steve's cooperating teacher, and he could tell by the quiver in her voice that she was very upset. "My father died last night." Steve did not speak into the ensuing pause and she continued, "I won't be in today, and I've requested you as the substitute. I can drop off lesson plans later this morning."

"Vicky, I'm so sorry! I didn't realize your dad had been ill."

"He wasn't. That's why this is such a shock."

Steve hesitated, not wanting to intrude on Vicky's feelings and not sure if he knew her well enough to ask too many questions. "I'm sorry," he said again, lamely. He retreated to the safety of their professional relationship. "Don't bother about the lesson plans. I can handle the class. Can I do anything for you?"

"I'll be OK. Thanks for your help. I'll call you tonight."

Steve walked out to the car, where his wife Pam was waiting for him. She was a teacher at Littleton High School, and they had commuted together almost every day since Steve began student teaching.

"Who called?" Pam asked.

"It was Vicky Falk. Her father died last night, and she asked if I would take over the class for her today. She didn't sound too good. I think she'll probably be out a while."

"Hmmm," Pam replied as she got into the car. "That's too bad. Do you need to talk about what you'll do?"

Steve could tell that she was already deep in thought about her own day at school. Last-minute mental preparation during their drive to work had become a shared habit since Steve began student teaching. He had decided to leave a career in industry after ten years to become a teacher, and this semester would conclude the master's program in elementary education which would launch him on his new career. He had chosen teaching in part because he had always envied Pam's experiences as a teacher, and he would have valued her input about his day today. But he knew that she needed the morning "think time" on her way to work, so he said, "No, I'll be OK."

As Pam maneuvered the car through early morning traffic, Steve thought about Vicky's news. He felt that he could handle the class on his own; he had been with these second-graders for the past six weeks and had been gradually assuming responsibility for all the teaching. Vicky, a twenty-year veteran, had been generous in turning over the class to him, but since this would be the first time entirely on his own with the group of nineteen students, he couldn't help feeling a little trepidation. He was most concerned about how to explain Vicky's absence to the children.

"I guess we're going to talk about death this morning," Steve spoke abruptly, breaking the silence.

Pam glanced over at him, then returned her gaze to the road. She did not seem irritated with his interruption. "Are you sure you want to talk about death with them?" she replied. "What are you going to say?"

"I don't know. But I think I need to tell them the truth about why Vicky's absent. That means I have to tell them that her father died."

"What will you say? Second-graders might be a little young to deal with this subject."

"I don't think so. We can talk about feelings and then maybe make sympathy cards for Vicky and her family. What do you think?"

Pam looked at her husband. "Do you think their parents have talked about death with them yet at home?"

Steve looked over at her with a "Who knows?" expression.

Pam nodded and spoke softly. "I guess you need to tell them."

Steve and Pam spent the rest of the drive in silence. Steve opened his plan book and made a few notes in it as Pam rounded the turn that led to the Roosevelt entrance. Steve walked into the building, trying not to be discouraged by her parting comment, "Good luck today. I'm not sure I'd want to be in your shoes this morning."

Steve continued thinking about how to talk about death with his class as he signed in as a substitute teacher in the main office and walked to Vicky's classroom. He glanced at the wall clock as he entered the room and felt his adrenalin flow when he realized the students would arrive in twenty-five minutes. He had the afternoon's lessons planned, as he had been slated to teach science and math anyway, but he needed to figure out what Vicky would have done this morning in language arts, as well as distribute writing folders, write the day's activities on the board, and decide about "the death talk"—all in twenty-five minutes.

As Steve sat thinking and making notes at Vicky's desk, Joan Ramirez, the second-grade teacher from across the hall, popped her head into Steve's room. "Isn't it terrible about Vicky's father? I feel just awful. I'm here if you need me. Anything you want, just let me know."

Joan had taught across the hall from Vicky for years, and they frequently merged their two classes for group lessons. They did all their planning together and usually taught the same things at the same time. As a result, Joan had become like a second cooperating teacher to Steve, and she always seemed willing to help.

"It's OK, Joan, I should be fine. Can I ask you a question about this morning, though?" Steve valued Joan's opinion and thought it would be wise to get her input.

He began to explain his ideas about the lesson he was planning for the morning. As he was talking, Phyllis Alberts, the school principal, came to the door.

"Steve, are you all set for today?"

"Thanks, yes. But I'm glad you're here, Dr. Alberts. I was just telling Joan that I might talk with the children about death and then make sympathy cards for Vicky. What do you think?"

"That sounds fine, Steve. I'm sure Vicky will probably be out for most or all of the week, so they're bound to find out what's happened anyway," she replied. "Call me if you need anything." With that, Dr. Alberts continued on her way.

"I guess that's all you needed to hear," Joan said.

"I guess so," replied Steve. "Here we go!"

The warning bell, which signaled the start of the school day, rang in the halls and in the playground. Steve stood in the doorway, greeting students as they tumbled in.

"Where's Mrs. Falk?" student after student asked.

"She'll be out today, and we have some important things to talk about this morning," Steve responded to the gathering mob.

"Who's the sub? I hope it's Mrs. Franklin or Miss Newman," chattered the students.

"Guess what?" smiled Steve. "I'm the substitute for today, and you all need to put your coats away since we have lots of things to do this morning."

Steve had established a good relationship with the second-graders, and he was pleased at their reaction to the news that he would be their substitute teacher. Some students clapped, and two of the boys ran over to give him a high five. The students put their things away and began to settle down as Steve went over the day's schedule. "We have a regular morning—reading and language arts—until gym at 11:30, and then we go straight to lunch. This afternoon we're going to observe and make entries in our bean journals, and then we'll have arithmetic. But before we get started, there's something I want to talk to you all about."

"Mr. Chandler, there's something I want to talk to you about! Where's Mrs. Falk?" asked Patrick.

Patrick, who always had a question, was one of the more difficult students in the class. Vicky had told Steve that she had heard that Patrick's father was an alcoholic. Furthermore, she told him that his mother often refused to acknowledge her son's behavior problems in school. Just prior to Steve's arrival, Patrick had disappeared from school in the middle of the day. When Vicky realized he was gone, she called his home. Patrick's mother answered the phone and acknowledged that he had come home early. She said that she was surprised it had taken them so long to realize he was gone and to contact her.

"It would've been nice if she had at least called us when he arrived home," Vicky had concluded. "It's as if she's testing us, trying to catch us making mistakes."

Patrick's desk was the only one in the room that was in isolation, separated from the horseshoe of desks that all of the other students in the class occupied. Vicky had separated him from the others because Patrick's behavior had been so disruptive to the rest of the class.

"I'm glad you asked that question, Patrick, because that's what I'd like to talk about this morning. Last night, Mrs. Falk's father died, and she won't be in today and probably not for the next few days. You can imagine how upset she is right now, and she needs our help."

"But what can we do to help, Mr. Chandler?" asked Carla. "Last year my cat died and I felt so sad that I cried all night. I don't know how anyone could have helped me, I was so upset!"

"I think it might be nice if we make some special cards for Mrs. Falk. Has anyone ever heard of a sympathy card?" Steve asked.

"Isn't that a card to say that you feel bad when someone dies or something?" asked Jason, an enthusiastic student who always seemed to know the answers.

"You're right, Jason. Very good! I think it might be nice if we all colored our own cards and wrote a message to Mrs. Falk letting her know that we're thinking of her. I'm going to see her after school today, so I can deliver them to her myself. I'm sure the cards will make her feel better."

"That sounds nice," Carla said. "I feel so bad for her. She must be even sadder than I was when Scruffy died."

"Maybe it would help us get some ideas for our cards if we talk about our feelings for a few minutes. Carla shared the feelings she had when her cat Scruffy died." Steve walked to the board and wrote the word "sad."

"Has anyone else ever lost someone close to them? It could have been a pet, a friend, a relative, anyone who you cared about."

Students began to share their stories with the class. Steve continued to write words such as "upset," "sorry," "scared," and "angry" on the blackboard. "I think it's good that we can all share how we feel with each other," he told them, feeling privately relieved that the discussion seemed natural and "safe" for the students. It was obvious that they were responding to each other's stories, and Steve began to move the discussion to Mrs. Falk's feelings when Patrick suddenly chimed in.

"I think it's funny when someone dies. It makes me feel like laughing."

"Patrick, why would it make you feel like laughing if someone you cared for died?" Steve asked him.

"I don't know, I just think it would be funny," he replied with a wide grin. Steve didn't know what to say. He knew that Patrick had many problems and assumed that he was just acting out as a result of his discomfort with the topic. The other students seemed upset by Patrick's comment, and Steve wondered if he should pursue the discussion with Patrick or try to divert him. Patrick was notorious for making up outrageous stories, and Steve wasn't sure what kind of response he might get. But he didn't want to ignore the reaction of the other students, nor to pretend Patrick hadn't spoken. So he asked a dangerous question. "Has anyone close to you ever died, Patrick?"

He was surprised when Patrick simply replied, "No." But just as Steve was about to call on Emily, a slight girl with blond braids, Patrick called out, "And I wouldn't care, anyway! I'd laugh!"

Steve continued the nod he had begun in Emily's direction, now deciding that the best way to deal with Patrick was to ignore him. "Emily, did you want to say something?" he asked.

"My goldfish die about every week," Emily volunteered somberly. "We keep getting new ones but they die."

"It's hard to keep goldfish, sometimes," Steve responded sympathetically. "I bet you take good care of them, too, Emily."

"Goldfish! We catch fish and eat them!" Patrick cried out. "We FRY them!"

Steve called on the patience he was rapidly developing in this new job. "Patrick, Emily is talking about pet fish. That's different."

"Fish is fish," Patrick grinned, seeming to relish Emily's unhappiness.

"Let's try to respect each other's feelings, OK? Talking about death makes us . . ."

"Laugh!" Patrick cried again.

"OK, Patrick, that's enough." Steve saw that the other students' willingness to explore their feelings had evaporated, and he knew he was losing control. Two boys in the corner of the horseshoe began to talk and giggle, and two others began making faces at each other across the center floor space.

Emily, meanwhile, looked about to cry. "I think I forgot to feed them," she whispered. Carla got up from her seat and put her arm around Emily. Two other students stood up and went to get drinks.

"Carla's cat was ROAD KILL!" Patrick laughed. He was now playing directly to the boys in the back of the horseshoe.

"Patrick, that's mean!" Steve said firmly. "You're skating on thin ice. The next step is upstairs to the office." Patrick stood up and began to pretend that he was skating around the classroom.

"That's it, Patrick. I've had enough." Steve walked toward the phone at the back of the room. Picking it up would connect him with the main office, and he looked at Patrick once more in an effort to avoid such a drastic measure. He knew Patrick didn't want to be sent to the office, but the child often had a "now that I'm knee-deep in it, I'm not backing down" attitude that he apparently decided to adopt on this occasion. Steve slowly picked up the phone, his expression betraying his wish that Patrick would begin to control himself.

"Hello, yes?" the voice on the other end of the line answered.

"Hi, this is Mr. Chandler. I'm having some trouble with Patrick Ritchey and was hoping I could send him up to the office for a little while."

"That's fine, Mr. Chandler. Just send him up. I'll tell Mrs. Fleming he's coming," replied the secretary. Audrey Fleming was the assistant principal who handled the discipline problems in the school.

Steve hung up the phone and turned to Patrick. "OK, Patrick, Mrs. Fleming is waiting for you upstairs."

"I'm not going, and you can't make me!" he screamed, running back into the cubbies, a favorite hiding place of his when he was upset or angry. The rest of the class watched with rapt attention.

Steve walked to the back of the room and knelt down in front of the child. "Patrick, Mrs. Fleming is expecting you. Let's not make things worse than they already are. If I have to call her to come down for you, it will only mean more trouble. Now I suggest you stand up and go to the office."

"I said I'm not going and I meant it!" Patrick replied, as he began to pull other students' coats out of their cubbies and throw them about the room.

"This is your last chance, Patrick. Does Mrs. Fleming need to come down herself, or are you going on your own?" There was no reply, so Steve walked back to the phone.

"Hello, yes?" he heard once more.

"Hi, this is Mr. Chandler again. Patrick refuses to go upstairs on his own," he explained.

"OK, I'll tell Mrs. Fleming."

Almost ten minutes passed before Mrs. Fleming arrived at the door of the classroom. During that time, Patrick sat huddled in his cubby while Steve regained control, calmed Emily, comforted Carla, and quickly sought refuge in the next activity.

Mrs. Fleming walked in and saw Patrick in the cubby. "Patrick, wait for me in the hall. I'll be there in a few minutes," she directed firmly. Patrick looked at her for a moment and walked out into the hallway with his head down. Mrs. Fleming turned to Steve. "Could you tell me what happened?" Steve tried to fill her in, including as much detail as possible.

"All right, I'll keep him upstairs for a while and talk to him. I know how difficult he can be."

"Thank you so much, Mrs. Fleming." Steve was relieved that she didn't seem upset that he was sending a student to her so early in the day. "Oh, one more thing, Mrs. Fleming. The kids have gym at 11:30. . . . "

Audrey Fleming cut him off. "I don't think Patrick will be going to gym today. I'm going to keep him in my office until after lunch, and then I'll send him back to your room. Patrick?" She addressed the child, who had snuck slowly back through the door. She took his hand and marched firmly toward the office.

The rest of the morning went well. The children all finished their sympathy cards and the planned reading activity. Steve took the children up to the gymnasium with Joan Ramirez's class, and he and Joan walked back to their rooms together.

"How did the morning go, Steve?" Joan asked.

"Do you really want to know?" She nodded and he told her the story. He was reassured by her interest and support, particularly when she reminded him that Vicky had lots of problems with Patrick and that Patrick would be a challenge for any teacher, experienced or novice.

At one o'clock, the children returned from lunch. As they entered the room, Mrs. Fleming appeared at the door with Patrick. "Patrick has something to tell you, Mr. Chandler," she stated flatly. "Go ahead, Patrick," she prodded. "What do you have to say to Mr. Chandler?"

Patrick looked down at the floor. "I'm sorry about the things I said this morning, Mr. Chandler. I didn't mean them."

"Anything else, Patrick?" the assistant principal asked.

"Well," he mumbled, "I don't think it's funny or anything like that when someone dies."

Patrick walked past Steve, still looking down at the ground. Steve felt so bad for him. He really wished Patrick could behave better on a more consistent basis. He knew Patrick was an intelligent child whose emotional problems and poor social skills were standing in the way of his success in school.

Steve's concern about Patrick was quickly superseded by a new worry, however. "Patrick's mother is coming in for a conference at 3:15 this afternoon, Mr. Chandler," Mrs. Fleming said. "I'd like you to be here to explain everything that happened."

Steve was not particularly pleased with the prospect of meeting Patrick's mother under these circumstances. "Mrs. Fleming, don't you think Mrs. Falk would want us to wait for her to be involved?"

"Well, Roosevelt's policy is that parents are notified any time a child is sent to the office, and when I spoke to Mrs. Ritchey on the telephone she asked to come in."

"Did you tell her what happened?" Steve asked. He had a sinking feeling; he felt his own doubts about the sensitivity of the morning's subject rising.

"Yes, briefly. That's when she asked for a conference."

Steve had found Mrs. Fleming taciturn in his other encounters with her, and he wished she would say more now. Her demeanor was so unfailingly professional that he could discern neither support nor criticism of his actions. He desperately wondered if she felt his decision to broach the subject of death with seven-year-olds had been unwise. Steve resisted the urge to ask her if she thought he had made a mistake, replying simply, "All right, Mrs. Fleming. Do you want me to bring Patrick to the office at dismissal?"

"No, we'll meet here. I'll be back then."

"Does Patrick know she's coming?" Steve asked a final question.

"Yes." Mrs. Fleming walked away down the hall.

The afternoon went much better than the morning. Even Patrick was a bit more relaxed, although he was reluctant to do his work. Steve just wanted to get through the day and was relieved that Patrick did not cause any major disturbances. Unfortunately, that all ended at 3:05 when Steve began to prepare the class for dismissal.

"Boys and girls, I'd like you all to take your homework folders out of your desks and sit up nice and tall. It's time to get ready to go home," Steve announced.

"Is Mrs. Falk coming back tomorrow?" Tommy asked.

"I don't think so, Tommy," Steve responded. He thought about what he would plan for tomorrow and realized that he was exhausted, and he still had to deal with Patrick's mother.

He resumed the dismissal process. "Team one, please walk back to the cubbies, get your coats and backpacks, and line up at the door." Steve watched the students do as he had asked. "Team two, go ahead. Patrick, if you want to get your things, that's fine. But then return to your seat because your mother will be here in a few minutes."

Patrick walked to the back of the room, picked up his things, and joined the other students lined up at the door.

"Patrick, you know your mother's coming, and I asked you to return to your seat. Please do that now," Steve said firmly.

"You can't make me stay. I'm not staying!" Patrick screamed. With this outburst, Patrick seemed to really lose control. He pushed some of the children and then swung his backpack around by the strap, hitting three or four others. Steve hurried over, took the backpack away, and gently guided Patrick by his shoulders toward his seat. Just then, Mrs. Ritchey appeared at the door. The resistance left Patrick's body immediately, and he quickly sat down. The bell rang and Steve dismissed the other students, leaving only Patrick, his mother, and Steve in the room.

"Where is Mrs. Fleming?" he wondered. He really didn't want to deal with Mrs. Ritchey alone. He smiled at her with feigned confidence and said, "I'm Steve Chandler, Mrs. Falk's student teacher this semester. Please have a seat," searching for one of the only two adult-sized chairs in the room. As he carried Vicky's desk chair toward the center of the room, Steve was relieved to see Mrs. Fleming at the door.

She greeted Patrick's mother politely. "Good afternoon, Mrs. Ritchey. Thank you for coming."

"Well, I wanted to. What happened? Is everything all right?" Mrs. Ritchey's gentle, concerned tone made Steve wonder whether the things he had heard about her were true.

"Mr. Chandler had a bit of trouble with Patrick today. You see, Mrs. Ritchey, Mrs. Falk's father died yesterday, and Mr. Chandler talked to the children about it. I'd like him to tell you what happened, but I think you'll agree that Patrick's behavior was really inappropriate."

Steve was appreciative of Mrs. Fleming's support, but he wished she hadn't opened the conversation quite so judgmentally. "Well, Mrs. Ritchey," he began, "this morning. . . . "

"Wait just a minute here," the mother interrupted, ignoring Steve and addressing Mrs. Fleming. "What right does he have talking to children about such a serious matter? Where was Mr. Cruz during all of this? Why wasn't he called in to talk to the children?"

Victor Cruz was the school psychologist, and Steve had, in fact, wondered why he hadn't come down to talk to the class. He was sure the school staff knew about Vicky's father early that morning, yet he had not seen or heard from Victor all day.

"Mrs. Ritchey, please just listen for a moment and hear the whole story," replied the assistant principal. "Please continue, Mr. Chandler."

Steve explained the rest of the story to Patrick's mother, although he could not tell whether she was really listening to him. She would look first at Steve, then at Mrs. Fleming, then at Patrick, then at her feet. She had an annoyed look on her face, and Steve wondered what she was thinking.

When Steve finished speaking, Mrs. Ritchey looked at her hands for a silent moment and then turned to Patrick. "No Boy's Club for the rest of the week, do you hear me?" she said to the child in a raised, threatening voice. "And you just wait until your father hears about this, young man!" Her son looked down, then ran out the back door and waited on the blacktop playground, just outside a classroom window.

Mrs. Fleming reacted quickly. "Mrs. Ritchey, I didn't notify you about Patrick's behavior so that you would punish your son. But we do think it's important that you know what goes on in school and that we all respond to his behavior with consistency."

Mrs. Ritchey spoke harshly, clearly angry with both of them. "How dare you lecture me about how to discipline my child. You people have been disciplining him all day. You make a public spectacle of a seven-year-old. You have no idea what Patrick is feeling. For your information, his uncle died about a month ago, and he has had a very hard time dealing with it. No wonder he reacted the way he did to Mr. Chandler's game about death. He acted out just the opposite of what he really felt."

Steve felt stricken. Why hadn't it occurred to him that Patrick's behavior might be explained so? He was glad Mrs. Fleming was controlling the meeting. "Perhaps you're right, Mrs. Ritchey," she rejoined, "but Patrick's inappropriate behavior still had to be dealt with. He was upsetting the other children."

Without responding, Mrs. Ritchey stood up and walked out of the classroom. Steve watched through the window as she held her hand out to Patrick and the two disappeared.

Steve finally met Mrs. Fleming's level gaze and still could not read her expression. Concern about dealing with parents instantly melted into worry about his discussion with the children about death. He hadn't known about Patrick's uncle, of course, but then he should have known that some of the children might bring painful experiences to such a discussion. How exposed was he? What should he say to Vicky, or to the children tomorrow?

"Hell," he thought, meeting Mrs. Fleming's cool look. "What should I say now?"

Jennifer Gordon

A mature woman beginning a second career as an elementary school teacher struggles during her student-teaching experience with how to deal with her cooperating teacher who treats her coldly and corrects her in front of the class.

The rain trickled down Jennifer Gordon's neck as she tried unsuccessfully to balance her open umbrella while locking her car. She splashed through the parking lot feeling the rain caught in the puddles kick up on her ankles and paused in the entrance vestibule, both to shake out her umbrella and to calm herself. She drew a deep breath and tried to shed the tension of her early morning rush.

This day began the second half of Jennifer's student-teaching placement. On Friday she had completed the first half of her student-teaching semester which had been in a third-grade class. It had been a wonderful experience. Her cooperating teacher, Gina Meyer, had modeled for Jennifer how to be a teacher. She welcomed her into her room from the beginning, making Jennifer feel comfortable and relaxed. Jennifer had felt useful there and had reveled in the atmosphere she felt she and the cooperating teacher created together with the children.

"Gina Meyer and I are teachers for the same reasons," Jennifer had often thought. Jennifer had an undergraduate degree in marketing and had worked in advertising for fourteen years prior to enrolling in a graduate program in education. She had changed careers because of her love for children and her desire to contribute. She enjoyed the sense of giving she felt in a classroom. She had two young children of her own, and the experience of both watching and helping them learn fascinated her. She felt very sure that a career in education was right for her.

"Good morning," Jennifer said as she walked into her new room. Martha Williams, the kindergarten teacher who would be her new cooperating teacher, was seated behind her desk and appeared to be looking for something in one of the drawers.

"Good morning," the woman replied, looking up from her search.

Jennifer looked around the room for a place to put her things, but didn't see one. "Is there somewhere I can put my purse and coat, Mrs. Williams?" she inquired.

"Please place them in the back corner, behind that bookcase," the cooperating teacher said, gesturing toward the back of the room.

Jennifer went to put her things down. Mrs. Williams seemed to find what she was looking for. She stood up and followed Jennifer.

"Our days are very full, Ms. uh . . . ?"

"Jennifer. Jennifer Gordon. I'm looking forward to our time together, Mrs. Williams." Jennifer smiled and hesitated, hoping that Mrs. Williams would use her first name.

"As I was saying, Ms. Gordon, our days are very full. It's important that you get here by 8:15 at the latest, so we can have some time to talk about the day ahead."

With that comment, Jennifer knew things were not going to start on the right foot. School didn't officially open until 8:30 A.M., and the final bell rang at 8:50 A.M. Furthermore, she assumed it took a few minutes for the children to put their coats away and get settled.

"Mrs. Williams, we need to talk about that. You see, I have two preschoolers at home myself. My baby-sitter doesn't arrive until eight in the morning, and I will do my best to be here by 8:30, but I cannot . . . ."

"Ms. Gordon, I understood from your school that you are to be treated like a teacher in every way possible during your student-teaching assignment. You wouldn't be late for school if it were your own class, would you?"

Jennifer did not know what to say. She knew that she was asking for a favor and that if it were her own class she would not have this luxury. And she definitely knew that she didn't want to have a conflict with Mrs. Williams within the first five minutes of their meeting.

"Mrs. Williams, I'll do my best to be here every day by 8:30, but I'm sorry, it is simply impossible for me to be here any earlier."

Mrs. Williams looked at her for a few seconds, then turned and walked back to her desk. Jennifer placed her belongings on the shelf behind the bookcase.

As she did so, a few students began to enter the room. Wet raincoats were being carelessly hung in cubbies, and the sound of children's voices made Jennifer feel better immediately.

"Boys and girls, please take your seats." Mrs. Williams spoke in a firm voice. Jennifer noticed name tags affixed to places at work tables, five or six children to a group. Children began to sit down. "Todd, could you move a bit faster this morning? Let's go!"

When all the students were seated, Mrs. Williams began. "Boys and girls, I want you all to listen carefully. Look and listen. We have a new student teacher starting today named Ms. Gordon. Please welcome her to our class."

"Good morning, Miss Gordon," the class sang in unison.

Jennifer looked around the room. There were twenty-one children in the class: ten boys and eleven girls. Roosevelt Elementary was a magnet school for the arts, and although it was in a marginal neighborhood its excellent reputation caused its student population to be more reflective of Littleton as a whole than of the surrounding area.

"Boys and girls, let's begin. Please stand for the Pledge of Allegiance," Mrs. Williams said. The students all stood and recited, as best they could, the pledge.

Jennifer, hand over her heart, was instantly awash with tenderness and patriotism. Children reciting the pledge were guaranteed to lift her spirits.

"Very good. Now everyone please take your seats so that we can proceed with our day. Ms. Gordon, could you help me here, please?"

Jennifer walked over. "Yes, Mrs. Williams?"

"Ms. Gordon, I'd appreciate it if you could run one copy of this worksheet for each of the children. There are twenty-one altogether."

"Sure, Mrs. Williams," Jennifer took the worksheet and left the room. The students watched her curiously as she walked out the door.

When she returned, the class was busy working on an art project. She walked over to Sonya's desk to see what she was doing. "Hi," Jennifer said. "What are you making?"

"I'm making a jack-o'-lantern. Does it look like a jack-o'-lantern to you, Miss Gordon?" It did look like one, and Jennifer told her so.

"Thank you, Miss Gordon," she replied, smiling.

The rest of the day went fairly well. Although Jennifer felt a coolness from Mrs. Williams, she became more comfortable with the students as she learned their names and spent some time with them. Mrs. Williams spoke to her in a tone that Jennifer was unable to identify. It was neither unfriendly nor friendly. It was just distant.

At the end of the day, students began to line up at the door. Many of them were bussed from other parts of town, but others were picked up by their mothers.

"Ms. Gordon, please walk the bus line out to the bus stop. Thank you."

"OK, girls and boys, let's go," Jennifer said. She walked out the door with a scraggly trail of fourteen students behind her. Littleton had instituted full-day kindergarten in its magnet schools two years earlier, and Jennifer knew that meant a long and tiring day for such young children, especially those who rode the bus. She was patient with their noise and rowdiness as they traveled the halls, realizing it was the natural consequence of fatigue. When they got to the bus, she said goodbye, trying to call as many children by name as she could. "Have a nice afternoon, everyone. I'll see you in the morning."

"Bye, Miss Gordon," they called. As he mounted the steps of the bus, one little boy turned back to Jennifer with all of the authority and assurance of an adult. "We really like you," he said seriously.

Jennifer laughed with delight. "Thank you, Robert!" she exclaimed. "And I really like you!" She waved as the bus departed and walked back into the school.

As she neared the room, she saw Carla walking down the hall, holding hands with her mother. "Mom, that's our new student teacher. She just started today, and I really like her. Her name's Miss . . . uh . . . ."

"Ms. Gordon, remember?" Jennifer said, laughing again. "Hi, you must be Carla's mother. I'm Jennifer Gordon, and I'll be student teaching in Carla's class for the next eight weeks."

"Hello, Jennifer. I'm Karen Roth. Carla sure seems excited about you."

"Well, Carla's a very nice girl. You should be proud."

"Oh, I am." Mrs. Roth smiled down at her daughter and then back at Jennifer. "Do you have any children?"

Jennifer nodded her head. "Two, in fact. Both preschoolers."

"How nice," Mrs. Roth replied. "Gosh, look at the time. I've got to run. It was very nice to meet you, Jennifer. Say goodbye, Carla."

"Bye, Miss Gordon."

"Bye, Carla," Jennifer answered, smiling.

Jennifer walked back to the room. A few parents and students were still left but most had gone by now.

"Ms. Gordon, may I talk to you for a moment?"

"Sure, Mrs. Williams." Jennifer was still smiling about her conversation with Carla and Mrs. Roth.

"Ms. Gordon, I really don't think it's appropriate for you to talk to the parents about their children. You barely know them yet, and you might say the wrong thing."

Jennifer's face flushed with emotion. "But, Mrs. Williams, I wasn't talking to Mrs. Roth about anything even having to do with school. It was more like a mother-to-mother conversation. I'm sure. . . . "

"Ms. Gordon, I feel very strongly about this." Mrs. Williams's voice was raised slightly. One of the mothers looked over for a second, obviously noticing the change in tone. "But it was my mistake to send you to walk with the students to the bus. I should have known you would be bound to bump into parents."

Jennifer couldn't believe what she was hearing. Wasn't her student-teaching experience to include some contact with parents? After all, she would have to deal with parents when she was a teacher herself. She couldn't think of anything to say. "Fine, Mrs. Williams. Is there anything else?"

"I think we're all set. See you tomorrow."

"Good night, Mrs. Williams." Jennifer picked up her things and walked out the door. "One day down," she thought to herself, closing the door behind her.

• • •

It was hard for Jennifer to believe that her student-teaching assignment with Mrs. Williams was more than half over. Jennifer had settled into a professional relationship with Mrs. Williams, which was foreign to Jennifer's nature but seemed to protect both of them from disagreement. Mrs. Williams's enthusiasm for art was obvious from her classroom and the activities she orchestrated for the students. Jennifer had learned no personal details from Mrs. Williams herself, but from other teachers she discovered that her cooperating teacher was a professional artist who, like Jennifer, had returned to college after several years for her teaching certification. She had been teaching kindergarten at Roosevelt for nine years. And in spite of their tense relationship, Jennifer knew she was learning a lot from the experience. Mrs. Williams was a skilled teacher.

It was Jennifer's relationship with the children that made it all bearable. As the days moved toward Christmas and holiday art projects proliferated, Jennifer's concerns retreated, and she could usually ignore Mrs. Williams's terse tone and distant manner.

"Miss Gordon, can you come here?" pleaded Jamie, a fragile looking, somewhat shy boy, had recently begun to trust Jennifer. A few weeks ago, he wouldn't even look up at her when she spoke to him, but now he followed her around the room, often initiating an interaction. Jennifer walked over to Jamie and put her hand on his shoulder as she knelt down beside him.

"Miss Gordon, I don't feel good."

"Let me feel your head, Jamie." She pushed his hair back and felt his forehead. He didn't feel warm at all. He looked up at her.

"Jamie, you are cool as a cucumber!"

"But, Miss Gordon, I don't feel good."

"Well, Jamie, you don't have a fever. Just hang in there and we'll see how you feel in a little while, OK?" She gave him a little hug.

"OK."

Jennifer looked up and saw that Mrs. Williams was looking at her.

"Boys and girls, let's all come back to the rug. It's story time," Mrs. Williams called. Story time, which was also snack time, was a morning highlight. The children hurried back to the rug.

"Would you like me to read to the children today, Mrs. Williams?"

"That's OK, Ms. Gordon. I'll read today."

Jennifer thought Mrs. Williams seemed annoyed. "Perhaps it's me," Jennifer thought. "Maybe I'm being too sensitive. Or maybe she just doesn't like me."

As the children settled, Jennifer's thoughts wandered back to recent conversations with her college supervisor about her tenuous relationship with Mrs. Williams. "Dr. Curry, I just don't know what to do. It seems as if everything I do isn't quite good enough. She hardly ever talks to me, and every time there's a break in the day she heads straight for the teacher's room."

Initially, Dr. Curry had encouraged Jennifer to give the relationship time, but after a few weeks he had been willing to seek alternatives. "Jennifer," he said, "there's still time to change to another class. I have no problem moving you in with another teacher."

Jennifer had often thought longingly of this option, but she felt that moving to another class would send a clear message to Mrs. Williams that she disliked her. Worse, she genuinely loved the children in the class, and the idea of hurting their feelings with an unexplained withdrawal was unacceptable. Furthermore, Jennifer was wise to the politics of student teaching and feared that her reassignment would imply failure, particularly if Mrs. Williams ever got a chance at commentary.

Jennifer returned to the present and saw that Jamie was sitting alone up on the table next to the rug. All the other children had brought their snacks and were sitting quietly on the rug. Jamie looked sad, so Jennifer walked over and sat up on the table next to him. Mrs. Williams began to read.

"*Danny and the Dinosaur.* Story and pictures by Syd Hoff," she began. "One day Danny went to the museum. He wanted to see what was inside." She held the book up so the children could see the pictures. She glanced at Jennifer and Jamie, then looked down at the book and continued. "He saw Indians. He saw bears. He saw Eskimos . . . ," she read.

"Miss Gordon," Jamie said quietly, looking up. "Could you feel my head again? I still don't feel so good."

Jennifer knew it had been no more than ten minutes since she last felt Jamie's head. He couldn't possibly have a fever, but she felt his head anyway. She pushed back his hair and lifted her hand to his forehead.

"Ms. Gordon," Mrs. Williams called in a raised voice. "Jamie is just trying to get your attention. If he were sick his mother would have kept him home from school today."

"Mrs. Williams," Jennifer began, not really knowing what to say, "he . . . ."

"And please get down from that table. We don't sit on the tables in this room."

Jennifer was shocked and embarrassed, and she knew the students were too. While Mrs. Williams was often bossy or impatient with her, this was the first time she had actually reprimanded her in front of the children. Jennifer smiled weakly, took Jamie by the hand, and slid him off the table. As they sat on the rug she patted his knee reassuringly, more for her own comfort than his. Mrs. Williams resumed reading, and Jennifer gratefully retreated into anonymity.

The calm expression on her face belied Jennifer's roiling emotions: shock turning to disbelief, confusion, and anger. "I'm just not sure how much more of this I can take!" she thought vehemently. Jennifer was irritated by her own meekness. It was not like her to accept such treatment, but she knew no other course. She felt trapped by her earlier decision. Now that she had decided to "stick it out" with Mrs. Williams rather than accept Dr. Curry's offer of reassignment, she was dependent upon Mrs. Williams's evaluation of her performance. "But," she agonized, "is it asking too much to be treated like a human being?"

• • •

"I can't believe this semester is almost over," Jennifer said to her husband, Jim, as they cleared the breakfast table. This Monday began her last week as a student teacher. "You know, there were times when I believed it would never end!"

"I know it's been hard on you. But you're right—only five more days."

"Thank goodness!" Jennifer turned from the dishwasher to the pile of papers, visual aids, and craft materials by the back door. "All I have to do is get through this observation and I'm home free!" On Wednesday, Dr. Curry was scheduled to observe Jennifer teach a lesson about holidays in Eastern Europe—a subject Jennifer thought ridiculous and irrelevant, but one that Mrs. Williams had insisted upon. Jennifer had fought the suspicion that Mrs. Williams was purposefully sabotaging her final observation and had shelved her own ideas for a seasonal lesson in the interest of tranquility. The consequence of this had been difficult research and forced creativity, but Jennifer thought it a small price to pay for a peaceful end to her student-teaching experience.

"Did I tell you she yelled at me again last week?" Jennifer asked Jim as he dried his hands. From the other room they could hear their boys singing along with some song on *Sesame Street.*

"Not in front of the class again?"

"Of course." Three days removed from the event, Jennifer could be casual; at the time, the incident had bothered her as much as the earlier one with Jamie. But one antidote for Mrs. William's irascibility had been Jennifer's ability to forget unpleasant incidents for a few days and then to laugh about them with her husband. "She yelled at me for talking to students from my third-grade class."

"I don't get it." Jim was trying to listen to her but was distracted by their two-year-old, who had entered the kitchen and was now tugging at his pant leg.

"Oh, a couple of my old students stopped at the door to wave and say hello on their way to a special," Jennifer explained. "When I went over to the door to speak to them, she got mad. Right in front of the kids she said, 'Ms. Gordon, I need you to attend to the children in this class.'" Jennifer unwrapped Bobby from his father's leg and hugged him tight. "I think she hates it that the children like me."

"Just get through it, OK?" Jim picked up his briefcase and keys and kissed Bobby and then Jennifer. "I'm tired of hearing about that woman."

As Jennifer drove to school, she thought about Jim's last comment. It had really hurt her feelings and resurrected her recurring confusion about her own passivity in the face of Mrs. William's abuse. "I am thirty-seven years old," Jennifer thought. "I am tired of letting that woman treat me like an undergraduate." Maybe it was her own fault for not trying to discuss their relationship, for not making more of an effort to communicate.

Jennifer also worried, for the hundredth time, about Mrs. Williams's evaluation of her performance. She honestly did not know what her cooperating teacher thought of her teaching. Dr. Curry's observations of Jennifer's teaching had been positive, but Mrs. Williams had never offered her feedback of any kind. Several times throughout their eight weeks Jennifer solicited Mrs. William's professional opinion about matters of content or style and had gotten some good ideas, but unless she asked for specific information, she had felt frozen out. So, her response was simply to try to get along. This morning, though, such behavior seemed overly submissive. "Maybe she doesn't like me because I'm a wimp."

Jennifer checked the time on the car clock; for once she was a few minutes ahead of schedule. "I'm going to talk with her about last Friday," she resolved. "I haven't been a terrible student teacher. Maybe we can end this in harmony."

Newly energized, Jennifer parked her car and strode through the playground, balancing the bulky materials she carried for Wednesday's observation. "Good morning, Miss Gordon," students called as they saw her.

"Good morning, Manny. How are you today? And you, Saul? Are you all ready for a busy day?" Jennifer loved interacting with the children outside the classroom; she thought it was important.

When she entered the room, Jennifer saw that Mrs. Williams was sitting at her desk, looking through some student work. It reminded her of their first day.

"Good morning, Mrs. Williams." Jennifer had given up on first names long ago. She put the supplies for Wednesday's lesson on the shelves in back.

"Good morning," Mrs. Williams answered.

Jennifer took a deep breath and returned to stand in front of Mrs. Williams's desk. "Mrs. Williams," Jennifer began quietly. "I need to talk to you for a minute." Mrs. Williams looked at her, and Jennifer thought she saw a mixture of irritation and curiosity on her face.

"I thought a lot about my student teaching with you over the weekend," Jennifer began. "I wondered if we could talk a moment about our relationship."

"I'm not sure I understand, Ms. Gordon." Mrs. Williams responded.

"Well, I thought a lot about the incident on Friday when some children from Mrs. Meyer's class stopped to speak to me at the door. . . ."

Mrs. Williams interrupted her. "Yes, that was unfortunate. We were in the middle of a math lesson. An interruption like that when you have a class of your own can be quite intrusive. You need to be aware of the things that have the potential to disrupt a lesson."

"But, Mrs. Williams, you seemed to think I had encouraged those children to visit me. Or that somehow I shirked my responsibility here."

"Well, if that wasn't your intention it was certainly the result," Mrs. Williams responded. "You encouraged the children in the hall by going to speak with them when a lesson that demanded your attention was going on. But let's get on with the new week, shall we?"

"Well, I . . . ." Jennifer's resolve was slipping. She blurted out, "Mrs. Williams, would you please try to discuss comments you have with me privately? I don't think it's appropriate for you to reprimand me in front of the children. I'm not comfortable in here when you do that."

Mrs. Williams seemed startled by Jennifer's tone. She hesitated a moment and then said flatly, "Ms. Gordon, if you're not happy here, you know where the door is."

Lauren Ross*

An enthusiastic young student teacher gets her first chance to "fly solo" for a full day with her fifth-grade class. Her cooperating teacher is very upset when she learns that Lauren has reported a mainstreamed student in her class for misbehavior during a fire drill.

As Lauren Ross negotiated through the Monday morning traffic she realized that at this time next week she might find herself longing for her students, but that she certainly would not miss this daily ordeal down Route 21. She thought fondly of the fifth-graders at Roosevelt School in Littleton she would be leaving when the first half of her fourteen-week student-teaching placement ended on Friday. Lively, energetic, and so ready to challenge her in September, they now seemed to accept her as their teacher. Lauren knew that this week, when she assumed full responsibility for the class while her cooperating teacher remained out of the classroom, would be the ultimate test of the degree to which her fifth-graders regarded Lauren as a real teacher, and she hoped she would pass that test with high marks. She was pleased at how her own perception of herself as a teacher had changed. A few weeks ago, she had anticipated making the transition from student to student teacher; now she believed she had actually begun to be the "professional teacher" her college professors talked about. She had grown in self-confidence and assertiveness, and she felt that she projected the air of authority that defined a professional teacher and that she admired in Barbara Milton, her cooperating teacher.

Lauren recalled her first meeting with Barbara several weeks before the semester began. Barbara had greeted her warmly and asked if she were nervous about student teaching. "A little bit," Lauren had replied. "But I've had some experience working with kids and teaching. I'm really looking forward to putting that experience to work in your classroom and learning more."

"Terrific! What kinds of experiences have you had with students?" Barbara had asked.

"Well, for two summers I worked as a counselor for our town's summer recreation program, once with the four-to-six-year-old group, once with the junior high drama group. That was when I was in high school. Since college I've

*Developed by Janet Stivers, Marist College.

been working at the Health and Fitness Club, and this year I'm teaching an aerobics class there twice a week. I really love it."

"Both of those jobs sound like lots of fun, but I'm not sure they have much in common with teaching the fifth-grade curriculum to twenty-nine ten-year-olds," Barbara had replied doubtfully. "Working with motivated adults and working with children in a relaxed environment like summer camp are really very different from working in a structured setting like a classroom, with students who are interested in anything but what you need to teach them. I think you'll find student teaching to be a totally new experience."

Lauren was a bit taken aback at Barbara's response, but she just smiled and replied, "Oh, I'm sure I will, and I guess that's why I'm looking forward to it so much. I feel ready for a new challenge. And I'm nervous, but I think people are pretty much the same everywhere, and I know I'm good with people."

"Yes. Good interpersonal skills are an essential prerequisite for an effective teacher," Barbara had agreed. "What about the curriculum? Are you comfortable with the topics we'll be covering during your seven weeks? I could show you copies of the texts and teachers manuals."

"I'd love to take a look at them. Can I take some home with me to look at when I have time?"

Lauren left the meeting with her arms full of materials, hoping she had begun to dispel doubts Barbara might have had about her readiness to assume the responsibilities of a teacher. It was important to Lauren that she create a good initial impression, because she had heard of Barbara's reputation as an excellent teacher from other students in her Elementary Methods classes who had volunteered in Barbara's room. Lauren also knew that Barbara had never agreed to take a student teacher before, even though she often accepted as volunteers college students who wanted to gain some practical experience before student teaching. Because of this, Lauren felt it was especially important for her to be a very successful student teacher. As she reviewed the past six weeks, Lauren felt good about her performance so far. She had made some mistakes, but she had worked hard and tried to incorporate all of Barbara's suggestions. She felt pretty sure that Barbara was pleased with her teaching, even though Barbara was not so effusive about Lauren's lessons as Lauren would have liked. Lauren looked forward to using this final week to demonstrate to Barbara that accepting her as a student teacher had been a wise decision.

She and Barbara had prepared very carefully for this week. They had first discussed Lauren's solo week at the beginning of the placement, when Barbara learned that Lauren's college supervisor, Alan McMurray, expected student teachers to assume full responsibility for the class for at least the final week of the student-teaching experience. On Dr. McMurray's first visit to the classroom, Barbara talked with him about this expectation, asking if it were actually a requirement of student teaching and suggesting that it might be better for both Lauren and the fifth-graders if she and Lauren spent the final week as colleagues, team teaching all of the content areas. But Dr. McMurray had said that it was important to give a student teacher enough time and space to allow her to find a teaching style that suited her best, rather than merely trying to find a style that was compatible with another teacher's. So Barbara revised the list of expectations and the week-by-week outline she had prepared for Lauren and added provisions for this solo week to the timetable.

As Lauren turned off Route 21 and headed toward Roosevelt, she thought about how thoroughly she and Barbara had prepared for this week. They had worked together at school until 6:30 Friday evening, going over all the details. Lauren found herself regularly having to adjust her schedule because she still wasn't used to staying to plan for the two hours or more that Barbara did each day after the children left, and she found it particularly difficult to stay late on Fridays. She had stayed willingly the previous Friday because she knew how important her solo performance was, but she thought that Barbara was more anxious about it than she was. She and Barbara had spent a long time planning for today's lessons, because the Monday schedule was a particularly difficult one. There were two specials in the afternoon, a forty-five-minute art period and a thirty-minute computer lab. Because the fifth-graders had a late lunch period anyway, the afternoon was fragmented. That, indirectly, caused problems in the morning schedule. On Mondays, all the children who left the classroom to go to speech, resource room, remedial reading, or remedial math had to be scheduled for those services in the morning. To further complicate matters, teachers had been notified on Thursday afternoon that the annual civil defense drill would be conducted at an unspecified time on Monday. Barbara had gone over the procedures with Lauren, even taking her into the hall and demonstrating the crouching position the students were to assume during the drill. Lauren had never participated in a civil defense drill, so she was grateful for the guidance, although she did feel conspicuous and a little silly as she knelt in front of the lockers with her head on her knees. When Lauren imagined how she must look and laughed self-consciously, Barbara said firmly, "That's one thing you want to be sure to avoid on Monday. The memo from the office couldn't be clearer about the seriousness of this exercise. The students will take their cues from you, so be sure not to allow any misbehavior."

As Lauren pulled into the faculty parking area adjacent to the school, she recalled the vague feeling of annoyance she had felt last night when Barbara had called her at her dormitory.

"Oh, Lauren, I'm glad to be able to reach you tonight, instead of trying to catch you on the run tomorrow morning," Barbara had begun. "Mostly, I wanted to let you know where I'll be tomorrow and to remind you of a few details. I've made plans to spend most of the morning in the teacher's room, meeting with Anne Finn and Susan Rivera." Anne was the director of special education who had mainstreamed Robert Silver and Joshua Richards into Barbara's science and social studies classes, and Susan was the special education teacher consultant who wanted to pilot an inclusion program with Barbara's class at the start of the next marking period.

"Anne and Susan are pleased with the way Robert and Joshua are doing," Barbara continued, "so we're going to go ahead and finalize plans for assigning them to my class full-time. It won't be as easy without you in the room, but Susan is promising to be very generous with her consultation time. We're still a little worried about Robert—there's a problem with his parents. They think he's better off in special education where he doesn't get into any trouble because the class is small and someone is always hovering over him. Also, Robert's really insecure about being in the fifth-grade class. Susan thinks it's because he's been in a self-contained special education class since first grade, so it will take him a little while to be socialized into acting like a typical fifth-grader. But, I think he's made a lot of progress."

"I'm sure it will be fine," Lauren replied, "although it will probably be a little crazy at first, until the kids get used to me being gone. They may have a hard time adjusting to a new teacher so soon after I leave."

"Maybe," Barbara replied. "Anyway, I wanted to remind you that Robert and Joshua should join the class as usual for science and social studies tomorrow. You may have to send for them; the civil defense drill may throw everyone off schedule, and they may forget to come on their own. Actually, that relates to another reason for my call. Do you have any questions about the drill?"

"No, Barbara," Lauren responded somewhat coolly. "Our practice session in the hallway did the trick. Actually, I'm not anticipating any problems tomorrow; we went over everything so thoroughly on Friday that I feel very prepared."

After hanging up, Lauren wondered if her tone of voice had offended Barbara. She hoped it hadn't, although she believed that Barbara's call had been unnecessary. Because of Barbara's anxiety they had spent three hours planning on Friday afternoon, and Lauren felt that Barbara's concerns about the day were unjustified. Dr. McMurray had observed her twice, and each time he had been full of praise for her lesson.

• • •

Barbara was in the room almost before the last student was out the door. "How'd it go? I've been thinking about you all day."

It was hard for Lauren to be annoyed with Barbara, since it was obvious that her cooperating teacher's concern for her was genuine. She smiled at Barbara and responded, "Well, things didn't go so smoothly as I'd hoped, but I think it went OK. It was my first solo day, so I shouldn't have expected things to be perfect."

Barbara looked a little worried. "Tell me what happened."

"Well, for one thing, I sent a group to remedial reading fifteen minutes early, and the teacher sent them right back with a request to return them at the right time."

"And did you?"

"Sure. But the students got a little rowdy when they came back. They couldn't settle down to work for the few minutes they had until they went back to reading, so I had a little trouble keeping them from disrupting the rest of the class. Then, probably because of the confusion those kids caused, I completely forgot to send the group to the math lab, but the office called and the students lost only a few minutes of their remedial math period."

Barbara smiled, a little thinly, Lauren thought. But her words were consoling. "These things happen. All the separate schedules are confusing. I thought you knew all the schedules because you follow them when I'm here with you, but I know it's hard to remember everything."

Lauren agreed. "I tried not to be too upset by my lapses. I know it would have been better if I'd been on top of everything going on during the day, but I figured it was OK to make some mistakes. I know no one expected me to be perfect when I assumed full responsibility. It was my first day all alone in the classroom."

Barbara nodded her agreement. "I think that's the right attitude. As long as you recognize what went wrong and figure out a way to keep those things from happening again. How did the civil defense drill go?"

Lauren felt she was on firm ground here. "I was really glad you told me how seriously to treat the drill. I was able to prevent what could have been a major problem by acting quickly."

"Oh, what happened?"

"Well, Robert apparently found the entire enterprise amusing and couldn't seem to stop giggling. I gave him a stern look, then moved closer and whispered sharply to him, but his giggling fit continued. Remembering how you stressed the seriousness of the drill and knowing that the laughter could easily spread to the rest of the class, I sent Robert to the office. It worked. No one else uttered a peep during the rest of the drill."

Lauren looked at Barbara for approval but saw only a frown. In a quiet voice that conveyed clearly the seriousness of the message, Barbara said, "I wish you hadn't done that. This is Robert's third disciplinary referral, and the school policy is that parents are contacted after a third incident. This will probably spell the end of Robert's regular ed inclusion, given how hesitant his parents have been about mainstreaming him this year. Now I don't know if we'll ever be able to convince them that he's better off in a regular class."

Emily Smith

An energetic student teacher requests and is assigned to student teach social studies in an inner-city high school. Her cooperating teacher gradually lets her assume control of the most difficult survey class, and she succeeds in reaching them until they find out her student-teaching assignment with them will soon end.

Emily Smith parked her car in the Alton High School West parking lot, dropped her keys into her purse, and headed for the nearest entrance, excited and at the same time a little scared. She had anticipated this moment for two years. She wanted to work with the sort of student she imagined attended Alton West. Now she was going to meet the principal for her student-teaching interview.

As Emily walked through the halls on her way to the main office, she noticed without surprise that most of the students were minorities. "The director of student teaching was right," she thought. "I stick out like a sore thumb." At one time Alton High School West served a white, middle-class student population, but over the past seven years the school district had been integrated through court mandate. The high school was now 85% minority, serving African-Americans, Hispanics, Asians, Indians, and a handful of other minorities.

Emily tried not to be self-conscious about the grins and stares she received as she headed for the office of Charles Green, the Assistant Principal. She looked back at the students lining the hallways with polite interest. Their body language and loud talk was intended, she knew, to convey an appearance of toughness. "They're doing pretty well at it, too," she mused, summoning reserves of willpower not to feel intimidated. She heard several languages in addition to English echoing through the corridors.

Charles Green was ready for Emily when she arrived, and after greeting her he gave her some background on the student population she had just observed. "Our students are functioning often with tremendous responsibility," he explained. "Those who manage to stay in school and perform are really surmounting many obstacles. Most of our students work after school, and some have more than one job. Many take care of younger siblings as well, and some contribute to the family income."

"Their effort is really impressive, when you think of it that way," Emily ventured.

"Yes, it is. But we also have a high rate of absenteeism and suspensions. Many of our students do not make good choices. Don't be surprised, for instance, to see pregnant fourteen-year-old girls in your classes. We have deans of discipline in the halls to keep order. Don't carry too much money, and be careful of your jewelry." Green paused and smiled. "After telling you all of the negatives, I want you to know that working here can be an invaluable experience. These kids really want to learn. If you get through to two or three real problem kids a year, it's the best feeling in the world."

"Can you tell me more about the classes I'll be teaching?" Emily asked, anxious to get some details.

"Sure. I assigned you to work with John Nolan. He teaches twelfth-grade Honors, eleventh-grade Honors, and three eleventh-grade Survey sections. He's been at Alton West for five years; before that he taught in Vermont, I think. He has a nice way with the kids, and they don't give him any guff. I think you'll learn a lot from him."

Emily knew that the students at Alton West were tracked into one of three programs: Honors, Above-Average, and Survey. She was glad to be getting some experience with the less able students in the school. "That sounds fine, Mr. Green," she replied. "I'm looking forward especially to working with the Survey classes. I got into education to make a difference in students' lives, and I guess they need difference-makers there the most." Emily cringed a bit at the kind but indulgent smile Mr. Green managed in reaction to this but was reassured by his reply.

"Welcome aboard, Miss Smith. We could use more young people like you!"

As Emily left the office she noticed that there were two police officers escorting five students down the hall. "Do I know what I am getting myself into?" Emily wondered as a custodian pointed her to the parking lot exit. She wondered if Alton was the place that would modify the enthusiasm and idealism about teaching that her friends and family kidded her about.

• • •

At the end of her first day of student teaching, Emily straightened the tablet desks back into neat rows and erased the chalkboard as she waited for John Nolan to return from bus duty. She had enjoyed the day and was making headway already as she struggled to remember the names of the 150 students and at least twenty faculty members to whom she had been introduced. As she had anticipated, she enjoyed the three Survey classes the most. Her favorite among these met second period. It was a class of ten girls and fifteen boys and was as racially heterogeneous, she supposed, as classes at Alton West could be considering the population it served and the fact of tracking. She had counted nine African-American students, eight Hispanic students, an Indian student, an Arab student, and six white students. There were some ESL students in the class and others who were freshly out of Special Education. But their personalities and energy, more than their demographics, had caught her interest and inspired her affection.

"God, bus duty is hell!" John Nolan sighed good naturedly as he strode back into the room. "One more year and I'm through with that!" He looked at her sympathetically. "Of course, first-year teachers have to serve cafeteria duty—now that's a real initiation!" Emily grinned back—already she felt an affinity with Nolan and a shared sense of the possible.

"Well, what did you think, Emily? How do you like my JDs?"

"A lot," she replied matter of factly. "My favorite group was second period. I'd like to take over teaching that group first."

Nolan looked at her thoughtfully. "I'm not sure that's a good idea," he replied quietly. "The kids in there tend to be difficult."

"Really? I liked the kids in second period. I think I'm drawn to remedial kids—if you can reach one of them, it seems like you could make a real difference in a kid's life." When she realized how naive she must be sounding, Emily amended her statement. "Or maybe you could get them to feel a little better about themselves as students."

John's smile was reminiscent of that indulgent look Mr. Green had settled on her two weeks ago. "Well, it's not so easy as your professors make it out to be, making a difference with a kid. But I guess that's as good a reason to go into teaching as any. Sure, you can take over the second period class. I'll back you up."

"Who would you say is the most difficult student in that class?" Emily inquired, not wanting to pursue a philosophical discussion so much as a practical one.

"No contest: Carlos Sanchez. He's the biggest problem in all of his classes. He gives every teacher a difficult time. He never does any class work and he's disruptive in class. In addition, he's a ringleader among his friends. He's a tough kid, hard to control."

Emily knew immediately which student Mr. Nolan was describing; among the hundreds she had met that day, only one had brought her coffee. She'd figured he was unique in some respect. "Ah, yes," she nodded. "Carlos. He brought me coffee."

"Probably his way of hitting on you. He's got a reputation as a ladies' man to uphold."

Emily smiled at the idea of a sixteen-year-old coming on to her. "Well, he seemed pretty well-behaved."

"Maybe because Desmond Walker, his big-mouthed friend, wasn't in class today. That kid has a comment for everything. One of his favorite topics is racism. He thinks all white people are racist and tells us that whenever possible. But despite his big mouth, Desmond does his work. He's a B student."

"Who was the slight boy with a bad complexion who sat behind Carlos?" Emily asked, concentrating on a mental image of the students in second period.

"You're probably thinking of Danny Riveria, another one of Carlos's posse. Actually, he's an excellent student. He usually gets 100s on all of his tests. But he's easily influenced by his friends and if provoked can become nasty and even violent."

"What about that sweet black girl?" Emily asked. "The tall one."

"Her name's Erline Cole. She's a good kid. She was just transferred out of Special Education. She's a hard worker and her attendance is excellent."

"Are any of the students parents? Mr. Green said that a lot of kids in this school have kids of their own."

"Mark Copitto, for one. He had a kid last year, which put a lot of stress and turmoil into his life. His grades suffered and he repeated his senior year. His attendance and grades aren't a problem this year, though," John replied.

"Is his girlfriend in this school?"

"Yeah, she's a junior now, and the kid is two."

"Wow!" Emily paused as this sank in. "What about the group of Mexicans that sit in the back?"

"Those kids stick together like glue, but they aren't behavior problems. They don't speak much English and their attendance is horrible. It's more than likely none of them will graduate," Nolan concluded matter-of-factly. "You know, let me say once more, you don't have to start with that class. One of my Honors sections would probably be a lot better place to get your feet wet."

"Thanks, but if it's OK with you, I've pretty much decided that's my class." It would be a challenge, but one that she looked forward to taking on.

Emily observed John's classes for the rest of that first week, and she began teaching lessons, using her cooperating teacher's plans, the beginning of her second week. For two more weeks, Emily and the second period class got to know each other. The first few days had been harder than Emily had anticipated, as students challenged her authority or simply refused to listen or follow directions. Each time she lost control John bailed her out without making a big deal out of the experience. Emily appreciated that he never said, "I told you so." Rather, he acted as a thoughtful observer of her teaching. He was able to point out what she was doing when things started to fall apart, helping her see her contribution to the problem. He suggested things she might try to keep the class on track. He was also quick to praise her when something she tried worked. He admitted that Carlos acted like a different student with Emily. "I'm not sure I can explain it," John had said one afternoon, "but Carlos responds more positively to you than to anyone else in the school."

"I really like him. He reminds me of my younger brother. You know, everyone in our family had been a whiz in school, and Jake never did very well. So he affected a tough-guy attitude, and most teachers thought he was dumb. But he wasn't—he just needed a different kind of teaching. Any teacher that took the time to get to know Jake, to talk to him, to find out why he wasn't doing the work ended up getting great results from him. I think that's what Carlos is like."

Looking at Emily, John laughed and said, "It's hard to picture Carlos as your brother."

Emily laughed back. "Agreed. We definitely don't **look** like brother and sister. But I mean it about really liking him. Maybe because of Jake, but he touches some chord in me. At first, he sort of scared me, you know? Because he's such a tough talker, and he looks pretty menacing. But now I think I've seen through that tough-guy role he plays. There's a vulnerable kid in there."

John nodded. "Well, it's clear that you've reached him. Whatever you're doing is working—keep it up."

Over the next few weeks, as she assumed more and more responsibility for different classes, Emily realized that students from all of her classes were asking her for extra help in school. Some of the girls even sought her advice on their personal lives. She found herself helping students with their college essays and English term papers. John commented that the students treated Emily more like a peer than a teacher, and he told her that he thought several of the students had crushes on her. While she laughed his comment off, after two students asked her out she became a little more formal with the students and made sure she behaved in ways that made her seem unavailable.

On the Friday at the end of her fifth week at Alton West, Emily and John were returning together to the room from bus duty. "Emily, why don't you think over the weekend about trying some different teaching approaches with the students? You've gotten much better at classroom control; the kids have pretty much stopped trying to take advantage of you. I think you have enough control over the situation to try some varied academic approaches."

Emily was delighted by John's encouragement. "I was actually thinking about organizing a debate over capital punishment. Do you think that would work with the second period class?"

"Well, I might start experimenting with first or third period instead," he replied dubiously.

"But the energy in second period is just what would make it work!" Emily's enthusiasm was palpable.

"OK," John laughed, his hands held defensively in front of him. "Your excitement is a wonderful thing. Why don't you try it the middle of next week. You can think about how you want to set it up over the weekend and fill me in on Monday."

"I can't wait! This should be fun. Something different than lectures and notes." As they entered their room and began packing up papers and plan books, Emily changed the subject. "By the way, I forgot to tell you that I had a long talk with Wencelseo Rodriguez. The reason he's been absent so much is because he's living on his own."

"What do you mean?" John asked.

"He moved to the United States when he was thirteen. He left his whole family in Mexico and lived here with his uncle's family. His uncle made him leave last year, so he's been living on his own in an apartment. He works at a restaurant to pay the bills. That's why his attendance is so poor. He's got to work to make it on his own. He asked me for extra help in school so he can graduate this June. Can you believe it? That poor kid," Emily sighed.

John said, "I've had him all year and never knew any of this. He must really trust you. Does he remind you of your brother, too?"

Emily flushed with pleasure at John's compliment. She couldn't resist saying, "I really do love teaching." She was pleased that John responded with a genuine grin and a thumbs-up sign instead of that indulgent look she'd come to expect. She felt, for the first time, as if he believed in the sincerity of her motives, so she went on. "But it's more than that. I really want to reach kids. Having a relationship with Carlos and with Wencelseo—understanding about their lives, seeing what they're about as people, that's what I really love."

The following week, John and Emily conferred over her ideas for a debate during second period. Emily decided to try it only in one class, opting for the more familiar terrain of lecture and worksheets in the other two Survey classes, and John did not object. He and Emily debriefed the debate over lunch on the day of the big event.

"Well, that certainly was lively," John commented.

"But I thought several of the participants made good points, didn't you?" Emily replied. She felt immediately defensive in response to John's implication that the class had been out of control; she had thought the lesson a great success. "And Carlos was as involved as he's ever been."

"True. But I wonder how much students retain from such a free-for-all."

"I'd like to think that the higher the emotional investment they have in a subject, the more they'll remember," Emily replied.

"Yes, but don't you think lots of them were play acting? Frankly, some of them have such a personal stake in this subject—relatives who've committed capital offenses, for instance—that they can't debate sincerely. It would hurt too much."

Emily was instantly angry with herself for not thinking about this before the debate, but for reasons other than those suggested by John's comment. An instinct told her she might have harnessed that personal investment in the topic. At the same time, though, she read John's feedback loud and clear: better safe than sorry in second period.

Emily's pleasure in her student-teaching experience was not diminished, though, by a return to more traditional methods, and she continued to refine presentation and management techniques until just after spring vacation. With the onset of spring and beautiful weather, attendance deteriorated dramatically. On sunny warm days fewer than half the students made it to class. Emily worried anew about how to motivate them. Various incentives, rewards, and deals generally worked well for John, and he used contracts with students a lot. Emily decided with two weeks left that she would plan her own farewell party and make it a reward for good attendance. With John's approval, she told the students in the second period class about the plan.

"Yo, miss, if we all sign a petition, do you think you can stay? You shouldn't leave." Emily was taken aback by Carlos's loud and almost angry reaction. He was using a tone she'd heard him use in the hall but not with her.

"Well, I don't want to leave either, but my student-teaching time is almost over."

"It doesn't seem fair that you have to leave," Mark chimed in. "Can't you just stay anyway?"

"Well, I have to get a job when my school is out," Emily smiled, certain that this group would understand that. "I'm not getting paid to be here, you know."

"Is that all this is to you, a job?" Desmond sneered. "Big deal, she's leaving."

Emily could not help but feel flattered by her students' reaction to her impending departure, but her announcement and the party idea did not have its intended effect. In fact, the problem seemed to get worse. Not only did attendance continue to decline, but the students who did show up became increasingly unruly. They were disruptive and rude in class, behaving in ways she hadn't seen since her first days of student teaching. Some students would play cards as soon as their class work was done. Others slept the whole period. In addition, Carlos resorted to the tactics John had described weeks earlier. He refused to do any class work, he carried on private conversations with his friends in class, and if his friends tried to ignore him, he would rap. It wasn't long before his behavior spread. Thinking of Jake, Emily stopped him after class one morning. "Carlos, I'd like to talk to you."

"No time. Got to get to third period."

"Carlos, don't walk away from me. It's important that we talk. You've stopped trying in class. Your grades are dropping. What's going on? Can I help?"

"Nothin's going on. School's school. Sometimes it's OK and usually it ain't. Now it ain't." He pushed passed her and joined his friends in the hall, shouting for them to wait for him.

Emily didn't need John's feedback to realize that she was losing control of the class. After three days of deteriorating behavior, she opened class in an uncharacteristically stern manner. "I have an announcement to make. I know you all know that I'm leaving soon, but that's no excuse for this class's behavior. Remember, I give the grades and right now you are all in trouble. I told you at the beginning of the term that class work and participation play an important role in your grades. If you come in and play cards, that's a zero for the day. This is not Atlantic City—I give no credit for card playing. If you come in and sleep, you get a zero. Start going to bed earlier. We don't have nap time in high school. If you continue to talk and not do any work, you get a zero. I expect you all to act like adults, and then I'll treat you like adults." She paused to make sure she still had their attention. "That's it. Got it?" Everyone nodded. For the entire class period the students were more attentive, and Emily hoped that her tough stance had put an end to the problems.

The following day it rained, and Emily knew that attendance would be better than usual. First period proved her right, and she anticipated a full house for the next class.

Even before the bell signalled the start of the period, Emily sensed trouble. Instead of coming to class, a few of her students were smoking in the courtyard, in spite of a light drizzle. As Emily watched helplessly they approached the window and literally jumped into the room. Another group of students started making derogatory comments about Arabs, directing their remarks at a new student in the class from Saudi Arabia. Emily wondered with rising panic when John Nolan would finish copying fifth period's exams and get back to the room. Meanwhile she sprang to Joseph's defense.

"You guys stop talking like that right now. You never know who you could hurt, and you wouldn't like it if someone talked that way about you," Emily warned.

"People always make jokes about Blacks, and you white people think it's funny," Desmond Walker yelled out.

"Desmond, I will not have this discussion with you again. Settle down and get to work," Emily responded.

"Yo, miss, you're prejudiced!" Desmond retorted. All eyes turned toward Emily to see her response.

"Desmond," Emily said calmly, "don't be ridiculous. You know that I haven't shown one bit of prejudice in this class."

Desmond grinned. "I know. I'm just bustin' your balls." With that Desmond laughed and started his class work. The rest of the class followed suit except for Carlos. He continued to talk to the student next to him.

"Carlos and Danny, get to work."

"In a minute, Miss, I just have to tell Danny something," Carlos said.

They continued to talk, and every few minutes Emily would tell them to get back to work. They ignored her until a student asked Emily for a pass.

"I wish I were white, then I could get a pass whenever I wanted to like Michael. You like those white boys better than us," Carlos yelled across the room.

"Carlos, you want a pass? Take one and go!" Emily said in an exasperated tone.

"Don't you be comin' in my face, Miss. I'll mess you up real bad!"

Emily decided to ignore Carlos. She turned to the class and said, "OK. Is everyone finished with the assignment?" Students nodded, and Emily began a review of the day's lesson. "How long does a mother have in the state of New York to decide if she wants to keep her baby or give it up for adoption?" Emily asked.

"Up to three months from the birth of the child," Tony responded.

"What happens if the mother waits four months and then tries to get her baby back? Before you call out I want the specific case we talked about yesterday." Hands shot up all over the class. Emily was privately congratulating herself on harnessing this class once again when Carlos and Danny erupted into loud rapping and swearing.

"Danny, move up here right now. If you two won't stop talking you can't sit together," Emily said.

"I'll move in a minute," Danny responded.

"I said now, and I mean now. You already have a zero for the day, and your average is falling rapidly. Why do you want to destroy a 92 average?" Emily asked.

"If you give me a zero and my average is lower than a 90, you won't be teaching anywhere next year!"

"Do not threaten me. I am not afraid of you. Move up front now!" Emily's voice was steely calm.

Emily broke her stare at Danny to quickly scan the room. The rest of the students appeared to be upset by the confrontation she was having with Carlos and Danny. She returned her glance to Danny, who after a few seconds broke off their eye contact and seemed through his body language to acquiesce. Although he had not obeyed her command to move, she decided to continue the lesson. "Four months—can I regain custody?" As she scanned the room for volunteers, Emily noticed that Carlos had pulled out a six-inch blade.

It did not occur to her to be afraid. She walked quickly to the back of the room. "Put the knife away immediately!" she told Carlos. As she finished speaking, the bell rang ending the period. He pocketed the weapon, rose nonchalantly, bowed politely in her direction, and walked out.

When the students had left the class, Emily sat down at her desk, feeling frustrated and exasperated. Desmond and Eric, Carlos's friends, came up to Emily to show her that they had done their work. She nodded. "Thanks, guys. I'm not upset with you."

Her comments were interrupted by Carlos yelling from the hallway, "Desmond's a brown nose. Eric has shit on his nose."

Emily waved the students from the room, closed her eyes for a moment, and thought, "How am I going to get through the next two weeks?" As she opened her eyes to smile at the entering third-period students, another thought surfaced. "Have I lost Carlos for good?"

PART SEVEN

Contemporary Teaching Issues

Ellen Norton

A high school teacher whose concern for a shy, underachieving student has caused the student to become her "shadow," learns that another student is being abused at home, and the teacher does not know if she should become involved.

"Hi, Miss Norton. Is this a good time?"

"Sure, Abby. Come on in. Just let me get these things cleared away." Ellen Norton smiled at the slight, dark-haired student who stood at the threshold of the classroom doorway. She stacked the papers she had been grading in order to clear a work space on her desk and made a waving gesture to indicate that Abby should come in.

"Pull up a chair, Abby. How did you do on the problems I gave you yesterday? Did you understand them?"

Rather nondescript in appearance and in behavior, Abby Maxwell impressed Ellen as an average high school sophomore. Abby's family had moved to Littleton recently, and Abby had not made many friends in her new school. She was withdrawn and shy—pleasant enough but always alone.

A few weeks ago, just after the Christmas break, Abby hesitantly approached Ellen for extra help in math. Ellen was touched that the child sought her out for help and tried to make her feel comfortable during their tutoring sessions. She attributed the child's shyness to the typical adolescent hesitancy about interacting with adults and sensed that Abby needed a more mature friend with whom to converse.

"Well, sure, I think I did all right. Here." Abby smiled tentatively as she slid her paper toward Ellen and sat down in the chair she had brought to the front of the room. She sat on its edge and leaned forward toward Ellen to look at the paper with her.

"OK, you had the right idea on the first problem, but you forgot to divide. Remember, to find the area of a triangle, you take half the base times the height. Do you remember why?"

"Oh, sure, I forgot. I guess I was going pretty fast on these," Abby replied. She hesitated and then abruptly changed subjects. "Miss Norton, did you decide to go into teaching when you were in high school?"

Ellen smiled at the question and leaned back in her chair. Abby's increasing tendency to want to discuss subjects other than math and her interest in Ellen's own life were the clues that made Ellen believe that Abby needed an older friend or role model. She knew little of Abby's family life, but she was young enough to remember that universal teenage need to identify with someone older than oneself but less "ancient" than one's parents.

"As a matter of fact, I did, Abby. I had a camp counselor the summer between ninth and tenth grades who taught English during the school year. She sort of befriended me, I guess, and I decided I'd like to make my living the same way."

"Do you like teaching?" Abby seemed encouraged by Ellen's response and began to let down her reserve.

"Very much, Abby. I like working with young people, and I like math. Which reminds me that we should get back to work." As Ellen steered the conversation back on track, she reflected that it was a good thing she liked her job, since she spent so much time at it. Besides teaching math at Littleton High School, Ellen coached the cheerleading squad, chaperoned dances, and volunteered for most extracurricular "duties," particularly those surrounding school sporting or social events. Ellen grew up in a community near Littleton and now lived at home with her widowed mother. She was a bright, attractive 25-year-old, and Littleton High School and her teaching responsibilities consumed a major portion of Ellen's time and energy.

This was Ellen's tenure year. In the Littleton school district, teachers were evaluated throughout their first three years of teaching, and at the end of the third year were either granted tenure or dismissed. Ellen's evaluations since beginning her career had been positive, and she had always been careful to adopt the suggestions her principal did make, so she had little concern about the administration's decision in the spring. Even so, she knew it didn't hurt to make herself as useful outside the classroom as she could. Besides, Ellen had few personal obligations that would compete with her career, since her fiancé, a law student, worked even longer hours than she did.

Ellen and Abby finished their review of Abby's work, and Ellen felt fairly confident that Abby understood the material. "Tomorrow in class we will be starting areas of geometric solids, so it's important that you feel comfortable with this chapter, Abby. Was this helpful?"

"Oh, yes, Miss Norton," replied Abby. "Thanks a lot!" Abby rose and pushed the chair back toward the front row. Ellen also stood and began to fill her briefcase with the papers she had not finished grading. "Are you going home now, Miss Norton?" asked Abby as she observed Ellen's activity.

"No, I'm headed for the gym," said Ellen as she locked the desk. "Cheerleading practice at 3:30." She smiled ruefully as if to minimize the importance of this responsibility. Ellen was always sensitive to the reaction cheerleading evoked in others. Some girls who were not on the squad desperately wished they were, while others thought cheerleading was a ridiculous throwback that mocked every advance feminism had achieved in two decades.

"Oh, can I walk with you? I left my English book in the gym before, and I have to go get it anyway."

"Well, I have to stop by the math department office and do a few other things first. I'll see you tomorrow in class, Abby." Ellen smiled again, and Abby, looking a little disappointed, took her cue and ducked out the door.

Ellen smiled to herself as she headed for the gym. She had felt slightly "crowded" by Abby's interest in accompanying her, but now she thought of Jane Caldwell—the camp counselor—and chuckled aloud. "I used to be poor Jane's shadow," Ellen thought as she took the stairs two at a time. She was a little late.

"Hi, Miss Norton!"

"Hi. Hello." Various greetings echoed through the cavernous gymnasium as Ellen entered through the locker-room door and met her squad. The girls were attired in gym clothes and ready to go.

"Hi, girls, thanks for starting without me. Sorry I'm late. Becky, have you received the schedule yet?"

Becky Kaplan handed Ellen a clipboard and nodded affirmatively. Becky was the captain of the cheerleading squad this year, and Ellen couldn't have asked for a more responsible leader. Becky, a senior, had been on the squad since enrolling at Littleton. Her dependability and her popularity with the other girls made her invaluable to Ellen. She had already covered the schedule of upcoming games with the squad, noting which members couldn't perform and jotting notes about routines in the margins.

As Ellen started the girls on their warm-up exercises, she watched Becky bend and stretch and felt the ache of sympathy swell again. Rumor had it that Becky had been physically abused by both parents since childhood. Her parents were now divorced or separated—Ellen wasn't sure which—and apparently the mother's new boyfriend was no improvement. Sometimes Ellen wondered if she should try to find out more about Becky's status at home; her knowledge was based only on hearsay.

The situation was the basis for gossip among the teaching staff, and Ellen and some of her colleagues had spoken about whether or not they should help or intervene. But Becky never displayed a specific need that would justify district action. She was tardy and absent more than other students, but her schoolwork was not adversely affected. Becky often lingered after practice as though hesitant to go home, but Ellen wasn't sure whether or not she was imagining that.

Last spring, Ellen discovered from another girl on the team that Becky wanted to go to the prom but that, because Becky's parents didn't allow her to date, she had no escort. Ellen enlisted the support of a young male teacher on the staff, and they arranged a date for Becky. Ellen called Becky's mother and explained that the "cheerleading captain-elect" really should be at the prom and that Ellen would be chaperoning. Mrs. Kaplan's reaction was supportive. But beyond this brief interaction, Ellen had no personal knowledge about Becky's home life.

Suddenly Ellen's heart skipped a beat, and she stared at Becky again. "Ten more windmills," she directed. The girls groaned and resumed the exercise they had just finished. As Becky bent at the waist to touch her opposite toe, the shadow Ellen thought she had seen before was clearly visible. Becky's motion bared the skin between her gym shorts and blouse, revealing a dark purple and yellow bruise spread across her waist from hip to rib cage.

Ellen could hardly breathe. "Five laps," she said as the girls finished the exercise. She desperately needed time to collect her thoughts.

"You're kidding!"

"What is this—September?"

"Is she mad at us?"

The girls griped loudly as they raggedly fell into a trot around the gym. Ellen hadn't asked them to do laps since the early days of the school year when conditioning was most important, but she needed the time to think. Suddenly the innuendo and rumor surrounding Becky's situation had become painful reality, and Ellen didn't know what to do.

As the girls ran, Ellen took several deep breaths and forced herself to calm down. "I cannot ignore this," she thought, and with that realization Ellen felt the courage of conviction. She led the girls through the practice she had planned, vowing to draw Becky aside later.

An hour later, as the girls headed toward the locker-room door, Ellen called to Becky, motioning with the clipboard as if she needed her help on a scheduling matter. "Becky, can you help me here?"

Becky turned back from her conversation with another cheerleader and retraced her steps to Ellen. "Come into the office with me a minute, will you, Becky?" asked Ellen.

"Sure." Becky looked puzzled but followed Ellen.

Ellen had developed a comfortable relationship with Becky and the rest of the team in the two years she had been coaching cheerleading. She was a competent coach and physically capable in her own right, and she felt she had earned the girls' respect. Besides, Ellen knew from her own experience that cheerleading was fun, and her youth and attitude were assets when the squad traveled to games on the bus or decorated the boys' locker room on game night. Several of the girls had even tried calling Ellen by her first name. She had resisted the urge to encourage them, but Ellen sometimes did feel as though she had more in common with her students than with her colleagues.

Becky had always seemed slightly aloof from the more raucous team activities, but her relationship with her peers was friendly. Now Ellen wished she knew Becky better personally in order to predict her reaction to the topic at hand. Her courage began to evaporate as she searched for a way to introduce the subject. "Becky, I hope you feel comfortable about coming to me if you need to talk about anything. You're a great asset to me, and I want to help if I can."

Becky looked apprehensive. "Well, thanks, Miss Norton, but I'm OK." Ellen decided to come to the point. "Becky, during warm-ups I couldn't help noticing the bruise on your left side. If you are in danger at home, I think someone should intervene."

Becky gazed at Ellen a moment, as if evaluating alternative responses. Finally she said quietly, "Miss Norton, everything is all right. I fell off my bike on my way home from practice last week."

Ellen was surprised by the matter-of-fact way in which Becky reacted. She had been concerned that her question would embarrass the child, but Becky's expression and tone of voice were calm and emotionless. Suddenly Ellen was the one who was embarrassed, concerned that she had made an improper assumption and reacted to innuendo rather than facts.

"Oh! I'm sorry. I thought. . . . " Ellen knew she was compounding the error. "Never mind, Becky. Please just know that I am here if you need to talk, OK?"

Becky smiled—a little sadly, Ellen thought—and turned to go.

• • •

Ellen looked out her classroom window at the drizzly March afternoon. Her mind wandered back to those first tutoring sessions with Abby Maxwell in early January, and she wondered where she had gone wrong. For in spite of all the extra time she had spent with Abby this semester, the child's performance in math was deteriorating. Abby was making obvious errors on homework assignments and seemed to make deliberate mistakes on tests. In fact, her grades were so bad that Ellen was worried that Abby would fail. Ellen guessed that she would be assigned to teach this class again next year, assuming the tenure decision was positive, and she frankly did not want to have Abby in class again.

Abby's demands on Ellen's time had gradually escalated. For a while, Ellen enjoyed their after-school conversations about teaching, growing up in the area, and math. Abby expressed an interest in cheerleading, and Ellen suggested some summer activities she might pursue to make herself more competitive at the tryouts next fall. Abby seemed so lonely and so buoyed by Ellen's attention that Ellen at first relished the opportunity to help the child adjust to her new community and school. But eventually Abby's constant presence became oppressive. It seemed to Ellen that Abby was everywhere she turned; it was uncanny how the girl could surface at Ellen's every move. She attended dances Ellen chaperoned and games Ellen coached. Abby always came alone to these events and hovered somewhere in Ellen's vicinity. Some of the other teachers began to joke about "Ellen's sidekick" or "the leech." Ellen knew she had a serious problem when Abby began leaving notes on her desk and driving by her house.

"What is it this child wants from me?" Ellen wondered as she watched the rain. Ellen was very worried that in befriending Abby she had encouraged an unhealthy emotional dependency, which she did not know how to sever. Ellen did not want to cause Abby pain, but she desperately wanted to be rid of her. Furthermore, Ellen was sure that Abby's poor performance in math was purposeful, staged in order to justify more tutoring sessions and even a repetition of the class with Ellen next year.

Ellen sighed and packed up for practice. She was anxious for the basketball season to end so that she could close down cheerleading for this year.

As Ellen walked toward the gym, half expecting Abby to appear at every hallway intersection, her thoughts shifted to Becky. Neither Ellen nor Becky had broached the subject of Becky's personal life since their conversation two months ago. Ellen had decided to respect Becky's apparent desire that she mind her own business, and Ellen's worsening situation with Abby made her wary of personal involvement with her students, anyway. Ellen had, however, helped Becky apply to colleges that granted cheerleading scholarships and had written letters of recommendation for her. She knew that Becky had been accepted at a good school in the midwest. "In two months she will graduate and be far from home," thought Ellen, "and I can stop worrying."

As Ellen approached the gym, she was surprised to see Becky standing in the hall outside the locker-room doors.

"Hi, Becky. How's it goin'? Let's get inside. You should be suited up by now," said Ellen. As she got closer to Becky, it seemed to her that the girl was hiding in the shadows created by the locker-room entranceway—*cowering* was the word that came to Ellen's mind.

"Miss Norton, can I ask you a big favor?" Becky whispered in spite of the fact that they were the only two people in the hall.

"Of course, Becky. What is it?"

"Can I go home with you tonight?"

The request caught Ellen totally off guard. She had become so comfortable with the idea that Becky was going to graduate and leave home that she had easily been able to deny the possibility of further danger for the girl. Now she didn't even know what to say. "What's happened, Becky?" Ellen blurted.

"I found out when I went home for lunch that my stepfather lost his job this morning. I think he'll be drinking, and I'm afraid to go home." Having asked her question, Becky was regaining her straightforward manner in spite of the horrible situation she was describing.

"Oh, Becky. I don't think it would be a good idea for me to take you to my home. Let me call the school social worker. She'll know what to do."

"No! Please don't do that, Miss Norton. She'll call the police or someone, and my stepfather will really go nuts. No, I just need to keep out of his way tonight."

Debby Bennett*

An experienced high school English teacher on hall duty during final exams challenges an obstreperous student in the hall without a pass. She is offended by the actions of an assistant principal who cajoles the student into leaving by minimizing his offenses and remarking on her need to "hassle" students.

The academic year was winding down in Stevenson, the large, rural high school where Debby Bennett had been teaching eleventh- and twelfth-grade English for seventeen years. It was June, and the ninth- and tenth-grade English classes were writing the composition portions of their final exams during class time. Those teachers on hall duty in that wing were trying particularly hard, therefore, to keep traffic during classes to a minimum and to reduce noise as much as possible. An unfortunate architectural design common to many schools had dictated that the hallways were also the location of student lockers. Students who arrived late or who had forgotten something were supposed to have hall passes allowing them to go quickly and quietly to their lockers during class time. Debby's assignment during second period each day was to insure that students who appeared in the hall after the late bell had legitimate reasons to be out of class and were going about their business quietly. Over the years, she had begun to believe that it was in the halls, dealing with unfamiliar students, that she had her most disturbing confrontations. In class, she rarely encountered a disciplinary problem that could not be managed; the halls in a school of 1800 students were another story.

In light of this, her approach to hall duty had always been to employ the principles of withitness and selective inattention. She always knew what was going on in the hall, but if students were quiet and orderly and did not appear too frequently, she allowed them to go by unchallenged. Some of her colleagues faulted her for not asking every single student for a pass for the sake of being consistent, but she preferred to treat the vast majority of students as young adults who had legitimate reasons to be in the hall.

On this particular Thursday morning, she glanced up from the student essay she was grading when she heard loud footsteps echoing in the stairwell. She watched the entry area until a young man appeared and walked to a locker directly opposite her desk. He was almost six feet tall, with sandy hair, grey

*Developed by Mara Goldstone and Janet Stivers, Marist College.

eyes, ruddy complexion, a moustache, and a day's growth of beard, all of which made him look much older than most students, even seniors. She didn't think she had ever seen him before. Reaching his locker, he started pounding on the door in an attempt to force it open.

Still seated, she quietly said, "Excuse me, but could you please be a little more quiet? There are final exams being given today."

The student ignored her, not even glancing in her direction or acknowledging that she had addressed him. Darlene Curtis, a special education resource room teacher who had been walking toward Debby, stopped near the desk. Debby, thinking that Darlene had come over to talk with her, threw her a look to say, "Just let me finish with this and I'll be right with you." The locker pounding continued as she approached the student.

"Excuse me, but do you have a pass?"

"I'm getting somethin' outta my locker."

"Yes, I see that," she replied, in what she hoped was a reasonable tone, "but do you have permission to be here? Where did you come from?"

"Social studies. My social studies teacher told me to get my book. She didn't give me no pass."

"I'm sorry, but you know the rules. If you have no pass, you have to go back to your class and get one."

"Mrs. Klein told me to get my book. I'm gettin' it."

This last comment was thrown over his shoulder in what seemed to Debby a very defiant manner. All the while the locker was clanging and rattling. The thought of the number of classes being disturbed worried her; the reality of Darlene Curtis watching as her authority was defied embarrassed her. She sensed that she was about to escalate the situation into a confrontation. Just as she was going to challenge the student, reinforcement appeared in the form of Fred Arnold, a vice principal. "Ah, thank goodness!" she thought as she relaxed and breathed a sigh of relief. She folded her arms and calmly waited until Mr. Arnold stood within hearing. All the while, Darlene Curtis stood by silently. The student, looming larger and more threatening, slammed books around inside the now open locker.

"Mr. Arnold," she said, "I need your help here. This boy . . . ."

"Who the hell are you calling 'boy'? I ain't a boy, you stupid . . . ."

Mr. Arnold stepped toward the student at once with a hearty smile and a hail-fellow-well-met air. He said, "Calm down here. Mrs. Bennett just wants to see your pass. She has to do that. It's her job."

Although the student continued to do exactly as he pleased by searching the locker, Debby felt relieved that the potential confrontation was over. Mr. Arnold seemed to know the boy; he was intervening in a nonthreatening manner, but in support of her position.

The student, having found his social studies book, turned to leave. In a loud voice he demanded of the vice principal, "What does she want from me? I had to get my book. Mrs. Klein sent me out without a pass. Tell her to leave me the hell alone."

Debby turned to Mr. Arnold, a kind-hearted man whose habitual expression that Debby read as "please like me" revealed how much he hated to reprimand anyone. At the moment, however, that look was focused on the student.

In a cajoling, conciliatory voice he said, "Mrs. Bennett has to do this. We tell her to do this. It's her job to hassle kids."

Debby's jaw dropped open. "Excuse me," she wanted to shout at Mr. Arnold. "What did you say?"

The student headed for the door, and no one tried to stop him. As he gained the stairs he shouted, and the words echoed in the stair well, "Just tell her to get off my back."

While Debby stood there, stunned, Darlene Curtis spoke for the first time. "His name is Scott Gould. He's one of my students. He has a long history of aggressive behavior and so did his older brother. They're both prone to violence when they're angry, which is most of the time."

Debby thought, "Well, thanks a lot for your help," as she turned back to the vice principal. "Is this where it's going to end?" she asked.

He hesitated, obviously considering what to say, then replied, "You **could** write him up, if you wanted to."

"**I** could write him up? Don't you see that he walked away feeling justified?"

"What do you mean? He left without a problem."

"He left thinking that he was right. Do you really think that my job here is to **hassle** kids? If you really believe that, I won't do this job. I don't **hassle** kids!"

"Oh, you English teachers. It's just a word. I use it all the time with kids."

"Well, I don't think you should. By using that word you validate his experience. He walked away believing that he had been needlessly *hassled* by a stupid teacher."

"No, he didn't. He didn't take it that way at all."

Debby struggled to control her temper by changing the subject. "Well, what about the social studies teacher? Are you going to remind her that all students need passes?"

"I will if you think I should. You decide. I'll do whatever you think is right."

Suddenly, the silent resource room teacher wanted to get chatty and reveal in gruesome detail all the crimes and violations in the Gould family history. Mercifully, the bell rang. Debby glared at her, turned, and stalked away.

She was stung by Fred Arnold's use of the term "English Teacher," which she felt had been used as an insult. But she was more angry that her concern about a student's behavior had been contemptuously dismissed as an argument about semantics. As she walked back to her classroom, she wondered if Fred Arnold could be right. Was it true that only an English teacher would be offended by the term "hassle" used to describe the purpose of hall duty?

Kate Sullivan

A principal faces the problems endemic to the students served by her school, which is located in a very low socioeconomic area. Issues of drugs, poverty, neglect, hunger, and homelessness are compounded by the underfunding for the school.

For a few minutes before school each morning, Kate Sullivan walked through the playground at North Hills Elementary School, talking with students and enjoying the youthful commotion. Her walks through the yard gave Kate the chance to mix with the students in a way that she still found reassuring after seventeen years as principal of the school. The walks also provided the students with a chance to talk to her about the issues in their young lives.

On this Monday morning early in spring, Kate's gaze across the playground was arrested by a handful of fourth-grade boys playing an unfamiliar game in a corner of the yard. Kate watched for a minute, then walked briskly toward them, nodding acknowledgements to a score of greetings and tugs at her sleeves as she cut through to the boys.

The boys shouted their own greetings as Kate approached, making no attempt to hide the crack vials they were passing among themselves. Several of the boys also held $20 and $50 bills.

"Gentlemen," Kate said, trying to catch the breath she had lost not from the dash across the playground but from the shock of her discovery. "What is this? I want these capsules. All of them. Where did you get these? Whose money is this?"

The boys only shuffled and collectively shrugged their shoulders. As she began to collect the vials, Kate realized with considerable relief that the vials were filled with chalk powder and that the boys had only been playing at being drug dealers. But the cash was real. A few questions more, and Kate traced the bills to the pockets of Miguel Aurillio, who had recently immigrated with his family from Mexico.

Kate instructed the boys to report to her office after school for a discussion about the seriousness of their game. She then took Miguel gently by the shoulder and steered him toward the building. "Miguel, you come with me. I want to discuss this large amount of money with your mother."

Miguel's command of English was superficial at best, and he knew to follow Kate more from her gesture than her words. Once through the hectic outer office and inside Kate's cramped but organized inner office, Kate called Miguel's home.

Miguel seemed to realize as she was on the telephone that Kate was calling his mother. Kate was not fluent in Spanish, but she had learned, out of obvious necessity, enough of the language to call parents to school conferences. Her intermittent use of Spanish words was enough to render Miguel distinctly uncomfortable.

While they waited for someone from Miguel's household to show up, the child fidgeted nervously in his chair. Kate offered him one of the several storybooks written in Spanish which she kept in her office, and she left him in order to attend to a few of the myriad details and minor complications that accompanied every new school day.

"¿Dónde está mi hijo?" Kate had been conferring with her secretary about morning announcements before picking up the microphone to lead the pledge, but she turned abruptly at the commotion created when a large, swarthy man burst through the outer office door, followed by two young men who resembled Miguel. The three men approached the two women, who were standing behind the counter that divided the employees' working space from a waiting area.

"Are you Miguel's father?" Kate asked quietly. The man clearly did not understand her; he barely seemed to hear her. He glanced around the room and, seeing the hinged gate in the counter, barged through toward Kate's office. The men, whom Kate took to be Miguel's brothers, followed.

"Louise, call Emilio and Barry," called Kate over her shoulder as she followed Mr. Aurillio toward Miguel, referring to the school security guard and the chief custodian. She knew she would need some help translating, and she hoped she would not need help protecting Miguel.

Even though he had only been a few steps ahead of her, by the time Kate reached her office Mr. Aurillio had Miguel on his feet and was gripping him roughly by his shirt collar. "¿Qué diablo crees que estás haciendo? ¿Dónde está el dinero?" Miguel only looked terrified and glanced pleadingly toward the two other men, who assumed positions at the door.

Kate's ignorance of Spanish was no handicap; the language of anger and retribution was universal. Kate had seen too many confrontations between parents and children, and she intervened immediately and without hesitation. Her gray hair and slight frame belied her determination to protect her students. She knew just how to buy time until Emilio and Barry arrived.

Purposefully, Kate stepped right up to Mr. Aurillio and the cowering Miguel, putting her face as close to the father's as she could given the one-foot discrepancy in height. She placed her left hand gently atop the father's hand, which was holding Miguel almost off the floor. Kate could not see what the two younger men were doing, but she hoped they were standing still.

"Put him down, Mr. Aurillio," Kate commanded softly, but with all the authority she could muster. "Put him down. We will talk." Mr. Aurillio seemed surprised that Kate would confront him so boldly, and he relaxed his grip more in response to this novelty than because he understood Kate's command. The instant she felt his grip relax, she pushed Miguel back into the chair and stepped between father and son.

Then she smiled. "Would you sit down, Mr. Aurillio?" Kate indicated another chair with an outstretched hand. "Siéntese." As she spoke, the school security guard, Emilio Sanchez, appeared at the door, and Kate breathed an inward sigh of relief.

"Hello, Emilio. Will you translate? First, introductions, please." As Emilio began one of the many responsibilities he performed outside his formal job description, Miguel's father sat down uncomfortably, and Kate moved to lean on the edge of her desk. She did not want any furniture separating her from this child.

The conversation that followed was a halting one, as Emilio translated between Kate, Mr. Aurillio, and Miguel, who held his chin against his chest and offered whispered, monosyllabic replies. The men in the doorway, whom introductions had established were indeed Miguel's older brothers, did not say a word. It was apparent to Kate that everyone was now lying and that Mr. Aurillio, although perfectly aware of the source of Miguel's wealth, was feigning ignorance. Finally, Kate asked Emilio to tell Mr. Aurillio that his son should not carry large sums of money in school, for the sake of order in the school and his own safety. Mr. Aurillio departed with a withering glance at his youngest son when Emilio escorted the three men out of the school.

Kate looked at Miguel with sympathy when they were alone. "¿Como te sientes?" She pulled a chair close to the child and touched his hand. He withdrew his hand reflexively and looked at the floor. After a quiet moment Kate stood and pulled Miguel to his feet with a gentle hand on his elbow. "Come, I'll walk you to class."

Kate returned from escorting Miguel and sat at her desk to complete the paperwork she had begun with Louise. From the window of her third-floor office, Kate had a clear view across the playground at North Hills and past the chain link fence that encircled it. Beyond the fence, looking south, Kate could scan the leaking rooftops and broken windows of the low-rise tenements of the neighborhoods that surrounded the school, built on the hills that gave the city its name. To the north, she could see down the city's broad commercial avenues, the arteries of a once vigorous business district that over the last decade had been drained by drugs and violence and the intense poverty of the community's disintegrating families.

At her desk every morning by seven o'clock, Kate often watched the prostitutes and drug dealers end their night's work only a half hour or so before the first school buses began rolling down the avenues on their way to her school. Against this inner-city backdrop, Kate and ninety other teachers, administrators, and support staff worked to teach 1300 children how to read and write and add and subtract, and how to defend themselves against the despair, neglect, and violence that broke like a wave at the doors of their homes and school.

The slow decline of North Hills began in the early 1970s, when a massive cooperative housing development designed to provide home ownership for middle-class families opened in a nearby suburb. The development drained North Hills of its middle class. In its place came a steady influx of immigrants from the Caribbean islands, Asia, and Eastern and Central Europe, fleeing poverty, natural disasters, or dictatorship. The new families, many with five or six children, placed enormous new demands on the city and its schools over the decade that followed. Many went on public assistance. Homes and apartments were subdivided and subdivided again to provide space in the crunch for cheap housing. North Hills's enrollment swelled to 500 over its design capacity. Nearly a quarter of the students in North Hills entered kindergarten speaking little English. Most of their parents spoke even less.

In the early 1980s, a public hospital opened a block from the school, attracting the city's poorest health-care clients and hastening the middle-class exodus. But the most devastating blow to North Hills came only a few years ago, when crack appeared on the streets. The crack epidemic finalized the middle-class flight from North Hills and helped to complete the city's transformation: North Hills was now 50 percent Hispanic, 20 percent black, 20 percent Asian, and 10 percent white.

Many businesses and industries followed the middle class out as the neighborhood deteriorated, taking jobs and tax revenues to the suburbs. Although state aid was increased to help the school district compensate for the loss of commercial tax revenues, the increase was never enough. The school districts in the wealthy suburban towns near North Hills were spending an average of $14,000 a year educating each pupil; in North Hills the expenditure per pupil was less than half that sum.

As a result, its teachers had become among the area's lowest-paid and worked in some of its most crowded classrooms. Most textbooks were ten or fifteen years old. Broken windows and leaking ceilings often took months to repair. The school's interior had gone eighteen years without paint.

A less visible but more ominous result of the poverty, and the one at the front of Kate's mind once she resolutely shed her thoughts of Miguel, was that both attendance rates and standardized test results had dropped significantly over the last several years. Kate had received the results of the most recent state standardized tests for elementary schools only two weeks ago. They showed that the steady decline in the North Hills's scores was continuing. In just over a decade, the scores had dropped from the top quarter to the bottom tenth of elementary schools in the state in nearly every category. Fewer than a third of North Hills's students were reading at grade level.

Kate withdrew her eyes and attention from the depressing cityscape below her window and turned to the business of running her school. Impatient with paperwork, she rose to make one of her several daily laps around the hallways before stopping in, casually, to observe a new teacher and then returning to finalize her thoughts about attendance rates and test scores in preparation for her meeting late that afternoon. Peter Warren, the North Hills school superintendent and Kate's boss, had received a request soon after the release of the damning state scores, suggesting a meeting between Peter, Kate, and officials from the state education department. Years of experience had taught her to be well prepared with facts and figures for any conversation with those bureaucrats.

• • •

After leading Nason Burns, the state education department's deputy commissioner for instruction, on a half-hour tour of the school, Peter Warren and Kate ushered him into Kate's spartan office. Each took a seat around Kate's desk, Nason settling where frightened Miguel had cowered a few hours earlier. He opened a briefcase and removed computer printouts of the test scores and attendance records. Kate leaned across her desk to flick on a countertop coffee machine. Nason was the first to speak.

"I think I have a good understanding of what you're trying to cope with here," Nason said, shifting his glance from Peter to Kate. "Your staff seems to be responding admirably against tremendous odds."

Kate's smile masked her skepticism; she had heard flattering remarks before. "Thank you, Nason. I am proud of my people. What questions do you have, now that you've seen our school?"

Nason leaned back in his chair. "Well, I am curious about a few things I saw. For example, I know that we gave you a special exemption so that you could convert your library and gymnasium to classroom space, but I think we still require some type of physical education and library programs."

"We're complying, of course, Nason," Kate said. "We've kept on a phys-ed teacher, who leads stretching and calisthenics over the public address system for ten minutes each morning. He held gym classes in the courtyard in warmer weather until two years ago, when we needed the space to build the eleven portable classrooms that you saw on our tour. Now we hold phys-ed in the cafeteria, when it's not taken by one of our six lunch sessions. And we have a rolling library, on carts, that visits each of our classrooms at least once a week."

Kate paused for a moment, then added, "But I think your question leads us to an excellent place to start our discussion—the issue of overcrowding. It's our most serious problem now. It is the root of a lot of our problems. A formula for failure."

Peter, as if on cue, opened a folder in his lap and leaned forward in his chair toward the deputy commissioner. "Here's a state policy regulation that we are violating. The cap for early childhood classes, K–3, is twenty-eight children. We've had as many as thirty-seven in a K–3 class. Here's another reg we come close to violating: We can't have regular classes meet in the halls. We don't, but several special programs do meet in the halls. The ESL program meets at the east end of the fourth-floor corridor. One of our remedial reading programs meets at the west end."

"That might help to explain some of these scores," Nason said, holding up a stack of printouts.

"Indeed, I think it does," Peter said. "It also might help you to understand why attendance is dropping so steadily here. And it's not just the remedial kids who are suffering because of what's happening to this school, to this city. You saw what had been our gym. Now, it's four third-grade classrooms, separated from each other by file cabinets and blackboards and the will of our teachers."

Kate picked up the day's attendance sheets from her desk. "One hundred twenty third-graders were in the classes in the gym today, Nason," she said. "Could you even hear yourself think above the din when you walked through it? And it's getting worse! Since the school year began we've enrolled forty-four students, half of them from overseas—from Haiti, Vietnam, Liberia, Lebanon, Russia. Wherever there is a problem in the world—a hurricane, an earthquake, a war, a coup d'état—families leave and end up here. When they come, they bring their problems: poverty, transience, family violence, chaotic home life."

"Tell me about the families, the parents," Nason interjected. "What are you doing to work with them?"

"We have two types of parents at North Hills, Nason. We have parents who truly love their children and want the best for them. Unfortunately, many of them can't work with us. Sometimes it's because both mother and father work long hours, as secretaries, clerks, drivers, hospital orderlies, city employees. Sometimes it's because it's just a mother at home who's got five or six kids and feels overwhelmed. Sometimes it's because neither parent speaks English."

Kate rose to pour some coffee as she continued; she didn't need her notes to recite the grim facts of her school and her life. "Here are some more statistics for you, Nason. Seventy percent of our students were born outside the United States, or were born to parents who were. One in five of our students is in ESL or bilingual classes. And 90 percent of our students are eligible for a free or reduced-cost lunch."

"You mentioned two types of parents," Nason interrupted. "What's the second?"

"Parents who are indifferent, or who continually work against us."

"What do you mean?"

Kate did not have to reach far back in her memory to illustrate her point. "Here's an example," she replied. "Miguel Aurillio is one of our most troubled students, a symbol of all in this school and community that is failing these children. He's on my mind because he was in this office just this morning. Often Miguel comes to school without having eaten and too late to receive the free breakfast he is entitled to. I worry that the federally subsidized lunch he receives here—the slabs of stale ham and surplus cheese between two slices of crust, with ketchup as his vegetable—is his most solid meal of the day. His teacher tells me that he comes to class every day without his homework or even a pencil or notebook, but with his pockets stuffed with gum and candy. I don't think he owns a winter jacket. And today I discovered that his father has him somehow involved with his cocaine business."

"What are you doing about that?" Nason asked.

"Worrying," Kate answered bluntly. "I have no proof—just a frightened little boy, an angry, almost violent father, and large-denomination bills in the hands of a 10-year-old."

"Well, how do you handle children from these problem homes in general?" Nason persisted. Kate could not prevent a private thought that this "expert" from upstate wasn't one.

"Nason, we try to teach them to read and write." Kate knew that the weariness of her day was reflected in her tone. "And while we do that, we work on their anger and, most especially, their self-esteem. These children are damaged by failure and by their home situations. They don't see themselves as learners and they don't see the point in becoming educated. We begin with a student like Miguel by being accepting, nurturing, and patient, and we go from there. We also try to keep our eyes open and to protect them.

"So, for $30,000 a year, teachers here have to be psychologists, social workers, and even substitute parents. The role of this school and its teachers has had to evolve as the community has changed. A lot of the responsibilities of the parents have been passed onto us. In the meantime, teachers start at $40,000 a year just half an hour north of here, in Raddison—a lovely, wealthy suburb." Kate ignored Peter's warning frown; she knew he thought she was overdoing it. But she didn't miss a beat: "We rarely have our pick of the best teachers, but still we have a staff I'm proud of."

"I admire your loyalty to them," Nason said. "But you know you're not alone in this. We have increased state aid to this district beyond what our formulas normally permit. And as for your teachers, I think you know that the federal government designated North Hills as a district where new teachers get a portion of their student loans forgiven for every year they teach here."

"Of course I know that, and we are grateful for it," Kate said. "And I know that we have a governor and a legislature that dole out special grants to impoverished schools piecemeal, yet refuse to make fundamental changes in the way education is funded so that we can eliminate the inequities between districts like North Hills and Raddison." Kate saw peripherally that Peter was really uncomfortable now.

Nason, too, seemed frustrated. He shifted in his chair and looked pointedly at his watch. "Mrs. Sullivan, our dialogue has to be more constructive if we are to help you in what you're trying to do here. I'm concerned that your focus is too much on the problems facing North Hills and too little on the programs in place to deal with them. I want to know how you intend to get these test scores up and deal with this atrocious attendance."

Kate looked at Peter with an openly incredulous gaze, as if to say, "This idiot hasn't heard a word I have said." To Nason, she replied tersely, "What sort of program might you suggest, Mr. Burns?"

"I have another appointment in thirty minutes," Nason said. "Obviously we need to talk a good deal more, particularly about exactly how you're dealing with the issues we discussed today. But before we meet again, I'd like a report from you outlining exactly that—how you're attempting to cope. Specifically, I want to know how your classroom teachers are dealing with all this—the overcrowding, the poverty, the language barriers." Nason snapped shut his briefcase, computer printouts safely inside, and reached for his suit jacket as he spoke. Suddenly, Kate felt like weeping as she realized that once again her paperwork had been increased, and the assistance she desperately needed was nonexistent. But seventeen years of experience had taught her to behave with dignity and control.

"Certainly, Nason. We are responding actively to the environment here, but I felt strongly that you could not appreciate our priorities until you were fully informed of our problems. When would you like this report?" Peter Warren seemed to relax as Kate resumed her bureaucratic facade.

"Is a month unreasonable?" Nason, too, seemed relieved to be back on comfortable ground rather than conversing about violence, drugs, and ketchup.

"Fine," Kate smiled as she held out her hand. She realized that one more month would put them within four weeks of summer recess, and that the report, and her requests for resources, would find a safe haven in a filing cabinet.

Nason and Peter left together for their car. Kate knew that Nason hadn't wanted to drive alone through the school's neighborhood and so had met Peter at district headquarters. Kate heard laughter and shuffling as she stood in the outer office and suddenly remembered the boys who had been pretending to deal drugs this morning. They were waiting in the hallway to meet with her. As she ushered them into her office, she looked out her window to the playground below and city beyond. The afternoon was turning overcast and gray; a slight drizzle had begun to fall. Kate looked down to the concrete play yard and saw Miguel, sitting alone on a broken bench.

Chris Kettering

A first-year high school social studies teacher finds to his dismay that his white, middle-class students are uninterested in becoming involved in social activism and suffer from narrow-mindedness.

Chris shut the classroom door immediately after the third-period bell rang; his students knew that his prompt action meant he would begin the class right away rather than let them take a minute to settle in. He walked into the middle of the semicircle of desks, where he usually stood to teach the class; quickly scanned the group of twenty-one seniors; and raised his voice a bit, as he always did when he began.

"How many of you know someone who has died from AIDS?"

Whatever quiet chatter there had been in the classroom stopped. After a moment, a few students shifted in their seats. Several looked around. No hands went up.

"That's good," Chris said, looking over the row of startled faces. He thought that for the first time in the ten weeks he'd been teaching this course, he had everyone's attention. "How many of you know anyone who has AIDS now?"

More silence. Several more students turned their heads to see if any hands were going up. None did. "We have a very lucky group of people in this room," Chris said.

"We're going to begin the second unit of this course today. We spent the first ten weeks researching and proposing solutions to what we've called 'public policy issues'—apartheid, the death penalty, abortion, teenage pregnancy. While we were researching and writing, several of you asked me why, if this course is called 'Participation in Government,' you weren't *doing* anything. You asked when you would start participating. The answer to that question is *today*.

"We spent ten weeks researching public policy problems so that we would have an understanding of what they are and how people work to solve them. For the next several weeks, we are going to take a few small public policy problems and work on them, not on paper but in real life. I have some ideas for projects we can work on. I want your ideas too."

Chris glanced around the semicircle at his students. They were looking at him curiously. He continued, "Obviously, we can't solve the AIDS epidemic.

But there is an annual walkathon that raised $3 million last year to help fight AIDS. I called the people who organize the walk, and they told me that twenty-five high schools sent teams last year, and they expect even more this year. Abbott Tech had the largest team last year. They sent about sixty students and teachers, and their team raised $5000."

Chris took a deep breath and continued. "I'd like to see this high school send a team to the walk this year. It's on Sunday, May 20. It's not too early to start planning for this, because all the projects will require a lot of work. We'll need to get the administration's approval for the things we decide to do, arrange for publicity in the school, figure out transportation . . . ."

Chris scanned the room again and felt he still had his students' attention, although he wasn't sure he had their interest. He glanced at the clock and saw he had thirty minutes remaining in the period, plenty of time to describe the other projects that the students could choose from to meet the participation requirement for the course. Among them, he suggested running a voter registration drive, designing and implementing a program to collect wastepaper from classrooms and offices for recycling, and organizing a Saturday morning footrace to raise money for the school's athletic department. He talked about the tasks that would have to be done in each of the projects.

There were five minutes left in the period when Chris finished, enough time to gauge his students' interest and to tell them to come to class the next day with their own ideas for projects. He answered a few questions and then asked students to indicate their preference for the projects discussed so far by a show of hands. They divided pretty evenly among three of the four projects. No one chose the AIDS walk.

Thirty minutes later, Chris was seated in the school's main office waiting for his appointment with Steve Helms, the principal at Fallstown High School. He'd need Helms's approval to go ahead with any of the projects in his government class. Waiting for the meeting, Chris went over his thoughts about the class. He was glad for the interest the students had shown for three of the projects, but he was disappointed that there had been no interest in the AIDS walk.

Chris found some clues about his class's response as he watched the faculty and student traffic move through the main office while he waited. The Fallstown school district was 98 percent white and solidly middle-class. Besides teaching the senior government class, Chris had three ninth-grade global studies classes at the high school and was an assistant coach on the school's track team. In all, he taught or coached 170 students, about 10 percent of the high school's enrollment. In his classrooms and at track practice, Chris's face was the only black one.

The town of Fallstown was insulated, Republican, and Roman Catholic. Although the town was located midway between two major cities in the northeast, about 50 miles from each, it remained mostly untouched by the social ills that had plagued its urban neighbors throughout the recent decades. Schools in the nearby cities were being overrun by crack and other cheap cocaine derivatives, but other than discussions about drinking and driving, school officials expressed little concern about drug abuse at Fallstown.

The town wasn't wealthy, but neither was there much poverty. Its small homeless population was housed in a handful of motel rooms, all of them out of town. Only one or two AIDS cases had been reported by local health officials. Indeed, the greatest threat to public health in Fallstown was the deer tick and the Lyme disease it carried.

The high school's curriculum was an indicator of the community's conservatism. English teachers long ago gave up trying to teach *Catcher in the Rye* because of the annual battle that would result with parents. *The Christian Science Monitor, USA Today,* and *The National Review* were available in the school library. *The New York Times, The Nation,* and *The New Republic* were not. The sex-education courses were the minimum required by the state and were taught separately to boys and girls. A well-attended Christian fundamentalist school in the town competed with the Fallstown public schools for students, a fact that department heads and administrators were keenly aware of when they planned curriculum.

Watching the stream of white faces and fashionably dressed bodies flow through the main office while he waited for his meeting, Chris thought of his own contrasting background. He was born and raised in the Red Hook section of Brooklyn. He earned a bachelor's degree from Howard University in Washington, D.C., and a graduate degree from Columbia University in New York. He spent seven years covering urban issues for a newspaper just outside New York; then he left the paper two years ago, thinking he could have more of an impact by teaching in a high school than by writing in a newsroom. This was his first year of teaching.

Chris knew a handful of people who were sick with AIDS or had died from it. Some of them he'd met while writing about AIDS; others were friends from college or graduate school or from the newspaper. Recalling them, Chris increased his resolve to have a group of his government students organize a team to do the AIDS walk. His thoughts were interrupted as Mr. Helms opened his office door and greeted Chris, waving him in.

• • •

"No."

"No?"

"I'm sorry, Chris," Mr. Helms said, leaning forward over his desk and taking off his glasses. "No. It's not a good idea. There's too much that will need to be done. You wouldn't be covered by the district's insurance policy because the walk takes place more than 40 miles away. And the transportation department schedules weekend buses the semester before. Besides all that, the school board doesn't meet again until May 21, four weeks from Monday. When is this walk?"

"It's on a Sunday. May 20."

"Well, that settles it, I'm afraid. The board reviews all requests for field trips, and this walk occurs before the board's next meeting. I'm sorry."

"Doesn't the board usually have work sessions between its regular meetings? Couldn't we present it to the board members then? Or couldn't we poll them by phone about this?"

"I don't think this is the kind of thing we should call board members at home about."

"OK. That's understandable. Could we call them at work?"

"You're missing my point, Chris. They wouldn't support you on this. I know this district, these parents. I know this school board. And I know these students. They won't support you."

"I'd like to give my students the opportunity to say so themselves, Mr. Helms. With your permission, I'd at least like to raise the possibility of the trip."

"How do your students feel about doing this walk, Chris?"

"Honestly, at this point, there's not much support for it."

"I didn't think there would be. So why are you pushing it?"

"Because I think I can build support for it."

"I don't think you'll get anywhere with this, Chris. I'm only trying to save you frustration."

"I appreciate that, Mr. Helms, but I'd like my students to be able to decide for themselves."

"Go ahead, Chris, if you feel that strongly about the issue. But I want you to know that I'll be talking to the superintendent today about it. I'm sure she'll agree with me that the board shouldn't be contacted."

"I don't understand, Mr. Helms. You said there would be a problem scheduling a bus to take us to the walk, but you said there wouldn't be a problem scheduling a school bus to operate as a shuttle for our Saturday morning run through town to raise money for the athletic department. And why is insurance a problem when students are walking a few miles in the city but not when they're running 5 miles against traffic on Route 47?"

"You're right, Chris. I don't think you understand. Let me be more clear: This is a very conservative community."

"Conservative? What's conservative got to do with this? We're talking about raising money to fight a fatal disease."

Mr. Helms leaned forward over his desk again, and his voice dropped almost to a whisper. "To this community, it's more than that," he said. Holding his eyes on Chris, he slowly leaned back in his chair. "I think you should drop the idea."

Chris gathered his papers and nodded a good-bye. He walked hurriedly from the office, feeling his resolve to do this walk increase once again.

• • •

Later in the afternoon, Chris had lunch in the faculty room with Larry Timber, a union representative and one of Chris's first friends among the faculty. "This isn't how teachers get tenure, Chris, at Fallstown or anywhere," said Larry. "This walk isn't worth it."

"What's tenure worth if you don't have some freedom in your classroom?"

"Tenure for you will be worth about $40,000 a year to start," Larry said. "And academic freedom comes with tenure, not before it. Wait a year, Chris. Then do the walk."

"One million people have this virus, Larry. Even in this county, out here a long way from anywhere, a few people have died. I don't think anybody should be talking about waiting. I think the least this school can do is send a busload of kids to this walk."

"But your kids don't want to do it. You said that yourself. More important for you, Helms doesn't want it. The school board won't touch it."

"Maybe I can change their minds. Maybe this is a chance to educate people, especially my students, about this disease. I feel that's my job. I'm a teacher."

"You're a first-year teacher without any job protection. Push this and Helms will see that the only walk you'll take will be out the front door forever in June. And there aren't many social studies jobs out there. Have you forgotten how hard it was to find a teaching job last fall? Don't be strident about this, Chris. Take Helms's advice. You want to walk? Do the March of Dimes walk. Or have the kids organize a bake sale or a car wash. Damn it, that's what the other government teachers have their classes do."

Chris started to laugh. "Look at me, Larry. I'm not exactly like the other teachers. You know, in a funny way, Helms did me a favor when he turned this idea down. He's helping me make this an object lesson in the political process. I'll bet his rejection of the idea will jump-start my kids' interest in the walk, even though I couldn't get them going. And it could be a great lesson: They'll learn how to oppose the system while working within it. The only way I'll give up on this is if my kids absolutely reject it. I really think I have to go with this now."

"I hope the students aren't interested, Chris," Larry said. "For your sake."

● ● ●

The door to Chris's government class swung shut again at the sound of the bell. Chris walked to the semicircle and handed a student twenty-one copies of a newspaper column written by a reporter Chris had worked with for several years before he left the newspaper to teach. As the article was being passed around, Chris asked one of the students to read it aloud.

"I lost my brother eleven days ago," Liana began. "He died of AIDS. A year ago today we were together in my car, inching through Easter traffic on the West Side Highway. We were headed home to see my parents. We sat in silence, our small talk swallowed in the blackness of my chest."

The column described the impact of AIDS on one man and his family. Chris had chosen it because, expecting that none of his students would know anyone with AIDS, he hoped it would help them put a face on one of its victims.

Chris moved back into the semicircle of desks as Liana continued reading. "So much has happened in the last year," she read, looking up occasionally at Chris. "My brother died on March 15, at the age of 31. Much of what we all experienced, of course, was horrible. AIDS is most cruel, not only in its indifference to youth but in how it inflicts an endless succession of scourges. Strength goes first, then flesh, then sight or reason—a vibrant person deactivated, one plug at a time. In a condensed span of months, my brother suffered a lifetime's pain and indignity.

"My brother is but one of more than 70,000 who have died of AIDS. Tens of thousands are now suffering as he did. Tens of thousands of families are suffering as we did. And the toll of this epidemic is only beginning."

Liana put the article down and looked at Chris, tears glistening in her eyes. Chris leaned against a desk and drew a breath, bracing himself for the forty minutes to follow.

"I met with Mr. Helms yesterday to get his approval for the projects we'll be doing, and he gave his okay to all of them except one. He said we couldn't organize a team for the AIDS walk. He said the school board wouldn't approve the project, and he said the community is so conservative that we couldn't get any backing. I know there wasn't much support in class yesterday for doing the walk, but let me ask a theoretical question: If we decide that we want the AIDS walk to be one of our choices, would it be our duty as citizens of the school community to try to change Mr. Helms's mind or to try to find some way to work around him?"

Liana spoke up first. "He can't stop us from doing this if we want to do it. We can do it on our own outside school."

"We could, Liana," Chris responded, "but the issue is doing it inside the school, as a project of this class, as a part of the school system."

Mike spoke up next. "Well, some of us could meet with Mr. Helms ourselves, or we could have our parents call him."

"Good suggestions," Chris said, marveling at how easy this was. "Could we do anything else?"

"We could go to the members of the school board. They could tell Mr. Helms to let us do this."

"All right. Possibly we could do all those things. But before we go to the board, we have to go to the superintendent, Dr. Hawthorne. We'll need to call or write to her asking for an appointment. Let's form a small group to do that. Who wants to be part of it?"

A long silence ensued.

"Anyone? Liana? Mike? What's the problem? I thought you were interested in this."

Another silence followed, broken after a minute by a voice tinged with sarcasm. "Thanks for the invitation, but I'm not walking next to any diseased faggots."

"Ron? I'm sorry, what did you say?"

"Those people have done it to themselves," Ron said. "Let them die. Or let somebody else save them. Besides that, it would be against my religion to raise money for those people. Look in the Bible. It says homosexuality is a sin. Sinners should be punished. They're getting what they deserve."

"Those are very strong words, Ron," Chris responded. "There may be others who feel differently." He scanned the semicircle. "What about the rest of you? I'm sure you don't all agree with Ron on this."

Greg spoke up next. "I think it would be dangerous. If we spent a morning with these AIDS guys, couldn't we get it? If we walk next to them, we'll probably brush against them. They're all sick and sneezing. I don't want to breathe that. No thanks. Put me down for the recycling drive."

Several students began speaking, all of them seconding Ron and Greg. Chris let his students talk, hopeful that the remarks would be self-correcting, that others more informed about AIDS would speak up and point out the inaccuracies. But after five minutes, when no one did, Chris cut off the exchange, afraid that the students' fear and misinformation would spread and destroy any chance of doing the walk.

He walked back to the center of the semicircle, angry that he had not been better prepared for this despite all the signals the day before that indicated the discussion might go this way. Under his breath, he cursed the school's health teachers for doing such a miserable job on AIDS education. "Before we go any further, I think I need to correct some misconceptions about AIDS so that we can have a more meaningful discussion," he said.

Chris spent the next ten minutes talking about how AIDS is spread, emphasizing that it is impossible to contract it by bumping into someone with the disease or breathing the same air as an infected person. He spent a few minutes more discussing the communities hardest hit by the disease.

He completed what had become a lecture by saying, "AIDS doesn't affect just homosexuals and drug addicts, although I think your perception that it does explains your reluctance to do the walk. Two thousand children under 5 years old have died from AIDS. Before a test was developed to screen the blood supply, half the hemophiliacs in America had AIDS. Think about Ryan White, the teenager from Indiana, who died, and all those celebrities went to his funeral. Did he deserve to be punished?"

Chris then distributed twenty-one copies of a brochure describing AIDS and the AIDS walk and asked the students to read it to themselves.

"What's this? The Gay Men's Health Crisis. What are you getting us into, Mr. Kettering?" It was Ron's voice again.

"What are you reading, Ron?"

"Here, on the back. It says that proceeds from the walk go to the American Foundation for AIDS Research, to the AIDS Action Council, to AIDS-Related Community Services, and to the Gay Men's Health Crisis. It sounds like a social club. And look at this! It says this gay group uses some of its money to run a 'buddy system.' A buddy system! I can guess what that is."

"You don't have to guess, Ron. I can tell you what it is. It's a system that provides a 'buddy' to shop or clean or run errands for anyone who's too sick to tend to the details of his or her own life. I also think we need to remember that we're trying to fight a disease, not a lifestyle. I think. . . . "

"Why did they choose that name—'Gay Men's Health Crisis'?" said Tara. "If they wanted to raise money, who's going to support a group with a name like that? It's stupid." It was the first time since the semester began that Tara had spoken up in class.

"Hemophiliacs and children with AIDS are innocent victims," Liana said. "Couldn't we raise money just for them?"

"I don't have a lot of prejudices, but this is one of them," said Janet, a Vietnamese girl whose family had immigrated to the United States several years ago and who was one of the brightest students in the class. Chris had thought she would be one of the supporters of the walk. "I think this is disgusting. I'm sorry these people have AIDS. But if they lived moral lives, if they weren't . . . you know, deviant, they wouldn't be sick. I'll do voter registration."

Chris thought of interrupting a second time. But for the few remaining minutes, he let the students express their views, hoping again that some student would speak up for the walk. None did. When the bell rang, he walked to his desk in the back of the room and began making plans for the voter registration drive, the 5-mile run, the recycling program, and the only new idea that had surfaced, a car wash to earn money for the senior class trip.